Ulysses in Focus

THE FLORIDA JAMES JOYCE SERIES

UNIVERSITY PRESS OF FLORIDA

Florida A&M University, Tallahassee
Florida Atlantic University, Boca Raton
Florida Gulf Coast University, Ft. Myers
Florida International University, Miami
Florida State University, Tallahassee
New College of Florida, Sarasota
University of Central Florida, Orlando
University of Florida, Gainesville
University of North Florida, Jacksonville
University of South Florida, Tampa
University of West Florida, Pensacola

Ulysses in Focus
Genetic, Textual, and Personal Views

Michael Groden

FOREWORD BY SEBASTIAN D. G. KNOWLES, SERIES EDITOR

UNIVERSITY PRESS OF FLORIDA
Gainesville / Tallahassee / Tampa / Boca Raton
Pensacola / Orlando / Miami / Jacksonville / Ft. Myers / Sarasota

Copyright 2010 by Michael Groden
All rights reserved
Printed in the United States of America. This book is printed on Glatfelter Natures Book, a paper certified under the standards of the Forestry Stewardship Council (FSC). It is a recycled stock that contains 30 percent post-consumer waste and is acid-free.

First cloth printing, 2010
First paperback printing, 2012

A record of cataloging-in-publication data is available from the Library of Congress.
ISBN 978-0-8130-3498-0 (cloth)
ISBN 978-0-8130-4172-8 (pbk.)

The University Press of Florida is the scholarly publishing agency for the State University System of Florida, comprising Florida A&M University, Florida Atlantic University, Florida Gulf Coast University, Florida International University, Florida State University, New College of Florida, University of Central Florida, University of Florida, University of North Florida, University of South Florida, and University of West Florida.

University Press of Florida
15 Northwest 15th Street
Gainesville, FL 32611-2079
http://www.upf.com

for Molly Peacock,
the first Molly

Contents

Foreword ix
Acknowledgments xi
Abbreviations xiii
Sources xv

Introduction 1
1. The Archive in Transition: The National Library of Ireland's New Joyce Manuscripts 14
2. When First I Saw, Part 1: Choosing and Being Chosen by *Ulysses* 32
3. From Monument to Mobile: Genetic Criticism and *Ulysses* 53
4. When First I Saw, Part 2: Discovering Joyce's Manuscripts 69
5. *The James Joyce Archive* and Hans Walter Gabler's Edition of *Ulysses*: A Personal History 81
6. Revisiting the "Cyclops" Manuscripts, Part 1: Wandering in the Avant-texte 105
7. Revisiting the "Cyclops" Manuscripts, Part 2: The National Library of Ireland Draft and Its Contexts 120
8. Mobile Pages: *Ulysses* in Print and on a Screen 144
9. Mobile Notes: Annotating *Ulysses* in Print and on a Screen 159
10. The Case of the Snuffed Footnote: A Report from the Stacks 174
Epilogue: Privacy in Bloom 185

Appendix 1. Remarks on the National Library of Ireland's Newly Acquired Joyce Manuscripts 195
Appendix 2. Extant Manuscripts for *Ulysses* as of Summer 2002: A Chart 199
Notes 205
Works Cited 221
Index 237

Foreword

The turn to autobiography, or "life-writing," in academia has value only in proportion to the general conclusions that can be drawn from the particular narrative, and just as all young intellectual would-be artists can see themselves in Stephen Dedalus, so all budding Joyceans can see themselves in Michael Groden, who has had the Zelig-like ability to be involved in seemingly every great Joycean event of the past quarter-century. It was Michael Groden who as a graduate student was handed the keys to the Joycean kingdom in Grand Central Terminal, and his story of how he ended up as the primary editor of the sixty-three volumes of the Garland Archive, still the single greatest printed resource for any scholar of any writer, is itself worth the price of admission. It was Michael Groden who served on the front lines of the so-called Joyce Wars and lived to tell the tale; and again Michael Groden who was called in September 2001 to ask if he could help identify what are now known as the National Library of Ireland's Joyce Papers 2002. Throughout the extraordinary story of his literary life, Groden keeps us grounded with a wry and self-deprecating wit: after his dissertation director tells him that his original idea for a thesis will never fly, Groden reports that "I spent about a month after that meeting lying in bed or sitting in a chair staring at a wall." It is enormously reassuring, for instance, to come upon an admission by the general editor of the *James Joyce Archive* that "even after putting the reproductions together I can't find specific passages in them." And editors everywhere will rejoice to learn that only when the bound copies of the page proofs for "Oxen of the Sun" arrived at Garland Press did someone finally notice that the title page read "Oxen *in* the Sun."

We are in the witches' kitchen, with the cauldron of Joyce's *Ulysses* coming to a boil: as the text reaches its perfect state, Groden has equally valuable insights to share about the process by which a text is created. This book is three things: a record of the growth of Joyce studies from 1970 to the present, a record of the genesis of the field of genetic criticism, and a testament to the evolutionary development of a Joycean. And it is more than all of these: Groden reports his observations with such felicity that as much pleasure comes from the presentation of the material as from the material itself. Again and again, Groden takes well-known points and phrases from the Joycean canon and recasts them so that they are re-sorted and restored, reversed and re-served. Love is not so much the "word known to all men" but "the means by which the Word was made known to all men." Stephen's thoughts on history in "Nestor" ("But can those have been possible seeing that they never were? Or was that only possible which came to pass?") become the first musings of a genetic critic. "The Parable of the Plums" is read as Stephen's greatest work of art in the book, an anecdote which is itself a parable of the need for interpretation. Reading the section genetically, Groden calls attention to Professor MacHugh's smile, which comes and goes in the drafts "like *Alice in Wonderland*'s Cheshire Cat's grin." Balanced by the headlines ("ANNE WIMBLES, FLO WANGLES") and the parallel lines of motionless trolleys bound for or from points around Dublin, Stephen's parable is memorably described as a "mobile," in which Nelson's Pillar and all that surrounds it are suspended for a moment in time. A mobile is a work of art that is "still, and still moving," as Eliot says in *Four Quartets*: Michael Groden's monumental work has the same kinetic facility. In its breathtaking attention to detail, it has the stillness of a violin; in its constant search for new dimensions of reading in *Ulysses*, it is a moving distillation of a lifetime's devotion to Joyce.

Sebastian D. G. Knowles

Acknowledgments

Much of *"Ulysses" in Focus* began as talks and lectures at various conferences, universities, and other organizations, and I thank the many people, unfortunately too numerous to mention individually here, who invited me to lecture and accepted my proposals for conference papers.

I also thank the editors of the journals and books in which the original versions of these chapters were published: Louis Armand, Michael Basinski, Wayne Chapman, Nicholas Fargnoli, Daniel Ferrer, Michael Patrick Gillespie, Almuth Grésillon, Sebastian Knowles, Sean Latham, Geert Lernout, Morton Levitt, Roger Lüdeke, James Maynard, John McCourt, Catherine Paul, Molly Peacock, Jean-Michel Rabaté, Christopher Ricks, Peter Stoicheff, Thomas Staley, Wolfgang Streit, Andrew Taylor, Cristina Urchueguía, and Hugh Witemeyer.

I thank the English Department at the University of Western Ontario for its continued support, both on this book and throughout my career over the past thirty-five years, and in particular the various department chairs under whom I've worked: Tom Collins, Patrick Deane, the late Paul Gaudet, Douglas Kneale, Jan Plug, Russell Poole, Alan Somerset, and the late Jim Woodruff. Work on this book was greatly helped by a research grant from the Social Sciences and Humanities Research Council of Canada, and publication was aided by a grant from the J. B. Smallman Research Fund of the University of Western Ontario's Faculty of Arts and Humanities.

I very much appreciate the three readers' reports that the University Press of Florida solicited, one from Florida James Joyce series editor Sebastian Knowles and two from anonymous reviewers, and also the work of copy editor Jonathan Lawrence. A writer could not ask for more careful and critical but also sympathetic and supportive help than I've received from these four people. I am also grateful for the efforts of acquiring editor Amy Gorelick, project editor Jacqueline Kinghorn Brown, rights and permissions manager Heather Turci, and sales and marketing assistant Ale Gasso at the Press. Any errors or infelicities that remain in this book despite the best efforts of all these people are mine alone.

For help in large and small ways on the chapters in this book, and for general and specific suggestions and encouragement, I am grateful to Stephen Adams, Louis Armand, Ruth Bauerle, Murray Beja, Mark Bernstein, Robert Bertholf, Ted Bishop, Jay David Bolter, Zack Bowen, Austin Briggs, Robert Cailliau, Luca Crispi, Vincent Deane, Jed Deppman, Nicholas Fargnoli, Mark Feltham, Daniel Ferrer, Anne Fogarty, Michael Gillespie, Eric Halpern, Colleen Jaurretche, Ellen Carol Jones, Michael Joyce, Christopher Keep, Sean Latham, John Lavagnino, Vicki Mahaffey, Timothy Martin, Paul Meahan, Jesse Meyers, Ed Mulhall, Hans-Harald Müller, Adrienne O'Henly, Paul Saint-Amour, Bunny Serlin, Carol Shloss, Sam Slote, James Henry Spohrer, Robert Spoo, Wim van Mierlo, and Michelle Witen.

No printed thanks can ever adequately acknowledge the importance that Molly Peacock has had in this book and in my life. I dedicate *"Ulysses" in Focus* to her with gratitude, awe, and love.

Abbreviations

Archive James Joyce. *The James Joyce Archive.* Photoreprint ed. General ed. Michael Groden. Ed. Hans Walter Gabler, David Hayman, A. Walton Litz, and Danis Rose. 63 vols. New York: Garland, 1977–79. Cited by volume:page number.

CW James Joyce. *Critical Writings.* Ed. Ellsworth Mason and Richard Ellmann. New York: Viking, 1959.

D James Joyce. *Dubliners.* 1914. Ed. Robert Scholes. New York: Viking, 1967.

E James Joyce. *Exiles.* 1918. New York: Penguin, 1973.

FW James Joyce. *Finnegans Wake.* New York: Viking, 1939. Cited by page:line number.

L James Joyce. *Letters.* 3 vols. Vol. 1. Ed. Stuart Gilbert. New York: Viking, 1957, 1966. Vols. 2–3. Ed. Richard Ellmann. New York: Viking, 1966. Cited by volume:page number.

Notes and Early Drafts James Joyce. *Joyce's Notes and Early Drafts for "Ulysses": Selections from the Buffalo Collection.* Ed. Phillip F. Herring. Charlottesville: University Press of Virginia, 1977.

Notesheets James Joyce. *Joyce's "Ulysses" Notesheets in the British Museum.* Ed. Phillip F. Herring. Charlottesville: University Press of Virginia, 1972.

P James Joyce. *A Portrait of the Artist as a Young Man.* 1916. Ed. Chester Anderson. New York: Viking, 1964.

SL James Joyce. *Selected Letters.* Ed. Richard Ellmann. New York: Viking, 1975.

U James Joyce. *Ulysses.* 1922. Ed. Hans Walter Gabler with Claus Melchior and Wolfhard Steppe. New York: Garland, 1984. New York: Vintage, 1986, 1993. London: Bodley Head, 1993, 2008. Cited by episode:line number.

Sources

All the previously published articles and chapters have been revised from their original appearances, substantially in many cases.

Chapter 1: The first section was originally published as "The National Library of Ireland's New Joyce Manuscripts" in *Joyce in Trieste: An Album of Risky Readings*, ed. Sebastian D. G. Knowles, Geert Lernout, and John McCourt (Gainesville: University Press of Florida, 2007), 13–35. Reprinted with permission of the University Press of Florida. That essay merged information from three earlier articles: "The National Library of Ireland's New Joyce Manuscripts: A Narrative and Document Summaries," *Journal of Modern Literature* 26 (2002): 1–16 (published by Indiana University Press); "The National Library of Ireland's New Joyce Manuscripts: A Statement and Document Descriptions," *James Joyce Quarterly* 39 (2001): 29–51 (published by University of Tulsa); and "The National Library of Ireland's New Joyce Manuscripts: An Outline and Archive Comparisons," *Joyce Studies Annual* 14 (2003): 5–17 (Copyright © 2003, University of Texas Press. All rights reserved). The second section was originally published as "'Proceeding Energetically from the Unknown to the Known': Looking Again at the Genetic Texts and Documents for Joyce's *Ulysses*" in *Variants: The Journal of the European Society for Textual Scholarship* 4 (2005): 183–95. Published by Editions Rodopi B.V.

Chapter 2: Previously unpublished.

Chapter 3: Originally published as "Genetic Joyce: Textual Studies and the Reader" in *Palgrave Advances in James Joyce Studies*, ed. Jean-Michel Rabaté (London: Palgrave Macmillan, 2004), 227–50. Copyright 2004, Palgrave Macmillan. Reproduced with permission of Palgrave Macmillan. A small section of "Genetic Joyce" is also in chapter 5.

Chapter 4: Partly originally published as "On First Looking into Joyce's Manuscripts" in *Discovering James Joyce: The UB Collection*, ed. James Maynard (Buffalo: The Poetry Collection, University at Buffalo, State University of New York, 2009), 53–61. Reprinted with permission of The Poetry Collection, University at Buffalo. Partly previously unpublished.

Chapter 5: Originally published as "Perplex in the Pen—and in the Pixels: Reflections on *The James Joyce Archive*, Hans Walter Gabler's *Ulysses*, and 'James Joyce's *Ulysses* in Hypermedia'" in *Journal of Modern Literature* 22 (1998–99): 225–44. Published by Indiana University Press. Reprinted with the rest of the issue in *Joyce and the Joyceans*, ed. Morton P. Levitt (Syracuse: Syracuse University Press, 2002), 32–50. The brief opening section comes from the beginning of an essay not otherwise reproduced in the present volume: "Before and After: The Manuscripts in Textual and Genetic Criticism of *Ulysses*" in *"Ulysses" in Critical Perspective*, ed. Michael Patrick Gillespie and A. Nicholas Fargnoli (Gainesville: University Press of Florida, 2006), 152–70. Reprinted with permission of the University Press of Florida.

Chapter 6: Originally published as "Wandering in the *Avant-texte*: Joyce's 'Cyclops' Copybook Revisited" in *The Future of Modernism*, ed. Hugh Witemeyer (Ann Arbor: University of Michigan Press, 1997), 181–99. Copyright 1997, University of Michigan. A slightly revised version appeared in French as "Divagations odysséennes dans l'avant-texte joycien: Retour sur le carnet du 'Cyclope,'" trans. Florence Meyerès, in *Genesis: Manuscrits/Recherche/Invention* 23 (2004): 27–41.

Chapter 7: Originally published as "Joyce at Work on 'Cyclops': Toward a Biography of *Ulysses*" in *James Joyce Quarterly* 44 (2007): 217–45. Published by University of Tulsa.

Chapter 8: Originally published as "James Joyce's *Ulysses* on the Page and on the Screen" in *The Future of the Page*, ed. Peter Stoicheff and Andrew Taylor (Toronto: University of Toronto Press, 2004), 159–75.

Chapter 9: Originally published as "Problems of Annotation in a Digital *Ulysses*" in *JoyceMedia: James Joyce, Hypermedia and Textual Genetics*, ed. Louis Armand (Prague: Litteraria Pragensia, 2004/Syracuse, N.Y.: Syracuse University Press, 2006), 116–32; also in *Hypermedia Joyce Studies* 4.2 (December 2003–January 2004), http://www.geocities.com/hypermedia_joyce/groden.html. This was a revised version of an electronic hypertext online article: "'James Joyce's *Ulysses* in Hypermedia': Problems of Annotation"

(Clemson, S.C.: Clemson University Digital Press, 2002), http://www.clemson.edu/caah/cedp/Tech%20Colloquium%202001/hypermedia-Groden.html.

Chapter 10: Originally published in *Literary Imagination* 6 (2004): 151–59. Published by the Association of Literary Scholars and Critics and Oxford University Press.

Epilogue: Originally published as "Privacy in Bloom" in *The Private I: Privacy in a Public World*, Graywolf Forum 4, ed. Molly Peacock (St. Paul, Minn.: Graywolf Press, 2001), 71–79. Adapted and reprinted with the permission of Graywolf Press, Saint Paul, Minnesota, www.graywolfpress.org.

Appendix 1: Originally published as part of "The National Library of Ireland's New Joyce Manuscripts" in *Joyce in Trieste: An Album of Risky Readings*, 21–25, and in "The National Library of Ireland's New Joyce Manuscripts: A Statement and Document Descriptions," *James Joyce Quarterly* 39 (2001): 30–33 (published by University of Tulsa).

Appendix 2: Originally published as part of "The National Library of Ireland's New Joyce Manuscripts" in *Joyce in Trieste: An Album of Risky Readings*, 28–33, and in "The National Library of Ireland's New Joyce Manuscripts: An Outline and Archive Comparisons," *Joyce Studies Annual* 14 (2003): 10–17 (copyright 2003, University of Texas Press. All rights reserved).

Introduction

"This monument of literature": so Stuart Gilbert honored *Ulysses* even before it could be legally purchased in any English-speaking country. The designation of "monument" certainly fits a work about which so many critical books and articles have been written, which headed a list of the most important twentieth-century novels and whose three main characters ranked among the century's top ten characters, and which can still command much popular attention and generate much controversy, even among people who haven't read it. The term recurs regularly in *Ulysses* criticism: S. L. Goldberg calls Joyce's novel "a literary monument of our age," Marilyn French refers to it as "a monument defining morality in a relativistic world," Vincent Sherry notes the "colossal monument of Joyce's work," and Derek Attridge its "massive monumentality." (Somehow combining monumentality with liquidity, Wyndham Lewis called *Ulysses* "a monument like a record diarrhoea.")[1] In writing yet another book on *Ulysses*, I can't help but acknowledge and contribute to Joyce's novel's monumental status.

Public monuments can serve, as John Pedro Schwartz has recently noted, "to represent history and ensure its continuity with the present," but they do so enmeshed in politics and ideology. Schwartz and Ellen Carol Jones both document the erection of monuments in nineteenth-century Ireland first to British imperialist interests and then to Irish nationalist ones, creating different kinds of (in Jones's words) "politicized public memory." A monument like Nelson's Pillar in Dublin can be both provocative in its sexual connotations—Stephen Dedalus refers to Nelson as "the onehandled adulterer" (*U* 7:1017–18)—and also irreparably inflammatory in what Schwartz calls its "imperial symbolism," as a member of the IRA demonstrated when he blew up the pillar on the Easter Rising's fiftieth anniversary in the mid-1960s.[2]

Apart from their political symbolism, however, monuments can be rather boring in their solid and stolid dominance of a cityscape or landscape. So Molly Bloom complains as she recalls her attempt to titillate Leopold Bloom by telling him about "some dean or bishop was sitting beside me in the jews temples gardens when I was knitting that woollen thing a stranger to Dublin," Bloom responding only by rambling on "about the monuments and he tired me out with statues" (*U* 18:90–93). Monuments suggest stasis, the young Stephen Dedalus's artistic ideal in *A Portrait of the Artist as a Young Man* and far removed from Molly's kinetic desires. Stephen argues that the mind is "arrested and raised above desire and loathing" by true, static art, unlike the "feelings excited by improper"—that is, kinetic—"art" (*P* 205). *Ulysses* moves beyond this hierarchy, however, as it balances Stephen's rather static picture of the women at the top of Nelson's Pillar in his "Parable of the Plums" at the end of "Aeolus" with Bloom's decidedly kinetic interest in the anatomical accuracy of the National Museum of Ireland's statues of goddesses.[3] It contrasts not only static and kinetic reactions to art but also stasis and motion, from the activity of the people on Dublin's streets during the day to the tumescence and detumescence of Bloom's penis as "He kissed the plump mellow yellow smellow melons of [Molly's] rump" (*U* 17:2241) to the description of the Blooms in bed at the end of "Ithaca" as both "At rest" and "In motion" (*U* 17:2307).

As I thought about Nelson's Pillar in Stephen's parable (for chapter 3 in this book) and more generally about *Ulysses* as a monument and as kinetic art, I read genetic critic Pierre-Marc de Biasi's claims that a work's drafts reveal "a mobile image, far more hypothetical and often richer than the one the published text will eventually give us to be read as its *truth* after many reworkings."[4] A mobile is a provocative counter-image to a monument. I looked at the sequence of changes in the Nelson's Pillar passage as Joyce revised it (my main concern in the chapter), and the two monuments—the pillar and *Ulysses*—both seemed to start to move.

"Mobile" can suggest the mobility of people in the modern world, whether Leopold Bloom unknowingly reenacting the epic, heroic wanderings of Odysseus as he walks around Dublin on June 16, 1904, or the decidedly unheroic Joe Hynes mocking Bloom's concept of a nation by declaring that he has continually moved around from place to place (*U* 12:1428–29). The word also names a small electronic device, a cell phone or mini-computer, even one capable of eliminating the novel's monumental bulk and containing the full text of *Ulysses* in tiny, weightless pixels. As a third and richer possibility, the term can evoke Alexander Calder's famous hanging mobiles, those marvels of balanced thin metal pieces, heaviness suspended in air, stillness interrupted by occasional movement in response to a chance draft.

Monument: heaviness, solidity, stability, fixity. Mobile: lightness, balance, motion, chance. By chance, while I was working on this book the Whitney Museum of American Art in New York mounted a large exhibition of Calder's works from his years in Paris, including his circus and many of his mobiles. Calder's light black and white (or sometimes black, white, and red) mobiles might seem far removed from the bulky, multi-colored *Ulysses*. But Calder, who wanted to "compose motions," produced, in the words of one scholar, "the first totally kinetic art." A Calder mobile seems to move even if it remains at rest. Art conservator Carol Mancusi-Ungaro, discussing the pieces of Calder's circus, considers another kind of movement: "Works of art move as they age—not only from place to place but internally."[5] A literary work ages differently from a sculpture or painting, of course, but it moves, too—in its changing words as editors produce new texts; its changing typefaces, pages, covers, and densities as publishers release new editions; its changing early history as genetic critics investigate its draft stages; its changing reception as readers at different points in time and with varying individual backgrounds encounter it; and its changing relationships to an individual reader during different periods of that person's life.

"Ulysses" in Focus considers some changing, moving aspects of Joyce's novel in three broad areas: genetic criticism, textual studies, and personal criticism. As the focus changes in various ways in these three views, the book's chapters attempt to show the monumental *Ulysses* turning into a mobile.

■

Beginning almost immediately after Joyce's death in 1941, what is now known as "genetic criticism" has been an important approach to his works. For over forty years it called itself, if anything, "manuscript study," its scholars investigating Joyce's surviving notes, drafts, fair copies, typescripts, and proofs, and producing much valuable work. (A "fair copy" can be defined as "a corrected and cleanly written manuscript, produced by its author or by a scribe.")[6] Work on Joyce's manuscripts has become increasingly sophisticated and prominent in the last couple of decades, however, for at least three reasons.

One is the publication in the late 1970s of *The James Joyce Archive*, the sixty-three-volume photoreprint edition of the raw materials for genetic study, which made scholarly work on the manuscripts much more possible than before. A second reason is the unexpected and stunningly large number of new documents that have come to light since 2000. Their very existence has provoked an increased interest in and resurgence of research on Joyce's manuscripts.

The third reason is that, for the last several decades, a group of French critics, thoroughly versed in the writings of Roland Barthes, Jacques Derrida, Hélène Cixous, Julia Kristeva, Jacques Lacan, and other leading theorists (many of them students of those theorists), have been working in an area they call *critique génétique* (the French original of the now-common English term "genetic criticism"), and they have brought subtle and wide-ranging models and methods to bear on manuscripts. They proceed from several assumptions: that the surviving documents for a work can be considered as texts (and not merely as preliminary states of a work) and, along with the work itself, as part of a textual system; that this textual system, the material that the genetic critic works with in the extant documents, is not simply a given but is constructed by the critic in relation to an endpoint (publication, termination of work, author's death), since not every bit of writing on a document necessarily forms part of the composition process for a work; and that the object of study is less the finished work or the documents that led to that work than the writing processes themselves or, more specifically, those aspects of the writing process that the extant documents can reveal.[7]

Genetic critics employ a term coined in 1972 by Jean Bellemin-Noël to designate the drafts' status as a text and the system's as a critical construct: avant-texte. I use this central term frequently in this book. Attempts to render it in English have been extremely awkward—formulations such as "pre-text" and "fore-text" are misleading and unattractive—and a foreign term presented as an English word can help to convey Bellemin-Noël's original sense of the avant-texte as the text's Other. So, as Jed Deppman, Daniel Ferrer, and I did in *Genetic Criticism: Texts and Avant-textes*, our collection of translated French essays, I have retained the French term throughout this book. I have also followed our practice in *Genetic Criticism* of not italicizing the term. When I quote an author who uses an English formulation or puts the term in italics, I have retained that author's usage.

Genetic critics often see movement as they investigate an author's writing processes, whether de Biasi's explicit "mobile image" or a more implicit series of possibilities, some of them eventually realized but others not. This is rather like Stephen Dedalus's paraphrase of Aristotle after he wonders whether events that didn't come to pass were ever really possible: "It must be a movement then, an actuality of the possible as possible" (*U* 2:67). In *"Ulysses" Annotated*, Don Gifford and Robert Seidman identify the source of Stephen's thought as Aristotle's *Physics*: "The fulfillment of what exists potentially, in so far as it exists potentially, is motion."[8] Genetic critics tend to see the movement while only partially considering a direct line from potential to fulfillment. Paul Valéry, a poet and writer often cited by genetic critics because he declared that to "create a poem is itself a poem" and expressed explicit desires to "transfer the artistry which is placed in a work to its process of production" and to "consider composition itself as the principal factor," finds movement everywhere in writing, seeing it "as a work, as a dance, as fencing, as the construction of acts and expectations."[9] (Contrast this dancing or fencing author with the clichéd film image of the frustrated writer at work, seated immovably at a typewriter, throwing one sheet of crumpled paper after another into a wastebasket or onto the floor.) We can imagine the author with the work in progress as a dancing partner: is the dance an arm's-length minuet, as in Jane Austen's day? a seductive waltz or even a tango? a more aggressive hip-hop dance? We know from Richard Ellmann's biography that Joyce could startle people on the Bahnhofstrasse in Zurich by spontaneously "flinging his loose limbs about in a kind of spider dance."[10] He didn't need a partner. In Valéry's couple, who is leading, the author or the work?

Even when they have tried, authors have—for many different reasons—not always described their own dance moves very well. In his 1846 essay "The Philosophy of Composition," Edgar Allan Poe calls for an author "who would—that is to say, who could—detail, step by step, the processes by which any one of his compositions attained its ultimate point of completion," and then fulfills his request with an account of how he wrote "The Raven." He promises to describe a writing process that was not "a species of fine frenzy—an ecstatic intuition" but rather involved a Valérian dance of "elaborate and vacillating crudities of thought," "true purposes seized only at the last moment," "innumerable glimpses of ideas that arrived not at the maturity of full view," "fully matured fancies discarded in despair as unmanageable," "cautious selections and rejections," and "painful erasures and interpolations." But as his retrospective account goes on, the recalcitrant dancing partner appears nevermore as Poe allows the mobile process he announced to harden into an inert monument and enumerates a series of problems conceived, considered, and overcome without any apparent effort: "the work proceeded, step by step, to its completion with the precision and rigid consequence of a mathematical problem."[11] The ominous raven proved to be an extraordinarily docile partner in one dance after another.

Scholars who investigate an author's writing processes engage in a different kind of dance, partnered with a sometimes compliant, sometimes resistant author who is unquestionably in the lead. The documents an author leaves behind cannot indicate everything about the way he or she wrote in general or composed specific works, but they can say a great deal, including much that is beyond an author's power to recall or desire to reveal. If Louis Hay's provocative statement that "Manuscripts have something new to tell us: it is high time we learned to make them speak" is at all accurate, we can continue to look to the avant-texte of *Ulysses* in search of fascinating commentary on Joyce's dance of composition.[12]

Five of the chapters in *"Ulysses" in Focus* are wholly or partly about genetic criticism or exercises in it. They include an overview of genetic criticism and its relevance to *Ulysses* (using Stephen's "Parable of the Plums" as an example), two different attempts to look anew at the "Cyclops" avant-texte that formed a central part of my 1977 book *"Ulysses" in Progress*, a general account of the new *Ulysses* manuscripts that the National Library of Ireland acquired in 2002, and discussion of three specific examples from those new drafts. Some of the chapters combine genetic with personal criticism. In those I recount my work on *The James Joyce Archive*, my involvement with the National Library as it acquired its Joyce documents, and my initial discovery of the *Ulysses* manuscripts when I was a graduate student.

■

"Textual studies" has become a common name for the expanded field of study that once was confined to the various branches of bibliography (analytical, descriptive, historical), textual criticism, and scholarly editing. Textual studies continues to include these specialties as vital elements, but it involves far more. The field experienced a sea change in the 1980s, when D. F. McKenzie positioned bibliography as part of the "sociology of texts" and Jerome McGann critiqued the dominant model of editing, one seeking to restore the author's final intentions, on the grounds that it ignores the possible contributions of other agents in the publishing process, and offered what became known as the "social theory of editing" as an alternative. McGann also called for "a more comprehensive study of textuality" that sees a work as composed of both a "linguistic code"—its words—and a "bibliographical code"—its previously under-discussed or ignored features such as its ink, typeface, page layout, paper, and binding.[13]

In the wake of McKenzie's and McGann's arguments and of developments that have arisen from them, a 1932 statement of principle from W. W. Greg, who as much as anyone established the paradigm for the earlier kinds of bibliography and editing, holds little appeal. For Greg, "what the bibliographer is concerned with is pieces of paper on parchment covered with certain written or printed signs. With these signs he is concerned merely as arbitrary marks; their meaning is no business of his." Instead, as Elizabeth Bergmann Loizeaux and Neil Fraistat, editors of a recent essay collection, put it, "textual studies provides a broad umbrella for a host of subfields concerned with the production, distribution, reproduction, consumption, reception, archiving, editing and sociology of texts," the texts under investigation including not only written and printed works but also digital productions, graphic works, film, music, and oral texts.[14] Textual studies' subfields often feature names with "history," "materiality," or "sociology" in them, especially the most common subfield, book history.

Modern textual studies can point to previously marginal or ignored aspects of a work, as Ted Bishop's *Riding with Rilke: Reflections on Motorcycles and Books* vividly displays. Bishop relates his experiences of working on Joyce and Virginia Woolf manuscripts and early book printings, especially at the Harry Ransom Center at the University of Texas at Austin, and also of traveling between his home in Edmonton, Alberta, and Austin, Texas, and back on a Ducati motorcycle. He gives his readers a clear sense of the manuscripts' and books' contents, but he especially conveys the look, feel, and smell of the individual pages and books, the atmosphere of the reading room, the emotional highs and lows of this kind of research, and what he calls the "archival jolt," which for him is "a portal to knowledge and, in itself, an assurance that we have connected with something real." Bishop offers a powerful and moving example of this jolt. In the British Library he started reading a handwritten letter from Woolf to Leonard Woolf, not realizing at first that he held her actual suicide note, the words of which he had seen many times in printed versions. On the back of the letter Leonard Woolf wrote a date that was more than five weeks later than Virginia's letter, startling Bishop into remembering Leonard's long wait between his reading of Virginia's note and the discovery of her body.[15] In Bishop's hands, McGann's bibliographical code comes alive as textual studies becomes lively, engaging, and, perhaps most surprising of all, personal.

Looking at *Ulysses* in light of the expanded field of textual studies is especially rewarding, and in four chapters of *"Ulysses" in Focus* I explore these areas. One deals with Hans Walter Gabler's edition of *Ulysses* from the perspective of my involvement with its production and in the controversy over it that ensued. Gabler produced his edition at almost exactly the same time as McKenzie and McGann were developing their ideas, and both its theory and its practice straddle a line between traditional editing and alternative models, both newer ones and ones from Europe rather than England and the United States. Another chapter is concerned with pages. Since Joyce wrote *Ulysses* as a novel that would ultimately be printed in book form, its pages—an example of McGann's bibliographical code—can usefully be explored in relation to changing media. Two other chapters involve those sometimes helpful, sometimes annoying ancillary features of editions: annotations and explanatory footnotes and endnotes. One considers the changing nature of annotations as the medium varies, and another contains a personal narrative about a triumphant and also maddeningly frustrating attempt to track down a reference for a footnote.

■

In "Aeolus," Leopold Bloom imagines writing a newspaper's advice column: "I'd like that part. Learn a lot teaching others. The personal note" (*U* 7:96–97). Despite this implicit endorsement, my book's third category, "personal criticism," requires more explanation than the other two. In 1996 James Atlas declared that we live in an "age of the literary memoir," and Sidonie Smith and Julia Watson have referred more recently to a "memoir boom."[16] Personal narratives are ubiquitous, and the furor that erupted over James Frey's *A Million Little Pieces* after the author was exposed as a fabricator of various central scenes indicates the important place that memoirs hold in today's culture. The academic study of memoirs and of autobiographical writing generally has grown apace, with such prominent critics and scholars as Paul John Eakin, Philippe Lejeune, Nancy K. Miller, James Olney, Sidonie Smith, and others, along with several anthologies of personal criticism, including Diane P. Freedman, Olivia Frey, and Frances Murphy Zauhar's *The Intimate Critique: Autobiographical Literary Criticism* (1993), H. Aram Veeser's *Confessions of the Critics* (1996), and Freedman and Frey's *Autobiographical Writing across the Disciplines* (2003).

The different terms that these anthologies' editors use to name their collections, however, reflect the uncertainty of the goals and even the identity of this kind of writing. So do the editors' shifts in their introductions from one name to another: personal criticism or personal writing; autobiographical criticism, autobiographical writing, or autobiography; confessional criticism; performative criticism; self-narration, self-portraiture, or self-referential writing; life narrative or life writing; memoir; or the unfortunate portmanteau construction "autocritography." These names constitute only a partial list: in an appendix to their book *Reading Autobiography*, Smith and Watson list and describe fifty-two kinds of life narrative. I have opted for the simple "personal criticism" as a category for several of the chapters in *"Ulysses" in Focus*.

In his introduction to *Confessions of the Critics*, Veeser lists nineteen actual and possible objections to personal criticism, including the charge that "everyone has subjective reactions to literature, and our job as professional interpreters is precisely to overcome those reactions and move beyond ordinary personal responses" (or, as the headline of a *New York Times* article about memoirs puts it, "We All Have a Life. Must We All Write About It?").[17] Assuming that many academics will find personal writing suspicious, distasteful, insufficiently serious, or simply irrelevant, Veeser mounts a defense against the objections by describing writing that is subversive, transgressive, and performative and that disrupts polarities and dichotomies such as neutral versus expressive writing, objective, logical thinking versus performance, intellect versus emotion, connected, teleological narrative versus discrete anecdote, centrality versus marginality, and concealment versus disclosure.

I found myself drawn to personal criticism not to be subversive, transgressive, or performative but rather to look at why *Ulysses* attracted me so much when I first read it and has continued to affect me so powerfully in the more than forty years since then. I quickly discovered that I couldn't do this without thinking and writing personally and without questioning some of the conventions of academic writing. "I'm tired of the conventions," Jane Tompkins declares in her pioneering 1987 personal essay "Me and My Shadow," conventions "that keep discussions of epistemology, or James Joyce"—

how nice!—"segregated from meditations on what is happening outside my window or inside my heart." The main segregation that concerned me was the one between the subject of my writing and the reasons for my choice. My desire to write about Joyce and *Ulysses* remained as strong as ever, but I wanted to stop taking the subject matter for granted, to build my motivations into my work itself, and to try to understand, in Diane Freedman's words, "how the writer came to read or write as he or she does," or, in Ruth Behar's, "what aspects of the self are the most important filters through which one perceives the world and, more particularly, the topic being studied."[18]

I also wanted to fill in the implications of a statement like Attridge's that a work of art "is experienced every time as a singular *event*, by an individual with specific (and changing) needs, expectations, memories, and associations, at a particular time and place" and to attempt to answer as completely as I could the deceptively simple question of why reading *Ulysses* was such a momentous event for me at first and repeatedly after that.[19] What "needs, expectations, memories, and associations" did I bring to my first and later readings of *Ulysses*? The answers are important to me, surely, but my gamble is that if I can articulate the various reasons for my own responses to *Ulysses*, my experiences will resonate with other people in relation to their own attractions to *Ulysses* or to other literary works or different kinds of art. I do this not from a conviction that my life story is so important or special that it needs to be aired (the opposite, in fact: in many ways, it's quite ordinary), and certainly not out of a desire to force readers to put their heads into the muck of my personal life. Rather, as Phillip Lopate has said, "I want to record how the world comes at me, because I think it is indicative of the way it comes at everyone."[20]

Various critics and scholars have described their ongoing responses to the works that matter to them. "When I reread *Middlemarch*," Peter Carlton writes, "I always end up rereading myself again," and Ellen Brown says that "I keep rereading *Jane Eyre* and revising myself." Can a life be plotted against a series of experiences with a single literary work? (In the last chapter of her amazing graphic memoir *Fun Home: A Family Tragicomic*, Alison Bechdel maps various aspects of her life, especially her relationship with her father and her understanding of both her own and her father's homosexualities, against different episodes of *Ulysses*.)[21] "Since I keep writing myself into the novel in my copious underlinings and marginalia," Carlton also remarks, "each rereading is both a new self-inscription and a rereading of previously inscribed versions of myself, more or less continuous with the self I currently know myself to be." He observes versions of himself, and Brown revises herself, both sounding almost like textual or genetic critics. So does Atlas when he describes people's formative years as "works in progress that reflect lives in progress, still waiting to be edited and shaped."[22] I wonder if one can look at one's past life as a genetic critic, discerning in those earlier self-inscriptions or unrevised states something like the drafts in an avant-texte. Philippe Lejeune has attempted to perform genetic criticism on autobiographies and even diaries, unpublished writing that by definition would seem to have no avant-texte, but maybe it is possible to engage in a kind of genetic criticism within a personal, autobiographical account and not as a critic looking in on someone else's work from the outside.[23]

If so, the double thrust of much genetic criticism also applies: a teleological movement toward the text's last stage, on the one hand, and a concern with process as distinct from the outcome, on the other. The opening words of Charles Dickens's first-person novel *David Copperfield* promise to treat the narrative as, ultimately, a line that will lead to the present, the novel's conclusion: "Whether I shall turn out to be the hero of my own life, or whether that station will by held by anybody else, these pages must show. To begin my life with the beginning of my life, . . ." Also, the thought entering Stephen Dedalus's head in "Aeolus" about "that striking of that match" (perhaps adapted from Wilkie Collins's novel *The New Magdalen*)—"I have often thought since on looking back over that strange time that it was that small act, trivial in itself, that striking of that match, that determined the whole aftercourse of both our lives" (*U* 7:763–65)—suggests a simple and single root explanation for complicated ensuing events.[24] Looking at the past as a genetic critic can't involve merely tracing a line between past and present: *Ulysses* savagely mocks Garrett Deasy in "Nestor" for seeing experience like this, and in the same episode Stephen recognizes the complex relationships between past and present when he wonders if events that never came to pass had "been possible seeing that they never were. Or was that only possible which came to pass?" (*U* 2:51–52). Looking at my life genetically involves both past-present relationships—the teleological question of what Atlas call "the journey from there to here"—and also the processes that I can discern in my life in relation to *Ulysses*, including paths not taken, possibilities not made actual.[25]

Discussing his rereading of *Middlemarch*, Carlton invites us to "imagine attending a professional conference where, instead of listening to hyperintellectualized, alienating papers, we talked with each other as much about ourselves as about literature—about how reading this poem or that novel or this play had helped us to reread ourselves." To some readers, his hypothetical meeting would be a horrible nightmare. Whenever I've made a gesture in the direction of personal criticism in a lecture or at a conference, however, either in a parenthetical aside or in a full presentation, my remarks seem to have struck a chord in other people. Some always start to speak personally no matter how scholarly and objective their subject matter might be, as if in at least tacit acknowledgment of Ruth Behar's desire "to recognize the autobiographical voice as a legitimate way of speaking in academe."[26] Maybe even academic audiences respond to movement away from neutral academic writing and toward personal criticism.

I've found that I can try to answer my questions about my ongoing relationship to *Ulysses* only if I write personally. To do so is to experiment. There is no fixed form for personal criticism and no clear set of expectations for this mobile form of writing. Smith and Watson call it "a moving target, a set of ever-shifting, self-referential practices that engage the past in order to reflect on identity in the present."[27] In five of the chapters in *"Ulysses" in Focus* as well as the epilogue, I write from my present identity—a reader of *Ulysses* for over forty years, a teacher and critic for more than thirty, early sixties, male, Caucasian, Jewish, married, citizen of two countries, survivor of a life-threatening illness—and experiment with various kinds of personal criticism. The most direct chapters offer narratives of my first reading of *Ulysses* and of my discovery of the manuscripts for Joyce's novel, and the epilogue is a short essay relating this kind of criticism to issues of privacy. In other chapters, as I've already indicated, I present personal accounts of my involvement with the National Library of Ireland's new manuscripts; my work on both *The James Joyce Archive* and Gabler's edition of *Ulysses*; and my search for the information to go into a single footnote, an attempt to demonstrate that even a common scholarly activity can be presented as an autobiographical narrative, even if a somewhat heightened one.

"Ulysses" in Focus is arranged as a kind of mobile image, interspersing chapters from the three approaches of genetic, textual, and personal criticism. Chapter 1 recounts from a personal viewpoint the scholarly, genetic activity of working with the National Library of Ireland as it acquired its new Joyce

manuscripts and also offers three short examples from the new manuscripts, while chapter 2 is a personal narrative describing my first reading of *Ulysses*, partly given from the perspective of genetic criticism. Chapter 3 presents an account of genetic criticism and its relevance to *Ulysses*. Chapters 4 and 5 mirror the first two, chapter 4 presenting a second personal narrative, this time concerning my discovery of the *Ulysses* manuscripts as a potential object of study, and chapter 5 an account of *The James Joyce Archive* and Gabler's edition of *Ulysses* based on my work on these projects.

The next four chapters form two sets of pairs. Chapters 6 and 7 present two different new looks at the manuscripts for "Cyclops," one in the light of changing approaches to manuscript study and the other in response to the new manuscripts in Dublin. Chapters 8 and 9 concern two elements of McGann's bibliographical code—pages and notes—and how changes in medium (print, digital) can provoke new thinking about them. Chapter 10, continuing the topic of the one before it as it recounts the search for the details to go into a footnote, depicts another scholarly activity as a personal account. To close the book, the epilogue offers a final personal narrative and makes both *"Ulysses" in Focus* and *Ulysses* itself "books with a Molly in them" (*U* 18:657–58).

1

The Archive in Transition
The National Library of Ireland's New Joyce Manuscripts

The list of new e-mail messages on that day in late September 2001 seemed unremarkable: the usual barrage of promises of better porn and lower debt, plus a few items of actual correspondence. None of those appeared to be particularly important. Among them was one from Noel Kissane, someone I did not know, who identified himself as the Keeper of Manuscripts at the National Library of Ireland. He asked if he could call me to talk about the manuscript of the "Circe" episode of *Ulysses* that the National Library had purchased the previous December and also about "recent associated developments." I knew a little about the "Circe" acquisition: it was a draft that Joyce had sent as a "curiosity" in April 1921 to John Quinn (*L* 3:40), who was purchasing the entire *Ulysses* manuscript in episode sections as Joyce finished each one, and the library had bought it for $1.5 million at a Christie's auction in New York. I hadn't seen the manuscript when it was exhibited in London, Dublin, or New York before the auction, however, and I had only skimmed the Christie's sale catalog, so I knew very little about it. I couldn't imagine what I could tell Mr. Kissane that he didn't already know or couldn't learn from someone else in much greater detail.

When he called me, it turned out that he didn't want to talk about "Circe" at all but rather about the associated developments. Some other Joyce manuscripts had surfaced, he told me in confidence, and the owner had given the National Library an exclusive opportunity to buy them. Would I consider coming to London, where the documents were now located, in the next month or so to look at these manuscripts and report on them to the library? My first reaction was to balk. This was two weeks after September 11, after all. I had just canceled an end-of-October commitment to talk on a panel at a conference in Houston because I didn't want to fly anywhere, and I had moved to Toronto four months earlier and was only a couple of weeks into my new routine of commuting to London, Ontario, for three days each week to teach my classes at the University of Western Ontario. The thought of flying at all, and of leaving home to go to my university's London from Monday to Wednesday, then to the London in England from Thursday to Sunday, and then again to the one in Ontario the next Monday to Wednesday, was distinctly unappealing. As I hesitated, Kissane said that he had prepared a short checklist of the documents and asked if he could at least e-mail it to me so that I could see what he was talking about. To that request it was easy to say yes.

I wondered what these documents might be, of course. Two manuscripts for *Ulysses* had surfaced in the past two years, and both were sold at auction for huge sums. One was the "Circe" draft, the National Library's new acquisition. People were surprised when this manuscript surfaced, but we quickly realized that we had been aware of its existence all along because of Joyce's reference to it in his letter. The second manuscript, on the other hand, came from out of the blue. It was a draft of "Eumaeus," one that, unlike the "Circe" draft, hardly anyone inside or outside of Joyce studies knew ever existed. Its provenance was less clear than that of the "Circe" draft. A French diplomat and writer named Henri Hoppenot possessed the document—he knew Adrienne Monnier and perhaps bought the manuscript from, or maybe was given it by, either her or Sylvia Beach—and after his death a French book dealer acquired it. Sotheby's in London auctioned it for that dealer in July 2001. An anonymous private collector bought it for over £850,000 (more than $1.2 million at the time), and the whereabouts of this draft, which is sometimes called "Eumeo" from the name written on its cover (possibly by someone other than Joyce), at present are unknown. People who saw this manuscript when Sotheby's exhibited it have described it as unique among the documents for *Ulysses*: according to Sam Slote, it features additions in red and green ink as well as the familiar pencil additions (the base text is in black ink), and before this draft came to light we had "never seen a *Ulysses* episode in such a primitive configuration."[1] No new manuscripts for *Ulysses* had come to light between the 1960s and 2000, and, after the news about these two documents, and like everybody else who paid attention to such matters, I wondered whether other materials might surface. The phone conversation suggested that there were indeed other manuscripts, but even so I wasn't expecting to hear about anything significant.

I couldn't have been more wrong. When I saw Kissane's checklist, I nearly fell out of my chair. None of my wildest speculations about the other manuscripts that might still be extant could have prepared me for what this list seemed to promise. Scholars who have worked with the manuscripts for *Ulysses*—and particularly with the extraordinary gathering in the Poetry Collection at the University at Buffalo, which has been in place since the early 1950s—know that Buffalo possesses a wealth of materials: intermediate and late notes for *Ulysses* (surpassed only by the larger and better-known set of *Ulysses* notes at the British Library), early drafts for "Proteus" and for six of the last eight episodes ("Sirens," "Cyclops," "Nausicaa," "Oxen of the Sun," "Circe," and "Eumaeus," with two stages for "Oxen"), various typescripts, and many sets of proofs that fit between the first set of placards (a stage equivalent to galley proofs) at Harvard University and final page proofs at the Harry Ransom Center at the University of Texas at Austin. But the holdings contain many gaps. Joyce must have taken and used other notes; several of the drafts are incomplete (Buffalo's "Sirens" and "Cyclops" manuscripts are each only half of the episode, and both stages of its "Oxen" drafts are fragmentary). Scholars studying these materials have been familiar with both the gaps and the odd circumstance that resulted when parts of a single draft became separated as Joyce moved from apartment to apartment and city to city. For example, Buffalo possesses the first part of a draft of "Nausicaa," which, whether by design or accident, moved to Paris with Joyce, whereas Cornell University has the other two parts, which presumably remained behind in Trieste.[2]

What first caught my eye in the checklist was the group of items for "Oxen of the Sun." They included three copybooks for the episode with Roman numerals for 3, 5, and 9 on their covers. One of Buffalo's sets of "Oxen" drafts consists of six copybooks numbered 1, 2, 4, 6, 7, and 8. The enormity of what I was looking at was obvious: these were long-lost documents that filled in some of the holes in the established collections. I was fairly certain about the identity of other documents on the checklist as well: a "Sirens" draft, identified as the first half of the episode, was probably the companion to Buffalo's second half, and a "Cyclops" draft might be the second half of Buffalo's fragmentary copybook. This was a pot of gold. I wondered about some of the other documents on the checklist. A copybook contained drafts of both

"Proteus" and "Sirens." How did those two episodes get together? Three copybooks featured a continuous draft of "Scylla and Charybdis." When Buffalo bought the first part of its collection from the Librairie La Hune in 1949–50, it thought it was acquiring a draft of "Scylla" along with the other materials, but that draft never reached Buffalo—was this it?[3] And two documents were described as drafts of "Ithaca" and "Penelope." Joyce mentioned in various letters from 1916 and 1920 that he had sketched, drafted, or written out parts of the end of *Ulysses* long before he turned to these two episodes in 1921 (*L* 1:141, 1:143, 2:387, 2:459, 3:31), but we have never had any early manuscripts for them; were these the lost evidence of that work? And what were all the notes?

The outline of the checklist was clear: the material included a couple of early documents from 1903 and 1904 and a few things for *Finnegans Wake*, but it mainly dealt with *Ulysses* and involved materials from the early stages of Joyce's work on the different episodes. It looked like an extraordinary collection.

By the time I finished reading the checklist, any reservations I had about flying to London or being inconvenienced by the trip were long gone. My main worry now was that I had been too ambivalent about taking on the assignment and Kissane might have turned to someone else. I couldn't call him back until the next day, but he hadn't looked elsewhere, and we started making plans for my inspection of the documents. It took a while to work out all the details, but I finally spent November 15 and 16 looking at the materials in Sotheby's offices in London.

My task for the National Library was threefold: to report to them on the documents' authenticity, contents, and value. As soon as I saw the checklist's indications of the Roman numerals on the "Oxen" manuscripts, I had few doubts about the collection's authenticity, and at least in general terms some of the documents' contents seemed clear just from the checklist. Judging their value did not mean putting a dollar amount on the documents—a task I wouldn't have been qualified to perform—but rather making a general recommendation, such as that the library should try to purchase the collection as a whole at any price, or should purchase it or parts of it if the price was right, or should pass it up. That determination, and the detailed account of the documents' contents, would have to wait until I saw the materials themselves.

I knew I was going to have to look at a lot of documents in a short period of time, and I prepared for the trip by rereading what I and others had written about the existing manuscripts (my own work in this area was more than twenty-five years old) and by gathering together photocopies of the known documents with which I'd likely want to compare the new ones along with other reference materials. I photocopied about five hundred relevant pages from the reproductions in *The James Joyce Archive* and the separate facsimile of the Rosenbach Manuscript (the manuscript that Joyce sold to Quinn, a beginning-to-nearly-end handwritten document that is partly a fair copy and partly a working draft), the Spielberg and Scholes catalogs of the Buffalo and Cornell collections, Phillip Herring's editions of the British Library notesheets and some of the Buffalo manuscripts, and some transcriptions of Joyce's early notes in Herbert Gorman's 1939 biography. I taught my classes in London, Ontario, on Monday and Tuesday and drove back to Toronto late Tuesday evening; my wife, Molly, and I took a Wednesday-morning flight from Toronto to London; and on Thursday morning I was led into a working area of Sotheby's to look at the documents. I took out and booted up my handheld computer with its primitive notetaking program as well as a searchable text of *Ulysses* that I had installed on it, connected its separate fold-out keyboard and prepared it for use, spread out the photocopies I had brought with me, and began to open the folders in the box that was placed in front of me.

It was an amazing experience. Wherever they had been, the manuscripts were in terrific shape, in much better condition than the materials in the existing library collections which have been handled by many people since becoming public. Some of the documents were less interesting than others, but for well over half of them I went from one thrilling experience to another. A very early notebook contained Joyce's handwritten versions of his aesthetic theories. This document included the so-called "Paris Notebook" and "Pola Notebook" that we have had only in Gorman's transcriptions and in subsequent printed versions in the *Critical Writings*, *The Workshop of Daedalus*, and the more recent *Occasional, Critical, and Political Writing*.[4] There were several sets of notes for *Ulysses*—most seemed to be late ones, similar to notes we already have, but one notebook appeared to be early, as Molly was spelled "Mollie" more than once in it.[5] A copybook contained a very early draft of "Proteus," an even earlier one than the draft of that episode at Buffalo, which had until then been considered the earliest surviving draft of any part of *Ulysses*. And, both thrilling and strange, following "Proteus" in this copybook was a very early draft of "Sirens." There was a draft for "Scylla and Charybdis," probably not Buffalo's missing draft but, nevertheless, something we had never before possessed. My speculations about the "Sirens" and "Cyclops" copybooks turned out to be correct: they were the other halves of the Buffalo documents. The "Oxen of the Sun" materials completely filled in both of the fragmentary stages represented by Buffalo's eight copybooks. There was yet another draft of "Circe" to accompany the one the National Library had acquired in December 2000. The "Ithaca" and "Penelope" manuscripts were almost certainly not, it turned out, evidence of Joyce's work on the episodes from as early as 1916, but they were fascinating nevertheless, the first pre–Rosenbach Manuscript evidence to surface for either episode.

There were other materials as well: early reading notes from Dante; a typescript of the *Ulysses* schema (with the same contents as the one Stuart Gilbert published in 1930 in his *James Joyce's "Ulysses": A Study*, but in a different typing from other known copies); and several sets of proofs and typescript fragments for *Finnegans Wake*, mostly for the printings of some of the chapters in *transition*, along with a few pages of notes.

Assessing the manuscripts' authenticity was easy: I had no doubt that they were Joyce's. Not only did several of them precisely fill in known gaps in the existing collections, but many of the *Ulysses* notes and drafts exhibited the writing and revising habits that we have been familiar with from the manuscripts we have been studying for the last fifty years: crowded paragraph-like units of notes with many items crossed out with a red, blue, or green crayon; drafts written on the rectos (right-hand pages) of a copybook, with the versos (left-hand pages) left blank for additions, the writing starting near the top left corner of the page and the margin gradually widening as the writing moves down the page, so that the last lines often cover less than half the page's width. Even the colors of the Roman numerals on the covers of the numbered "Oxen of the Sun" drafts matched those at Buffalo. Everything fit together.

In all there were twenty-six documents, not counting the many loose proof pages for the *Wake*. I looked them over one at a time during the two days I had, feeling at times like a mature genetic critic fitting pieces together in a way only a few other people would be able to do and at other times like a child let loose in a magical candy shop: often I felt like both at once. I noticed what I could, given the average of half an hour I had available for each document. By 5 P.M. on Friday I was both exhilarated and exhausted.

In addition to the contents of the materials, I learned some other facts in London. I found out who owned these materials, a question that had nagged me from the start. Kissane didn't want to mention the owner's name in any of our phone conversations before we met, and from the minute I saw his checklist I wondered who might possess a collection of this scope and magnitude. He now told me confidentially that the owner was Alexis Léon, son of Joyce's Parisian friends Paul and Lucie Léon. (Paul Léon, a Jew, was killed by the Nazis in 1942.) Journalists who interviewed Alexis Léon after the sale was announced provided additional information: one reported that he "was not aware of the treasure trove he possessed until 2000" because "the effects of his mother, who had died in 1972, . . . had for a long time been placed in storage," and another wrote that "the manuscripts acquired this year formed part of Lucie Léon's own so-called 'Joyceana'—a special collection of books relating to Joyce."[6]

Because of the delicate negotiations between Alexis Léon and the National Library that were already ongoing and would likely soon intensify, I was asked to keep the manuscripts' existence completely secret. In London, though, I also learned that my friend Daniel Ferrer in Paris had already seen the documents and had been asked not to disclose anything about them until the sale was accomplished. We were both greatly relieved to learn that someone else had seen the manuscripts, since each of us knew that the other had taken notes and made some determinations regarding the manuscripts' contents and significance and also that there was one other person to whom we could talk about them. Ferrer helped me to determine several of the relationships between these new documents and existing ones, especially for "Proteus," "Sirens," and "Circe."

I faced the first test of my agreement to keep my knowledge of these materials secret almost immediately. After I finished investigating the documents on Friday afternoon and met briefly with Kissane to summarize my findings, Molly and I went out to dinner with two friends I had known since graduate school thirty years earlier, Ron Bush (who had recently moved to England to take up a professorship at Oxford) and Bill Quillian (who was on sabbatical from Mount Holyoke College and visiting Ron). Both of them work on Joyce and would be very interested in what I had seen, and both, naturally, wanted to know why I had popped up in London without any warning for two days in November. I was bursting with an eagerness to talk about the manuscripts, and especially to tell Bill that there was a draft of "Scylla and Charybdis" (the episode in which he specialized) among the documents. But I told them only that I had been looking at really exciting Joyce materials and resisted saying anything more about what the documents were or who had asked me to look at them. They prodded, but not too strenuously. After that, keeping the secret was easier, even at the Modern Language Association convention six weeks later in New Orleans and the Sarasota Joyce conference the following February, mainly because no one had any reason be curious or to suspect anything.

After one free day in London, I returned to Toronto on Sunday, taught my classes in London, Ontario, from Monday to Wednesday, and, back in Toronto on Thursday, began to prepare my report on the manuscripts for the National Library. Over the next couple of weeks, with the help of my notes from my two days at Sotheby's and all the photoreprint editions, transcriptions, catalogs, and scholarly works—as well as e-mail correspondence with Ferrer—I produced my report and sent it to the library in early December.

It was easy to make a general assessment of the manuscripts' value. I recommended that the National Library try to acquire the entire collection if it possibly could. If the library could purchase this phenomenal new group of Joyce materials, then it, Dublin, and Ireland would instantly become a major center for Joyce studies. After describing the collection in general as enthusiastically as I could, I went on to discuss each document individually in as much detail as I thought would be useful for the library to make its case that it should try to acquire the collection and then, if it decided to go ahead, to raise whatever huge amount of money it would need to purchase the manuscripts.

I knew that the negotiations that would go on after the library received my report would take quite a while. When I needed something to get anxious about in the next few months, I worried that the sale would not go through and that, somehow, the manuscripts would disappear before I was able to see them again or anyone else ever got to look at them at all.

After I submitted my report, Kissane told me that the next stages in the sale would take several months, and that the entire deal could very easily fall through. He would get in touch with me again when there was any news. I didn't hear from him until early May 2002, when he called to say that most of the details had been worked out and that the sale would probably be completed and made public sometime in late May or early June. A national election was taking place on May 17, and the sale wouldn't be announced until after that. Confidentiality was still important: the final negotiations were sensitive, and the agreement could fall apart even at this late stage. He also asked if I would come to Dublin for the press conference announcing the library's acquisition of the materials and read a short, maybe ten-minute, statement at the event. In mid-May he called again to say that the dates for the announcement had been set. The manuscripts would be brought to Dublin from London (where they had remained all the time since I had seen them) on May 29, and the press conference at the National Library would occur the next day. In a coincidence that of course delighted me, the press conference was scheduled to take place on my fifty-fifth birthday.

Molly and I arrived in Dublin around noon on May 29—at almost the exact time, we learned a little later, that the plane carrying the manuscripts from London landed in another part of the Dublin Airport. Their arrival was announced on television and the Web later that day and in print newspapers the next morning. The National Library had agreed to pay £8 million, which converted to about €12.6 million or $11.7 million. It would pay the costs over three years, with over €5 million coming from the Heritage Fund set up by the Irish Ministry of Arts, Heritage, Gaeltacht, and the Islands ("Gaeltacht" refers to the Irish-speaking regions of Ireland) and the remainder from the Allied Irish Bank Group, operating under the Irish government's tax credit scheme. "At one bound," Terence Killeen wrote in the *Irish Times*, "the National Library, which already had impressive Joyce holdings, has established itself as one of the world's major Joyce repositories." Introducing what he called a "vast and previously unsuspected archive of manuscript material by James Joyce," Killeen also reported that "frustratingly enough, only a glimpse of the collection was offered" at the airport.[7]

Early the next morning I was awakened in my hotel room by a phone call from Stephen James Joyce, who, like almost everyone else, had just learned about the manuscripts' existence and also about their sale to the National Library of Ireland. He was furious that he had been kept in the dark during the preceding months, and he told me that, because of my involvement with the library and my silence regarding the manuscripts, I should consider becoming a garbage collector in New York City because I'd never obtain his permission to quote a Joyce text again. I was so flabbergasted by the remark that I wrote it down immediately after the phone call ended so that I wouldn't forget it.[8]

After that, the day improved immensely. Enticed by the partial information that was available, the couple of hundred people who gathered for the press conference at the National Library at noon were eager for more details. The speakers included Brendan O Donoghue, the library's director; Síle de Valera, the Minister of Arts, Heritage, Gaeltacht, and the Islands, who had made the library's purchase of the manuscripts possible; Dr. Tony Scott, chair of the library's Council of Trustees, which in the beginning and at several other points during the long process authorized the library to try to purchase the manuscripts (I had been involved with the manuscripts for eight months since Kissane's first phone call and for six months since I had seen the documents, but for the library the process had been going on for more than sixteen months); and me. Also present were Lochlann Quinn, chair of the board of the AIB Group, and Mr. and Mrs. Alexis Léon. In my talk I tried to describe the manuscripts in a way that would make sense to nonspecialists, and I also wanted to convey the excitement of these materials. (Appendix 1 contains my remarks from the press conference.) A beautiful and beguiling exhibit of a few manuscript pages—all the more impressive given that Kissane and his staff had only part of one afternoon and part of the next morning to assemble it—permitted the audience at least to sample the new collection. As I talked with people while we looked at the pages, it was obvious how amazing they found the manuscripts to be, of course, but it was also clear that they were uncertain whether to be more surprised that the National Library now possessed such a major collection of Joyce documents or that the secret had been kept from everyone in Dublin for well over a year.

After the press conference, the manuscripts received a great deal of attention as newspapers, radio and television stations, and Web sites started to cover the story. The next day John McCourt, organizer of the Eighteenth International James Joyce Symposium, which was about to take place in Trieste, called me to ask if I could fill in for one of the plenary speakers who had withdrawn and talk about the new manuscripts. Now released from my vow of silence, I was glad to do that, and on June 18, 2002, I presented a version of what I have written here, illustrated by a chart comparing the extant *Ulysses* manuscripts from before 2000 with the archive from after 2002. (Appendix 2 presents that chart.) Amazingly, the manuscripts became the main topic of interest at the symposium—manuscript study, often considered an arcane bypath of Joyce scholarship, now seemed to inspire mainstream interest. After that, the National Library made the materials available for scholarly investigation. Unlike in the past, when Joyce manuscripts sat unread in library collections for years, the interest and enthusiasm demonstrated at the symposium quickly extended into scholars visiting the National Library to look at and study the documents. A new phase of *Ulysses* scholarship had begun, inspired by these fascinating new manuscripts.[9]

■

Near the end of *Ulysses*, just before Leopold Bloom and Stephen Dedalus part, the encyclopedically voluble "Ithaca" narrator tells us that Stephen Dedalus "affirmed his significance as a conscious rational animal proceeding syllogistically from the known to the unknown and a conscious rational reagent between a micro and a macrocosm ineluctably constructed upon the incertitude of the void" (*U* 17:1012–15). Barely understanding what Stephen has said, Bloom takes comfort from the fact that, again in the narrator's words, "as a competent keyless citizen he had proceeded energetically from the unknown to the known through the incertitude of the void" (*U* 17:1019–20). Stephen moves abstractly out from what he earlier called "the now, the here" (*U* 9:89), whereas Bloom progresses experientially into what once was an unknown future but now is a known present.

Stephen's void is the gulf between the known and the unknown, Bloom's between the present and the future (or, eventually, the past and the present). Genetic critics—scholars who study an author's manuscripts and writing processes—face voids of various kinds as they confront the gap between the manuscript archive, the avant-texte, and the text as it was published, and especially the gap between the traces of the creative process that the documents permit them to study and the process itself. They attempt to reconstruct the process from the work's origins and early stages, when its future was unknown, to its published state, trying, like Bloom, to proceed energetically and experientially along with the author. But also, like Stephen, they start from the known, published work and attempt to discover whatever there is to know about the work's earlier states and the author's writing, both of them unknown and unpredictable, graspable partly through tangible observation but partly only through reasoning, extrapolation, and Stephen's syllogizing. The process, the writing, is knowable only to a degree. Bloom counters Stephen's thinking when he is described as concluding that there is "no known method from the known to the unknown" (*U* 17:1140–41). In a parallel way, the writing process will always to some extent remain a void.

Louis Hay memorably describes the "moment of the writing itself" as "stretched out between the author's life and the sheet of paper like a drumskin on which the pen beats its message."[10] Hay's drumskin, in some ways like Stephen's and Bloom's void, is a border between the known and the unknown, between the author's conception and the words that he or she can get onto the paper or screen and also between the existing text and the scholar's attempt to reconstruct and interpret the writing process. Unlike the void, however, the drumskin does not have to remain silent. Genetic criticism lets us hear the music of the manuscripts, the drumbeat of the drafts.

What happens when the unknown becomes more known not because we proceed more energetically or with better syllogisms but because the record itself changes? Can we hear a new drumbeat rhythm from Joyce's pen? Three details that I noticed during my first encounter with the newly available manuscripts for *Ulysses* can suggest the beginnings of some answers.

My first example comes from the very end of *Ulysses*. We have known for a long time that Joyce only gradually built up the rhythms of the last words of Molly Bloom's monologue—tapping out yeses with his pen on the drumskin of the proofs. The fair copy of the book's last words reads "and first I put my arms around him and drew him down to me so he could feel my breasts all perfume and I said I will yes."[11] He added "yes and his heart was going like mad" after "perfume" on the typescript, "yes" after "I said" on the first placards, and another "yes" before "I said" on the second placards, where he also capitalized the final "Yes." On the fourth placards and first page proofs he added more yeses a few lines up.[12]

The National Library's "Penelope" draft contains a big surprise at the end: Joyce originally wrote "and I said I would" before he crossed out "would" and, in a *currente calamo* revision (a change made on the fly, in the process of writing rather than later on), wrote "will" next to it on the line, followed by the closing "yes."[13]

Richard Ellmann claimed long ago that Joyce came up with "yes" as the last word of *Ulysses* only in mid-1921 as he was drafting "Penelope," and our sense of any genetic instability lying behind the ending of *Ulysses* has focused for the most part on that word.[14] The new draft reveals something else: even after he had presumably settled on the concluding "yes," Joyce's sense of the ending's grammar, and hence of the emotional force of Molly's closing memory, was in flux. The draft's original ending is grammatically smoother than the revised version, since it continues Molly's thoughts in a consistent verb tense, but it is also much less dramatic. The switch to "will" turns the last words into a memory of spoken dialogue as it changes the ending from the subdued subjunctive "would" to the decisive indicative "will." This revision of one simple word to another says as much to me about Joyce's genius as anything else I know about how he wrote.

In discussing three different texts of Marianne Moore's "Poetry," Jerome McGann notes that we probably still "read" the longer thirty-line version even when we see in front of us the three-line poem she published in her *Complete Poems*, and he argues that the "interplay" of the texts is "at the centre of the reading experience."[15] Thanks to the National Library's "Penelope" draft, "will" no longer stands as the only possible penultimate word of *Ulysses*. The superseded "would" now appears just under it in the palimpsest and allows the reader who sees or knows about it to experience the oscillating mobile of the alternatives.

My second example, an especially appropriate one in the light of Hay's metaphor of an author's pen beating out a text on a drumskin, comes from the "Sirens" episode. The National Library collection contains two new documents for this episode, one a very early draft (in the same copybook as an early draft of "Proteus") and the other a later draft of the first half of the episode. (As I've mentioned, this is the first half of a draft that is continued in a Buffalo manuscript.)[16] The early document is quite startling: ten pages of a very early draft of part of the episode, followed by more than fifteen pages containing fragmentary scenes. Most intriguingly, this draft of the episode that both deals with music and is written in the form of verbal music is pre-musical—it contains musical effects in some of its words, but the musical structure that intrigues, bewilders, fascinates, and sometimes infuriates readers of the published text is completely absent. The draft suggests an episode substantially similar to the first nine episodes of *Ulysses*, with their combination of narration, dialogue, and interior monologue plus local variations in language and imagery based on each episode's particular theme. In that sense, the "Sirens" draft seems like the early parts of the first draft of the "Cyclops" episode, which, as I argued in *"Ulysses" in Progress*, indicate that Joyce at least briefly planned to continue using the narration-dialogue-interior-monologue technique before he eliminated it from "Cyclops" and, except for the second half of "Nausicaa," from *Ulysses*.[17]

The later of the two new drafts is most immediately noteworthy because of its inside front cover. There Joyce wrote and underlined the words "Fuga per canonem," followed by eight numbered Italian terms, including "soggetto," "contrasoggetto," "esposizioni," and "pedale." In both his 1920 and 1921 schemas for *Ulysses*, Joyce named the "technic" of "Sirens" as "fuga per canonem," and in an August 1919 letter to Harriet Shaw Weaver he wrote that various passages she had mentioned in a letter to him "are all the eight regular parts of a *fuga per canonem*."[18] Critics have been puzzled and vexed by what, if anything, Joyce meant by these words. The copybook, contrary to some of the earlier speculation, indicates that Joyce was serious about writing a verbal fugue. His list also suggests what he meant in his letter by the eight "parts" of a fugue. Critics have usually been frustrated in their attempts to locate eight musical voices in the episode, but the list indicates that by "parts" Joyce meant something like structural sections.[19] What is clear is that he imposed a musical structure onto an episode that was already partially drafted, somewhat parallel to the way he superimposed the newspaper heads onto the "Aeolus" episode to break up the episode into a series of small article-sized units. (In "The Mystery of the Fuga per Canonem Solved," Susan Brown has identified Joyce's source for his list of terms as Ralph Vaughan Williams's entry on "Fugue" in the 1906 edition of *Grove's Dictionary of Music and Musicians*, and she has also demonstrated that Joyce mistook *fuga per canonem*, a specific type of fugue mentioned in the entry, for the more general musical form.)

At the top of the later draft's first recto, Joyce wrote the words "Repeat phrases episode." The draft does not include the bizarre, and notorious, series of fragmentary phrases that open the published version of the episode and that are usually interpreted as something like a musical overture or an orchestra tuning up before a performance, and this note might be Joyce's reminder to himself to extract some phrases in order to construct that opening.

The two "Sirens" documents have the potential to significantly affect our sense of how Joyce wrote *Ulysses*. The earlier one, located as it is in the same copybook as a very early version of "Proteus" (which now becomes the earliest extant draft of any part of *Ulysses*), suggests that "Sirens" was drafted quite early, perhaps even as early as the first three Stephen Dedalus episodes. This might be what Joyce meant in a letter from October 1916, almost three years before the fair copy of "Sirens," where he said that he had written part of the middle of the book (*L* 2:387). I had always assumed that he was referring to the fourth Stephen episode, "Scylla and Charybdis," but he might have been speaking about "Sirens" and maybe even other episodes in addition to, or instead of, "Scylla."

The "Sirens" drafts also confirm speculations about Joyce's writing of *Ulysses* that Rodney Wilson Owen made in the early 1980s. In *James Joyce and the Beginnings of "Ulysses,"* Owen studied the few documents from the period 1912 to 1918 that were extant at the time in an attempt to piece together what Joyce might have done in those years. In particular, he compared some notes at Cornell with the few *Ulysses* drafts from those years and concluded that "the first third of 'Sirens' was earlier and more complete than the rest" and that "the presence of the notebook echoes in 'Proteus,' 'Scylla,' and to a lesser extent in 'Sirens' and 'Wandering Rocks' suggests these episodes were among the earliest planned."[20] After twenty years, the new documents show that Owen was correct to put "Sirens" into the group of early written episodes (his largely ignored book should be read seriously now for its suggestions as to how *Ulysses* might have developed), with implications yet to be discovered.

My third and final example involves the most prominent restored passage in Hans Walter Gabler's edition of *Ulysses*. In the "Scylla and Charybdis" episode, as Stephen discusses his wound-and-the-bow theory of *Hamlet* with three skeptical listeners in the National Library of Ireland, he refers to the major tragedies and then asks "how the shadow lifts" in Shakespeare's last plays (*U* 9:402). He names Pericles and his daughter Marina (in *Pericles*) before his thoughts and spoken words get briefly deflected. When he returns to the topic, he again names Marina and also daughters from *The Tempest* and *The Winter's Tale*:

> —Marina, Stephen said, a child of storm, Miranda, a wonder, Perdita, that which was lost. What was lost is given back to him: his daughter's child. *My dearest wife*, Pericles says, *was like this maid*. Will any man love the daughter if he has not loved the mother?
>
> —The art of being a grandfather, Mr Best gan murmur. *L'art d'être grandp*. . . . .
>
> —Will he not see reborn in her, with the memory of his own youth added, another image?
>
>   Do you know what you are talking about? Love, yes. Word known to all men. *Amor vero aliquid alicui bonum vult unde et ea quae concupiscimus* . . .
>
> —His own image to a man with that queer thing genius is the standard

of all experience, material and moral. (U 9:421-33 [Joyce's italics and ellipses])

The text in the Gabler edition includes a line of dialogue and a paragraph of interior monologue (from "—Will he not" to "*concupiscimus . . .*") that are not in any previous printed texts of *Ulysses*. Gabler explains the absence of these lines from the previously published texts by speculating that, after typing one phrase from the lost final working draft ending in an ellipsis and underlined to signal italics (ending with "*grandp. . . . .*"), the typist jumped to another phrase also underlined and with an ellipsis (ending with "*concupiscimus . . .*") and omitted the words between the two ellipses.[21] The restored phrase, "Love, yes. Word known to all men," is especially intriguing in the light of Stephen's questions from earlier and later in *Ulysses* as to what the word known to all men might be (*U* 3:435, 15:4192-93).

The passage exists in the National Library's "Scylla and Charybdis" manuscript, but, interestingly, only "Love, yes" forms part of the draft's original text. "Word known to all men" is an addition. The original paragraph of Stephen's interior monologue in the new draft thus reads, "Do you know what you are talking about? Love, yes. *Amor vero aliquid alicui bonum vult unde et ea quae concupiscimus. . . .*" (The first of the two underlined/italicized phrases, "*L'art d'être grandp. . . . . ,*" is not in the Rosenbach Manuscript fair copy. Gabler speculates that it is present in the lost final working draft, since it is part of the typed text on the typescript).[22] This forms an unbroken string of thoughts. Stephen's mind darts from detail to detail: from Marina to Miranda to Perdita, then to Pericles and to Shakespeare and his (according to Stephen) troubled relationship with his wife and daughter, which brings in the question of love. Stephen resists being deflected a second time when Richard Best picks up not the idea of love but the role of the grandfather and then answers "Love, yes" as the answer to his self-interrogation regarding whether he knows what he is talking about. The fragments from St. Thomas Aquinas, which Don Gifford and Robert J. Seidman identify as conjoining various phrases from one sentence in *Summa Contra Gentiles*, distinguish between true love and desire: "love wills something to someone . . . will some good . . . when we want a thing . . . desire it . . ."[23] In their form, these fragments resemble Stephen's skimming of Deasy's letter about foot-and-mouth disease earlier in the book, where a few prominent phrases registered in his mind (*U* 2:332-37). In their content, the fragments and the sentence they come from establish a contrast between selfless love, which "wishes something to somebody," and more selfish desire, in which "we rather love ourselves for whom we desire" the something. (The full passage is "For love wishes something to somebody: hence the things that we desire, we are properly said to 'desire,' not to 'love,' but in them we rather love ourselves for whom we desire them.")[24] Stephen then picks up his last spoken words about a granddaughter and "another image" as he talks about the artist whose standard of experience is "his own image," a phrase that William T. Noon, in his study of Joyce and Aquinas (published in 1957, long before Gabler restored Stephen's quotation from Aquinas to the text of *Ulysses*), links to Aquinas's "idea of man as an image of God."[25]

What, then, about "word known to all men"? Since the publication of Gabler's edition in 1984, critics have focused on it as the core of the restored passage. They have usually seen the phrase as a deliberate echo of the earlier passage in "Proteus" where Stephen thinks, "Touch me. Soft eyes. Soft soft soft hand. I am lonely here. O, touch me soon, now. What is that word known to all men? I am quiet here alone. Sad too. Touch, touch me" (*U* 3:434–36). They also connect it to Stephen's later plea to his mother, in one of the "Circe" fantasies, to "Tell me the word, . . . if you know now. The word known to all men" (*U* 15:4192–93 [my ellipsis]). His boast to Bloom in "Ithaca" notwithstanding, Stephen here seems to want to proceed from the unknown to the known—or from what he thinks is known to everyone but him—not by syllogism but by interrogation, by catechism, by recognizing Bloom's strategy of relying on personal experience. If Joyce at least sketched out "Scylla and Charybdis" around the time of "Proteus," a conjunction between those two episodes would not be surprising. But "word known to all men" appears in very different contexts in each of its three appearances in *Ulysses*: guilty and erotic in "Proteus" and guilty and anguished in "Circe," but theological and artistic in "Scylla."[26] This suggests to me that the three phrases have little connection with each other.

It is possible, of course, that Joyce added "word known to all men" in order to restore some text that he neglected to copy into the draft. As an insert, however, it seems to throw the passage off balance, disrupting the movement from "Love, yes" to the "*Amor*" of the Aquinas quotation. Isolated as an addition to an already consistent passage in the "Scylla" draft, the phrase can be interpreted in at least three different ways. First, it may be what it is often assumed to be: Stephen's answer to himself that "Love" is the "word known to all men." Second, the phrase is itself part of Stephen's answer to his question, "Do you know what you are talking about?" He first answers "Love, yes," but, as if recognizing the inadequacy of that response, adds that love is a word known to everyone. Interestingly, Stephen seems to assume that the word's being known to everyone demonstrates that he knows what he is talking about, whereas the original problem that he seemed to recognize was that he has not experienced a father's love for a daughter. (Gifford and Seidman say that "the key to the mystery seems to be not the word itself but the word-made-manifest. Only in the experience of love can the word known to all men be truly *known*.")[27] Third, "word known to all men" might be a quotation that pops into Stephen's head, perhaps a response to the word "love" that he thinks of as if by rote association. (Earlier, in the "Aeolus" episode, he listens to Professor MacHugh quote John F. Taylor—"I heard his words and their meaning was revealed to me"—and a phrase from Augustine enters his mind, as if involuntarily: "It was revealed to me that those things are good which yet are corrupted which neither if they were supremely good nor unless they were good could be corrupted. Ah, curse you! That's saint Augustine" [U 7:839–44].) If a quotation, it might be a phrase from the Bible or from any of the biblical commentators that Stephen knows so well, including Aquinas. Rather than identifying love as the word known to all men, it might mean something like love as the means by which the Word was made known to all men. "Word known to all men" thus appears more like a momentary, isolated mental intrusion than as an answer to Stephen's questions.

To appropriate Louis Hay's metaphor one last time, the new *Ulysses* manuscripts at the National Library of Ireland are allowing scholars to begin to develop a more detailed and subtler sense of the drumskin on which Joyce tapped out his book. In the rhythms of Molly Bloom's concluding yeses, the fugal structure of "Sirens," and the concordance or dissonance of the "word known to all men," they provide us with a better opportunity than we have ever had before to listen to the *Ulysses* manuscripts. The gap between the known and the unknown will never be fully closed, but in small and large ways, the new manuscripts will help scholars of Joyce's writing processes move a little farther toward the known.

2

When First I Saw, Part 1

Choosing and Being Chosen by *Ulysses*

I first read *Ulysses* when I was nineteen, in the fall of 1966 at the start of my sophomore year at Dartmouth College. I had been miserable during much of my freshman year there, to the point of considering transferring to another college. Because during my high school years I had planned to become a mathematician and my teachers told me about Dartmouth's outstanding math department, it was the school I most wanted to attend. No one in my family had gone to any college, and I was stunned and thrilled when I was accepted there. But I came from a working-class Jewish family in suburban Buffalo, and I felt overwhelmed by the wealth, privilege, and New England WASP-iness that seemed to be everywhere around me once I arrived. My high school was a large public one, and I had a particularly hard time adjusting to tiny, isolated Hanover, New Hampshire, and to the absence of women at the college. I felt lonely for my high school girlfriend, Molly Peacock, who was at a college three hundred miles away in New York State, especially as our relationship was falling apart. Dartmouth's academic life was almost everything I could have asked for. Only almost, though: my math courses disappointed me, but I found myself increasingly attracted to my English classes. As I finished my freshman year, I had many doubts but decided to return to Dartmouth in the fall, and as I signed up for my fall courses I officially switched my major from math to English.

Back in Hanover in September a few days before classes started, I was only slightly less unhappy than I had been the year before. But then on a Monday afternoon, I went to a large lecture hall for the start of a course on the twentieth-century European novel. At 2:00, a smallish, thin man, balding and with wire-rimmed glasses, looking quite formal in a jacket and tie, came into the room holding a large three-ring binder, which he opened at the podium. Professor Peter Bien handed out a class schedule and many pages of blue mimeographed notes on Joyce's *Ulysses*, the first book on the course, and started to speak in a somewhat high-pitched voice, clear, articulate, and serious, as he read a lecture from the large binder. He wasted little time, was thoroughly organized, packed even the first class with a great deal of information, rarely made small talk or told jokes—and held the audience, well over one hundred of us, completely spellbound from almost his first word.

That initial class set the tone for all the others. During each hour, Mr. Bien was full of information and interpretations, intense, serious, rarely funny but far from humorless. I remember hardly ever being bored. We covered an amazing amount of material: works by Joyce, Marcel Proust, Franz Kafka, D. H. Lawrence, Thomas Mann, André Malroux, and Nikos Kazantzakis. The first three weeks, the ones that covered *Ulysses*, turned out for me to be the meal; the other classes dealing with all those other wonderful novels were only side dishes. I dutifully read the assigned pages about Stephen Dedalus for the first couple of classes, wondering a little why people made such a fuss about Joyce's book. I even got through the third episode, although I barely understood a word of it. In his lectures, Mr. Bien surprised me by talking about what I had treated as routine reading assignments with an extraordinary amount of enthusiasm, finding much more humanity in the episodes than I had seen and also (at least in the first two) much more humor. But even though Stephen Dedalus was like me in many ways—college age, unhappy and confused, moving away from his family, no longer practicing his childhood religion, lonely without a girlfriend—he hardly interested me.

Things started to happen when we got to the fourth episode, though. Leopold Bloom in many ways lived precisely the kind of life I was trying to avoid: no university education; moving from job to job; full of half knowledge; married to a woman about to betray him by having an affair; and, a Jewish man in Catholic Dublin, an outsider in the only home city he ever knew. And, at a time when people were telling us never to trust anyone over thirty, he was nearly my father's age. Despite all this, he riveted me.

I devoured the episodes that dealt with Leopold Bloom, looking forward to each afternoon's class and anticipating what Mr. Bien would tell me that I hadn't noticed on my own. The classes were as full of information and interpretation as ever, but I noticed something else now as well: Mr. Bien wasn't just analyzing *Ulysses*, he also seemed to like Leopold Bloom a lot. In many different ways, he was demonstrating that *Ulysses* was worth reading and that Leopold Bloom was a fictional character worth knowing and spending time with, even a great deal of time. I dutifully wrote down everything I could catch as he read his lectures, even though I doubt whether I understood much of what I was recording. I noted that he described Joyce as one of the healthiest authors of his period—well, who wouldn't look healthy next to Lawrence and Kafka?—because he saw human vice as funny and not as tragic. And Mr. Bien talked about *Ulysses* and Leopold Bloom in terms of acting effectively in the world without overlooking the fact of problematic human motivation and in terms of preserving optimism and even lyricism in a life where things are often very different. At the age of nineteen, I wasn't at all prepared to confront issues like complex reactions to vice and betrayal or the multiple facets of human motivation. But I heard what I wanted and needed from both Joyce and Mr. Bien, and what I heard was enough.

My enthusiasm for *Ulysses* grew and grew as the novel progressed and the class sessions went by. Each new episode offered an unexpected and different kind of thrill (well, almost each one: "Oxen of the Sun" put me to sleep several times), and I was elated when we got to the last episode and Molly Bloom's sleepy, sexy, unpunctuated closing monologue, although also a little disappointed to realize that the book had come to an end.

I lost myself in *Ulysses* and in the classes, and allowing that to happen was wonderful. I had never thought about Dublin at all before, but now Hanover seemed like a tiny version of Joyce's city. Like Leopold Bloom I saw a POST NO BILLS sign on a wall (or did it actually say POST 110 PILLS, as Bloom mentally rewrites such a sign? [*U* 8:101]), seeming to prove to me that *Ulysses* was everywhere and that any place could be the setting for *Ulysses*.

Those three weeks changed me forever. But why did *Ulysses* appeal to me so strongly? I didn't think too much about this then, engrossed as I was with reading about Leopold Bloom, discovering that everyday modern characters in an ordinary city could be equivalents of Homer's classical heroes, meeting the challenges of the novel's length and demands, and enjoying its puzzles and games. Those responses were the only answers I needed. Just getting through *Ulysses*, no matter how much or how little I was understanding, felt like a triumph, but its comedy and humor, even the silly puns and fart jokes, made it a pleasure much more than an endurance test, and its passages of direct and graphic sexiness provided an added treat, well worth the tedium of some turgid pages on Aristotle and Catholic heretics that preceded them. In ways I could never have imagined a year or even a month earlier, I was smitten by a book.

■

Now, more than forty years later, *Ulysses* is always with me. I reread it often and talk, write, and think about it regularly. Every year, I guide students at the University of Western Ontario and also adults in New York City and Toronto through it. The adults in particular have often asked me why I spend so much of my time with this one novel. Standard, potted answers have always been easy to supply: besides repeating my explanations from when I was nineteen, I can explain that *Ulysses* is a groundbreaking work of fiction and also that in various best-of-the-twentieth-century lists it was named the greatest novel, Joyce was designated the top writer, and Leopold Bloom, Molly Bloom, and Stephen Dedalus were all in the first ten among the hundred best characters.[1] These responses usually ward off further prodding. But they've stopped satisfying me, and other questions have joined the original one in my mind. How did I end up as an English professor and not the mathematician that throughout most of my teenage years I assumed I would become? Why *Ulysses* and not, say, *The Canterbury Tales* or *Paradise Lost* or *Emma* or *Moby-Dick* or *Middlemarch*, all of which I read at about the same time? Why *Ulysses* when I was twenty and thirty but not something else when I was forty or fifty or sixty?

Characters in *Ulysses* often wonder why Molly chose Leopold Bloom. "Why did she me?" Bloom asks himself, simply and eloquently (*U* 11:732), and various characters offer many different possible answers depending on who is responding and when during the day the question is posed, with no single or overarching answer ever given. Just before he thinks of the question, and incorporating words from the opera *Martha* that Simon Dedalus is singing, Bloom recalls his initial glimpse of Molly: "First night when first I saw her at Mat Dillon's in Terenure. Yellow, black lace she wore. Musical chairs. We two the last. Fate. After her. Fate" (*U* 11:725–26). Fate, coincidence, fortuitous circumstance? These explanations, while perhaps true to some extent, are far too simple. For one thing, they may say something about Bloom's attraction to Molly, but they completely ignore the issue of why she chose him. *Ulysses* trains its readers to put aside expectations of simple or even complicatedly single answers to questions, unless the query involves why café workers put chairs upside down on tables at night (*U* 16:1709–10). And as I've pondered my parallel question about *Ulysses*—"Why did I it?" or maybe even "Why did it me?"—I've realized that it too resists a simple or single answer.

My memory of my first encounter with *Ulysses* is like a draft of a work. That work can be my life, and I can look back at those few weeks in 1966 as a first draft of the Joyce scholar and teacher I became. But I can also, from the perspective of the present, investigate that draft from various angles to try to see what each new glance reveals about my initial response to *Ulysses*. "Me. And me now," Bloom movingly thinks as he eats his lunch at Davy Byrne's pub and recalls lying with Molly on Howth Hill sixteen years earlier (*U* 8:917). I can look back at my young self, or my various young selves, when the forty years to come were an unknown void and, with a mixture of satisfaction, nostalgia, and embarrassment, compare the people I see and trace the process of how the then-unknown future became the now-known present and remembered past.

But it isn't as simple as that. During the Shakespeare discussion in "Scylla and Charybdis," Stephen makes two mental observations about his present and past selves, one somewhat contradicting the other: "In the intense instant of imagination, when the mind, Shelley says, is a fading coal, that which I was is that which I am and that which in possibility I may come to be. So in the future, the sister of the past, I may see myself as I sit here now but by reflection from that which then I shall be" (*U* 9:381–85). Finn Fordham, who quotes these thoughts, goes on to conclude that "the self of the past is continually refracted to produce multiple sibling selves."[2] These earlier versions of myself, those sibling selves, are, to other people, I hope, as well as to me, worth viewing on their own, apart from their place in a historical process that led somewhere. A person's relationship to a work of art is just as complicated as one person's relationship to another or a writer's to his or her work, and my dissatisfaction with my easy explanations about why I've spent so much of my life with *Ulysses* makes me want to look at and understand as many aspects of my first reaction to Joyce's novel as I can. The details will be different, of course, but everyone who responds strongly to a work of art has a similar story to tell.

Can Louis Hay's provocative suggestion that the "moment of the writing itself" is "stretched out between the author's life and the sheet of paper like a drumskin on which the pen beats its message" also apply to a life?[3] Can the moment of living be seen as stretched out like a drumskin, with memory in all its plentitude but also in its gaps and distortions supplying the drumstick? If genetic criticism can let us hear the music of the manuscripts, can observing a life through genetic criticism's models and metaphors help us hear the music of memory?

■

I mentioned that when I first read *Ulysses* I felt almost totally indifferent to Stephen Dedalus and his plight, even though there were many similarities between his situation and mine when I first encountered him, and this lack of interest in Stephen has often puzzled me. I was just a few years younger than he is in the novel, and like him I was experiencing an intellectual awakening, which for me meant a profound shift from a working-class life to a middle-class one focused on the mind. But perhaps because of his angry arrogance and self-protective intellectualizing, or his Catholic upbringing, or the external circumstances of his family life, which were so different from my early Jewish life (his mother had recently died, his father was a shiftless alcoholic, there were nine or ten children in his family), I saw no connection between our lives. Or, more likely, at the time I didn't think there was anything wrong with my family, and my resistance to even thinking about possible problems was so well developed that I perceived no connections. Stephen seemed like an alien being who left me cold.

In fact, as I was growing up I thought I was experiencing a perfect childhood. I was born in 1947, my parents' first child (with two more to follow in the next five years). In many ways we were a typical post–World War II working-class family, first in the city of Buffalo and then, beginning when I was eleven, in the suburb of Tonawanda. We weren't rich or well off, but we were secure and happy, and for several years we were relatively comfortable. My father worked on swing shifts as a laborer at Bell Aircraft and had a second job as owner and proprietor of a used paperback and comic-book store around the corner from our house. He was serious and very smart, and he seemed able to do anything, whether mental or physical. He was a large man, just under six feet tall and weighing around 220 pounds, and until a couple of years before he died he smoked heavily, usually two packs of cigarettes or more a day. In contrast, my mother was small, around five foot two and about a hundred pounds, and a nonsmoker. She was loud and funny, always smiling or laughing and routinely cracking jokes, and she could be foolish and silly. Dad was often the earnest but bemused straight man to

Mom's manic comedian. They weren't exactly like Lucy and Ricky Ricardo on *I Love Lucy*—Dad rarely got as overtly exasperated as Ricky often did—but they came close. Like Lucy, Mom made mistakes and messed things up. She joked around with friends and was the life of a party. When she was around, we never knew what complication she would cause or what unpredictable event would happen. Dad and especially Mom often mentioned how happy a family we were and how much we all loved each other. I could see that this was true. My parents hardly ever spent a night apart from each other; they rarely yelled at each other or at us children, and hardly ever got angry; there was no spanking or hitting of any kind; no one had a drinking problem. Our home was secure and safe. To me it was perfect.

From an early age I was very good at arithmetic, and through all six years of junior high and high school, each aspect of math that I encountered delighted me: arithmetic, geometry, trigonometry, algebra, calculus. I could easily do many kinds of arithmetic calculations in my head, quickly becoming a very good, even elegant, solver of mathematical proofs. During these years my future seemed certain to involve math and numbers in some way. The challenges from the numbers and proofs, sometimes easy and sometimes difficult ones, were invitations I eagerly accepted. I wanted to be a successful and accomplished boy but also an emotionally stable one—that was important. I never got riled up or angry, and the numbers and proofs didn't upset the even keel of my moods. Getting the right answer or solving a proof offered me pure, uncomplicated satisfaction. Math and I were made for each other.

I always had a small group of good friends, but I also spent a lot of time alone, including amusing myself with my math problems. However, I hardly ever enjoyed that other solitary activity that is so important to many children who end up where I am now: reading. Our house had few books in it, and my parents weren't readers. They rarely read aloud to me when I was a small child, and most of the standard classic children's books passed me by. As I grew a little older I occasionally visited Dad's bookstore, which seemed like a den of strange and slightly unsettling mystery to me. Budding textual scholar that I now realize I was, I became intrigued by the names of the authors and titles on the book covers and spines, and sometimes by the covers themselves, even if I rarely felt tempted to open the books. When I was curious I had to restrain myself. Dad didn't allow me to read or even open any of the books in his store. They were only for grown-ups, he said.

Life changed in 1957, when I was ten. The growth of television, and especially an economic recession which hit that year and affected the Buffalo area especially hard, eliminated much of the bookstore's business, and Dad had to sell the shop. More drastically, he was laid off from his job at Bell Aircraft. Despite reassurances that the recession would be short and expectations that his job would be restored, he never did get it back, and for a couple of years he couldn't find any other employment. Mom went to work full time, something she continued to do for over twenty-five years, and we had much less money than before. As we moved to the suburbs, Mom was the principal breadwinner, and even when Dad found work again he didn't make enough money to support us on his own. He became more withdrawn, and Mom's antic clowning quieted down somewhat. In my teens I involved myself more and more with my schoolwork and with extracurricular activities, and when I was sixteen I started going out with Molly and spent as much time as I could with her.

When I was younger I had felt miserably homesick whenever I spent even a single night away from my house, but even though I felt no strong desire to move away from home, I never seriously considered staying in Buffalo for college. I applied to Dartmouth and was accepted there with a full scholarship. Throughout my unhappy freshman year, I counted the days until I could escape and go home, but as the year ended I made my decisions to return in the fall and to switch my major from math to English. Molly and I broke up at the beginning of the summer, and then during my first week back at Dartmouth in the fall I started to read *Ulysses*.

I don't think Stephen Dedalus could possibly have resonated with me at that time. I was totally invested in not rocking the boat with my parents or feeling anything remotely negative toward them. I tolerated my brother, two years younger than me, but largely ignored him, and certainly didn't feel any need for a bitter, arrogant, and more rebellious fictional sibling. Nor did Stephen provide a mirror, even a cracked one, that I had the slightest interest in looking at. His education and intellectualizing give him no help in coming to terms with his mother's death or with his guilt over his refusal to kneel at her bedside as she was dying, and the last thing in the world I would have wanted to face at the time was the prospect of a university education leaving me unprepared to deal with problems. (Declan Kiberd argues that parts of "Proteus" constitute "a cautionary tale about how a college degree in arts may unfit you for the world.")[4] It wasn't so much the inadequate preparation, however, as the problems themselves. Except for my unhappiness with Dartmouth and the end of my relationship with my girlfriend, I didn't think I had any problems.

■

If *Ulysses* had remained primarily about Stephen Dedalus, I doubt it would have appealed much to me, if at all. That novel was my first encounter with Stephen; only during the semester following Mr. Bien's course did I read *A Portrait of the Artist as Young Man*. Even though *Portrait* interested me, most strongly in its presentation of the vulnerable young boy in its early sections, I remained mostly indifferent to Stephen, especially the university student of the later parts.

Joyce's first version of *Portrait*, a short sketch he wrote in 1904 with the similar but not identical name of "A Portrait of the Artist," begins by defining a verbal portrait, claiming confidently that "the past assuredly implies a fluid succession of presents, the development of an entity of which our actual present is a phase only."[5] In her essay "Modern Fiction," originally written while Joyce was at work on *Ulysses*, Virginia Woolf contrasts "materialist" writers such as Arnold Bennett, who provide detailed depictions of characters' faces, clothes, and houses, with "spiritual" ones—"several young writers," she notes, "among whom Mr. James Joyce is the most notable"—who "record the atoms as they fall upon the mind in the order in which they fall," "trace the pattern, however disconnected and incoherent in appearance, which each sight or incident scores upon the consciousness," and do not "take it for granted that life exists more fully in what is commonly thought big than in what is commonly thought small."[6] Joyce sounds a lot like Woolf when he declares in his essay that the world knows "an entity" mainly through external details, "the characters of beard and inches," and rejects the heroic creators who seek "by some process of the mind as yet untabulated, to liberate from the personalised lumps of matter that which is their individuating rhythm." For these custom-defying writers, Joyce's opening paragraph concludes, "a portrait is not an identificative paper but rather the curve of an emotion."[7]

Leopold Bloom recalls first seeing Molly during a game of musical chairs. Many hours later, a sleepy and hungover Stephen Dedalus asks his question about chairs on top of tables at night. Bloom's thought, "Me. And me now," and especially Joyce's presentation of the past Bloom through the memories of the present man, suggest chairs not so much functionally and statically lined up in rows on their tables as in motion, active props in a musical game, shifting points on an emotional curve. When I consider what it was about *Ulysses* that appealed to me so strongly, the possible answers that suggest themselves don't involve straight lines from me to *Ulysses* or from past to present so much as curved, even wavy, ones.

∎

In the *Odyssey* Telemachus yearns for his long-absent father, Odysseus, to return, but Joyce famously reverses the genders in the opening episodes of *Ulysses* as Stephen reacts to his mother's death. In a reversal of Joyce's gender reversal, my father died when I was twenty-three, almost exactly Stephen's age in *Ulysses*. This happened at the end of 1970, just after I had finished my first term of graduate school at Princeton University. He was forty-nine. I learned that he was dying from a phone call, not a telegram, but only a couple of hours before he died. Until then I didn't even know he was sick. When I reached Buffalo he was already gone. His death should have saddened me, I know, and both his death from lung cancer and my not being told beforehand that he was dying should have shocked and angered me. Instead, I felt a sense of dislocation, wondering if I was really there, and numbness—but also relief. From the time I had heard about his illness, I couldn't imagine seeing him at his bedside. I didn't know him well enough to say anything to him or to hear anything from him.

I don't think I ever knew him. He hardly ever told me anything about himself or seemed to really want a close relationship with me. He never let on that anything was troubling him, and, even though he didn't turn me away or refuse to help me, I didn't think I could go to him when I needed advice or consolation or support.

My father seemed to know everything and be able to do anything. I could never keep up with him. If I attempted to talk to him about something he knew, I'd always get part of it wrong. When we played a game like horseshoes, table tennis, or badminton, I could never win. If I went to his bookstore and tried to assist him, I'd mostly be in the way. When I helped him with one of his building projects, I'd usually work too slowly, or make some kind of mistake. He hardly ever yelled at me, but I could see that he wasn't pleased.

But he reinforced me in many ways. If I was faced with a school assignment I couldn't do by myself, he'd suggest how I could look up information on the topic or work with me until I came up with the answer. When my teachers gave me A's on my report card, he seemed genuinely pleased and proud.

All his and Mom's friends were Jewish, and he wanted, and expected, me to have a Jewish-centered life as well. I considered myself thoroughly Jewish. I looked through a book in our house called *They All Are Jews* by someone named Mac Davis and cherished the profiles of earlier Jewish achievers, even though I hadn't heard of most of the people who were mentioned. I'd fill with pride when I learned that someone famous was Jewish, deflate with disappointment when I realized that someone I thought was Jewish actually wasn't. My family joined a synagogue when I was about eight so that I could take Hebrew School classes in preparation for my Bar Mitzvah, and when I had a good teacher there I enjoyed learning about Jewish history, traditions, and beliefs. For a while I even thought that I might become a rabbi when I grew up. I stayed in the synagogue until my Bar Mitzvah when I was thirteen but then quietly stopped going and never returned.

When Dad lost his job in 1957 and Mom went to work full time, he was always around the house. He saw my brother, my sister, and me off to school in the morning after Mom left for her work, and he was there when we came home at lunchtime and after school. Often he was sitting in a gray Barcalounger chair, and as it reclined into something like a bed he usually fell asleep. He sat around at home a lot, smoked even more than before, and gained a great deal of extra weight. When we moved to the suburbs shortly after I turned eleven, he occupied himself with many building projects on our new home, including a basement recreation room and a garage. But more than ever he was stretched out on the chair in our living room with the television on, asleep and snoring with a lit cigarette that my mother had to butt out. If we tried to turn the TV off or change the channel, he would wake up just long enough to stop us, and then he would fall back to sleep. Even after he found work again, my main image of him during my teenage years is of a man sleeping and snoring, TV and cigarette going, in that gray chair.

What was going on inside his head? That question rarely if ever occurred to me. I didn't have much of an imagination, living almost entirely as I did in the world that I could see and hear and in my math exercises, and Dad gave me hardly any materials out of which to construct any sense of his interior life. Even while I was still living in our house with him, and especially after I moved to Dartmouth, it was easy to just drift away and accept the sleeping man in the chair as the entire reality.

But then I encountered Leopold Bloom. My strong response to him when I first read *Ulysses* must have been connected to my relationship with my father. Bloom's unassuming demeanor is similar to my father's quiet personality, and his partial Jewishness isn't all that far removed from both my father's and my own inactive Judaism. But his incredibly rich and varied inner life was a revelation. I didn't think of Dad as I read about Leopold Bloom, but here was a male character about his age, partly successful and partly not, happy in some aspects of his life but certainly not in all, and, in the end, decent, humane, resilient, and positive. Dad was a cipher, but Bloom is full: multiple and manifold, divided and ambiguous, composed of human limitations and imperfections, strengths and weaknesses. Unlike my father, Bloom can be deciphered, particularly through the small details that make up his outer and especially his inner life.

The package that is Leopold Bloom, the combination of minutiae, comes all of a piece. He defies any neat or stereotypical idea of what a person is or should be, as *Ulysses* depicts him at one point as a "new womanly man" (*U* 15:1798-99) and at another as having a "firm full masculine feminine passive active" hand (*U* 17:289-90). Goaded into stating what he believes in, he answers simply, "Love," which he defines only as "the opposite of hatred" (*U* 12:1485). We witness the love he feels for people close to him: his daughter, Milly; his dead son, Rudy, for whom he would have acted as a teacher: "I could have helped him on in life. I could. Make him independent, Learn German too" (*U* 6:83-84); his father, who died, a lonely suicide, eighteen years earlier; and especially the unfaithful Molly. His simple credo is shorthand for a complexity that *Ulysses* convincingly portrays, since love comes in many forms in the book, including masochism, pain, and betrayal—multifaceted human desire that is irreducible to something neat and tidy. When I first read *Ulysses*, I wanted my life to be just that, neat and tidy, although much in it wasn't and couldn't be. I responded to Bloom and the messy world Joyce puts him in, however, like a starving person who is suddenly and unexpectedly presented with a gift of a meal, even if a partly burnt grilled kidney.

At some level, I must have seen Leopold Bloom as a kind of substitute father, or at least as the role model my father never was or tried to be for me. I never had and never will have access to Dad's dreams and hopes or losses and disappointments, and I can't know his quirks and flaws, but I can know Bloom's intimately. He can even offer me a possible, even if an idealized, picture of my father. What better thoughts could I have imagined Dad having than Bloom's? I never think of Bloom as a contemporary of mine or even as someone younger than me (as he is now, and by many years), but always as what he was when I first encountered him, a father figure, something I needed much more than the openly rebellious sibling I could have found in Stephen Dedalus. And unlike Stephen, who politely but firmly declines Bloom's invitation to stay the night and walks away to an unknown future, I stuck with him until I grew enough to appreciate what he could give me.

He's a fictional character, of course. Like the young lovers in John Keats's "Ode on a Grecian Urn," he can't change, but he also can't leave. I change, though, and I see Bloom a little differently each time I meet him, so he is never quite the same. One of the reasons, I think, that this work of imaginative literature became vitally important to me is that it says things I didn't hear any living person utter, even things I would have run away from had anyone said them aloud to me. At some level, and in ways I couldn't recognize when I first read his story, I very much needed to hear what Leopold Bloom had to say.

■

If my father was emotionally absent, my mother was very present, and as I was growing up I was extremely grateful for that. My sense of our family being perfect came almost entirely from her. When I was young—but also well into adulthood—I didn't think there could be a better mother. She was pretty and funny. She kissed my brother, my sister, and me a lot and told us how much she loved us. She reminded us often that, even though we had a lot less money than other people, we were as close to ideal as a family could be. As I got older, I realized that we weren't ideal at all, but I still saw Mom as the unblemished center that held everything that was good in our family together and also as the victim of some terrible injustices.

Unlike Dad, who was quiet, serious, and smart and who graduated at the top of his high school class, Mom was loud and silly, ending up near the bottom, something she treated almost as a badge of honor. From my earliest memories of her, she was happy and funny. I loved to watch her clown around, although sometimes she'd go on too long, and occasionally she'd do something to embarrass me. I could joke around, too, if I was with people who made me feel comfortable, but I would be quiet to the point of almost invisible silence, hunched over biting my fingernails, if I didn't feel at ease. I never tried to be funny around Mom, recognizing early on, I'm sure, that there could be only one comic in a room and making no attempt to compete with her.

Mom kept almost all unpleasantness out of the house. We watched mainly comedies and variety shows on TV and went only to funny movies. If people got sick, as did Nana—my mother's mother, who lived with us until I was twelve or so—Mom wouldn't tell us what was wrong or let us visit her wherever she had gone or attend her funeral. Somehow, after Nana died, I learned that she had suffered from liver cancer, and "cancer" became a terrible word that I knew shouldn't be uttered. No one ever said anything about her after she died or even mentioned her name again.

Mom never followed orders or instructions. If anyone in a position of authority—a doctor or pharmacist, a salesperson describing how an object should be used, even Dad—tried to tell her to do something in a particular way, she'd rebel and act as she pleased. I enjoyed watching her defy authorities like this, although it also made me nervous. When I was eight, my family planned a weeklong summer vacation in various parks and towns in the Adirondack Mountains in eastern New York State, our first trip away from home. With excitement and with Dad's help, I wrote away for brochures about the various towns and sites to visit and motels to stay in. A few days before we were scheduled to leave, Mom took my brother, my sister, and me to a cousin's birthday party at a roller-skating rink. Don't put on any skates, Dad joked to her as we left, but as soon as we got there she did exactly that, and after whooping it up and clowning around as the center of attention for a little while, she fell. When she didn't get up right away, an ambulance was called. She was taken to a hospital, where we learned that she had broken one of her legs quite severely, and we spent our vacation week making trips back and forth to the hospital to visit her. We finally did make the trip to the Adirondacks the next summer, but it was somewhat disappointing. Perhaps the vacation never recovered from the year's delay, or maybe a trip envisioned by an eight-year-old wasn't quite the same thing to a more mature boy of nine.

Mom was proud of me when I did well in school. She made a fuss when I brought my report cards home and told her friends about my achievements. Very early on, she started talking about me as someone headed for college. But occasionally she'd say something negative about relatives who had gone to college or were professionals of any kind. This one was having trouble in his marriage, that one had suffered a nervous breakdown, another's children were spoiled. I grew up with strong mixed messages: I was an outstanding student who was headed for college and life as a professional, and I knew from what my parents said that they wanted me to achieve this. But I could make people who weren't doing as well as I was feel bad, and none of my college-educated, middle-class relatives could be relied on or trusted as much as my high-school-graduate, working-class parents and their friends.

Mom's words told me that people could be dangerous in far worse ways than this, and so did my own eyes and ears. I knew, for instance, that I couldn't trust my other grandmother, my father's mother, and shouldn't like her very much. Grandma doesn't like me, Mom often said. She doesn't think I'm good enough for your father. Mom told me that Grandma preferred my uncle, Dad's older brother, who had gone to college and was a lawyer in New York City and whose wife had also gone to college. And so when my father, my brother, my sister, and I visited my grandmother each Sunday in her apartment, Mom didn't come with us. In fact, she had no contact with her at all. During our visits, Grandma asked about Mom in a polite but distant way that I could see came from someone who didn't like her.

Mom had an older sister, and they were good friends, but she also had an older brother who had moved to Florida years before and had done something to her, causing a total estrangement. I met him only once, when he came to Buffalo for a distant relative's funeral sometime in the 1950s. He wasn't the monster I expected to find, but I didn't try very hard to like him or to get to know someone who had done whatever he did to Mom. She never did speak to him in the next sixty years before he died in 2006, at the age of ninety-one. I didn't think much about these ruptures—I simply assumed that they took place in every family—but I felt very sorry for my mother for being hurt by these terrible people. I wondered how my grandmother, my uncle, and probably many others could have treated such a wonderful person so badly. At some level of my being, I must have clearly resolved that I would never do such a thing to her.

As I grew older, the ruptures became more numerous and hit much closer to home. Mom became estranged from people who had been her good friends and off and on from her sister, and after Dad died from my brother, her second son. I suspect she would have cut off my father, too, had he not died when he did. "Molly. Milly. Same thing watered down," Bloom thinks of his wife and daughter (*U* 6:87). In my family, the ruptures have continued unabated in my own generation.

What caused these many cut-offs? I never knew. Mom always claimed that the other person didn't like her, was a bad person, or had done something to her that she didn't want to talk about, and I never heard the other side of the story. For many years, well into my late thirties, I simply took it for granted that Mom—so happy, so good, so perfect—needed to be protected against her dangerous world. I was totally incapable of feeling angry at her, even when she did things like ruin our vacation. Such a thought would have been impossible for me to articulate when I was young, but I almost certainly feared that if I didn't watch out, I could also become a danger to her and, worse, could be the next person she stopped talking to. Without knowing I was doing it, I trained myself well, becoming careful never to say anything that might upset her or to think that she might be even partly responsible for all the severed ties. I also learned very early on not to say what I really thought to anyone, or even to think anything that could be dangerous. Extremely unsure of myself, I didn't trust other people very much, especially any people I found myself getting close to. My homework, especially the math problems, probably satisfied me so much because I felt safer with it than with any of the people around me, and these solitary activities reassured me that at least part of my world fell into an order that I could see and understand. And if that order was pure, clean, and emotionally neutral, as my math proofs reliably were, so much the better.

I succeeded in avoiding my mother's cut-off—if "succeed" is the correct word—but at a tremendous cost. I never developed much of an imagination. The absence of many books in our house is one reason why I didn't read much, but also, I'm sure, I didn't want to risk being exposed to other lives, perhaps ones that seemed more alluring than my own. I think Mom worked hard to ensure that I wouldn't question anything about our home and family and especially not compare our lives to other people's, whether in reality, in books, or in fantasy. When I was in high school I started to admire a friend's family. They seemed more cultured than mine, and the parents listened to their children and engaged them in serious and respectful conversation. When I came home after eating dinner one evening at this friend's house and mentioned this to Mom, she got so upset that she started to cry. Making her feel so bad caused me to feel terrible. I was almost relieved when, during another dinner a little later, my friend's father became enraged over something minor that had happened, and I couldn't wait to get out of his house. After this, there wasn't any way I wanted to exchange my home for that one.

Reading about or imagining other houses, parents, or lives made my world dangerous. And danger for me meant, most of all, the possibility of being cut off from Mom.

I protected myself against myself, but in high school two important intruders slipped through my fortress. First came reading and literature. When I was partway through tenth grade, my English teacher took me aside and said he didn't think his class assignments challenged me enough. He offered to direct me through a program of independent reading and suggested several modern American plays. I started reading dramatists and plays unknown to me before: Eugene O'Neill's *Desire under the Elms*, *The Great God Brown*, and *Mourning Becomes Elektra*; Arthur Miller's *All My Sons* and *Death of a Salesman*; Arthur Kopit's *Oh Dad, Poor Dad, Mamma's Hung You In the Closet and I'm Feelin' So Sad*; and Edward Albee's *The American Dream*, *The Sandbox*, and, when it was published during the year, *Who's Afraid of Virginia Woolf?* I never thought about any connection between these plays and my own life, but I couldn't put them down. In my late fifties I reread all these plays, realizing to my astonishment how much I had been immersing myself in dysfunctional families, unrealized dreams, ineffectual fathers, and strong and dangerous, even deadly, mothers while I thought that my family life was perfect. After I encountered these plays when I was fifteen, I began reading a great deal on my own, especially works that weren't nearly as safe as those assigned in my classes or that I had occasionally chosen on my own.

If I perhaps responded to Leopold Bloom as a way of indirectly reaching my father, I see a different connection with my mother. *Ulysses* is relatively silent on mothers. Stephen's is dead, and I didn't react to his grief or to his now tortured relationship with her. Bloom, surprisingly, hardly ever thinks of his mother, and this might have helped me in my initial response to the book, since I was years away from being prepared to reassess my relationship to mine. But Bloom and also Molly, as well as all of *Ulysses*, connect to my mother in a crucial way.

As important as anything else about Leopold and Molly Bloom for me is that, in contrast to my family, where people said so little to each other, where no one ever expressed what they were feeling, and where everyone was guarded about what disruption any misstep might cause, they are in a novel that seems to spill out everything. Deepest feelings are conveyed, all thoughts are exposed, and no one gets hurt or punished for anything they think or feel. Thoughts are cherished and safe. No sky comes falling down;

no one stops talking to anyone else. Nothing much happens at all, which is quite something to say for a day on which an act of adultery takes place.

■

The second disruption to my self-protected life in high school involved Molly Peacock. Each other's first girlfriend and boyfriend, Molly and I were together for two and a half years, from the ages of sixteen to nineteen. She was as unlike me as could be. I was calm and even-tempered, and I didn't think my moods varied much, but her emotions were all over the place. I never knew what she would be like from one day to the next, or even from one hour in school to another. If my family life seemed perfect, she made it clear that hers was a mess. I never understood what she saw in me—"Why did she me?"—and nothing she said when she tried to tell me really convinced me. I always worried that she would suddenly and inexplicably end everything between us. But for much of our junior year and our entire senior year in high school we were inseparable.

Neither of us had experienced much beyond our families and Buffalo, but when we were with each other new worlds opened up. She was a devoted reader, and both to keep up with her and because her enthusiasm was infectious, I started reading more; she gave me a second reason for doing that. We went to films, concerts, and art exhibits together, and once we drove ninety miles to Rochester for an afternoon—it was our vacation in Paris. Sexually, I was as repressed as a child of the 1940s and 1950s could be, but we were also full of curiosity about each other's bodies, and after a long delay, when we were in college and living away from our homes, we became each other's first lover.

My parents spent almost every ounce of energy they had trying to break Molly and me up. She wasn't Jewish, they complained. We'd get too close and she'd get pregnant, ruining my future. We'd decide to get married instead of going to college, and I'd ruin my future that way. They'd never succeed, we knew, and we were correct, but as we moved through our lives away from home at different colleges, we broke up on our own at the end of our freshman year.

When I read *Ulysses* a few months after our breakup, I unexpectedly met a new Molly. Meeting another one at that time wasn't anything I expected or really wanted, but so it goes. And this one was thinking words I had never thought I'd be reading: "I wished he was here or somebody to let myself go with and come again like that I feel all fire inside me" (*U* 18:584–85); "whats the idea making us like that with a big hole in the middle of us or like a Stallion driving it up into you because thats all they want out of you" (*U* 18:151–52). Did women really think things like that? I was at Dartmouth College—the movie *Animal House*, based on a fraternity at the college from around my time there, indicates that calling the prevailing attitude toward women Neanderthal would be making it sound a lot more mature and enlightened than it was. I was amazed at, and probably also a little frightened by, the directness and frankness of Molly Bloom's thoughts, but as with so much else in *Ulysses*, I was startled to see that she doesn't get punished for her openness and especially for her infidelity. Instead, she's alive at the end, her husband doesn't stop talking to her, and life presumably goes on. Given where I was both in my own development and at my college, it was easy at first to see Molly primarily, even only, as a sexual being, and much of the published criticism that was available then reinforced this attitude. But Leopold Bloom doesn't. His thoughts about Molly throughout the day evoke a full human being, one who, I eventually realized, was willing to wait several years until I was ready to see her as a much more complex character, even if she waited all that time in her bed.

■

I can now look back at my initial encounter with *Ulysses* from various later points in time, years that unfolded in many curves and waves, even if a quick summary here reduces them to a line. I went on to graduate school at Princeton University and wrote a dissertation that was supervised by A. Walton Litz, becoming a manuscript scholar and writing *"Ulysses" in Progress* and editing *The James Joyce Archive*. The University of Western Ontario hired me to teach in its English Department, and in 1975 I made what turned out to be a permanent move to Canada.

My late twenties, thirties, and early forties had their ups and downs. I was in a short first marriage that I ended, followed by several years of brief, unsuccessful affairs in which I would become obsessed with a woman who didn't want a relationship with me or feel indifferent to someone who did. When I was thirty-three and thirty-four I suffered two bouts of melanoma, and after the second one I was given a poor prognosis of surviving five years. That prognosis turned out to be wrong, fortunately, but that once unspeakable word "cancer" now became an always present reality in my life. For several years I wasn't able to write anything, including about *Ulysses*, nor did I read or teach the novel very often. One experience that started in the down column eventually switched, however: after the recurrence of melanoma, I began seeing a psychotherapist, initially in an attempt to come to terms with my cancer. Eventually I started talking less and less about it and more about my childhood and my relationships to my family and to other people I knew. When I turned to *Ulysses* again during those years, it was as wonderful as ever but in many ways a new and even richer book for me than it had been before.

My life changed again in the 1990s, when I was well into my forties. As I worked on a digital presentation of *Ulysses*, I found myself turning in unexpected ways to Joyce's novel and to issues of reading and teaching it, many of which I had never really thought about before, and the opportunity to work with the National Library of Ireland in 2001 and 2002 as it acquired its collection of Joyce papers took me back with delight to my earliest work on the manuscripts. Most important, though, was my reconnection with Molly Peacock eighteen years after we broke up, the resumption of our love affair seven years after that, and our marriage a year later, in 1992. Molly Bloom, who became relegated to the "second Molly" in our household, says that she doesn't "like books with a Molly in them" (*U* 18:657–58), but in my book, life with two Mollys is wonderful.

■

My initial encounter with *Ulysses*, the first draft of my life with Joyce's novel, reveals several possible reasons why the novel and I bonded strongly when we found each other, even if none of them alone or even all of them together can be the complete story. Other novels and art works appealed to some of my aesthetic, emotional, and psychological needs, but *Ulysses* satisfied many more of them, both when I was nineteen and could articulate some of them but not many others, and also as I grew older and my needs evolved along with my awareness of my past and present selves. I'd like to think that by the time I reached my forties and fifties I had become someone much more receptive to the gifts that *Ulysses* began offering me when I first read it. I still struggle all the time to balance the insecurity I inherited from my mother's habit of cutting people off and my father's remoteness with whatever confidence and security I'm able to feel. I'm very fortunate to have twice found Molly Peacock and to have encountered a teacher like Peter Bien at such a formative moment in my life. (I reconnected with Peter as well as with Molly. That happened in the late 1990s, when I discovered him to be the same prodigiously intelligent and learned, and also warm and humane, man that I remembered from those years at Dartmouth College in the late 1960s.) These crucial parts of my life are all intimately tied to *Ulysses*, with its struggling but surviving, very decent ordinary extraordinary characters living their everyday heroic lives. Why do I spend so much time with this one novel? I don't know all the reasons, or maybe even most of them, but as long as *Ulysses*, and Leopold and Molly Bloom, keep speaking to me, I'll never put the book down.

3

From Monument to Mobile

Genetic Criticism and *Ulysses*

As the "Aeolus" episode of *Ulysses* nears its conclusion, Stephen Dedalus comes to the end of his short vignette about two old ladies who have climbed to the top of Nelson's Pillar. Feeling dizzy from the height, the women "pull up their skirts" and "settle down on their striped petticoats, peering up at the statue of the onehandled adulterer." The text continues:

> DAMES DONATE DUBLIN'S CITS
> SPEEDPILLS VELOCITOUS AEROLITHS, BELIEF
>
> —It gives them a crick in their necks, Stephen said, and they are too tired to look up or down or to speak. They put the bag of plums between them and eat the plums out of it, one after another, wiping off with their handkerchiefs the plumjuice that dribbles out of their mouths and spitting the plumstones slowly out between the railings.

A few lines later, the focus shifts briefly from Stephen's oral story to Dublin's tram system:

> HELLO THERE, CENTRAL!
>
> At various points along the eight lines tramcars with motionless trolleys stood in their tracks, bound for or from Rathmines, Rathfarnham, Blackrock, Kingstown and Dalkey, Sandymount Green, Ringsend and Sandymount Tower, Donnybrook, Palmerston Park and Upper Rathmines, all still, becalmed in short circuit. Hackney cars, cabs, delivery waggons, mailvans, private broughams, aerated mineral water floats with rattling crates of bottles, rattled, rolled, horsedrawn, rapidly.

Finally, as "Aeolus" draws to a close, Stephen names his tale "*A Pisgah Sight of Palestine* or *The Parable of The Plums*." One of his listeners, Professor MacHugh, reacts ("We gave him that idea") and then, like the trams, stops his motion:

> He halted on sir John Gray's pavement island and peered aloft at Nelson through the meshes of his wry smile.
>
> **DIMINISHED DIGITS PROVE TOO TITILLATING FOR FRISKY FRUMPS. ANNE WIMBLES, FLO WANGLES—YET CAN YOU BLAME THEM?**
>
> —Onehandled adulterer, he said smiling grimly. That tickles me, I must say.
>
> —Tickled the old ones too, Myles Crawford said, if the God Almighty's truth was known. (U 7:1013–75)

Critics have analyzed this short scene in many different ways. First, it parallels one in the *Odyssey*: Odysseus and his men are stuck on Aeolia after Aeolus's winds blew them almost home to Ithaca but then back to the island, and in *Ulysses* the women are motionless and silent, the men have stopped walking, and the trams are short-circuited. At the end of an episode full of noise and movement, almost everything is quiet and motionless.

Second, Stephen's parable calls out for interpretation. His short tale is full of realistic detail and strong language, and, unlike his anemic vampire poem from a few pages earlier (or the villanelle in *A Portrait of the Artist as a Young Man*), it obeys Myles Crawford's request that he produce "something with a bite in it. Put us all into it" (U 7:621). Stephen weaves several details from *Ulysses* into his narrative: the two midwives with their umbrellas whom he saw on Sandymount Strand (U 3:29ff); Fumbally's lane, where, he recalled on the strand, he once met a prostitute (U 3:379) and where his two climbers live; Garrett Deasy's "little savingsbox," which finds an echo in the women's "red tin letterbox moneybox" (U 2:218, 7:932); Nelson's Pillar, toward which Stephen and Professor MacHugh walk after they leave the newspaper office; Buck Mulligan's song about Mary Ann "hising up her petticoats" (U 1:384, 3:462), clothing that becomes part of Stephen's story; and, in his title, Seymour Bushe's speech about Michelangelo's statue of Moses (U 7:768–71) and John F. Taylor's about "the youthful Moses" (U 7:833), which provokes J. J. O'Molloy's remark that Moses "died without having entered the land of promise" (U 7:873; C. H. Peake discusses these and other echoes in *James Joyce: The Citizen and the Artist*).[1]

Harry Blamires discusses Stephen's story as a study in frustration and disappointment; Daniel Schwarz considers it a metaphoric presentation of a sterile Ireland in which two old women "spit potential seeds upon concrete where they cannot grow" and Paul Schwaber a picture in which the women are "representative of sterile Ireland and [Stephen's] own self-censure"; and Peake emphasizes the linking of politics and sex, since the Irish women are transfixed and paralyzed by the English conqueror Nelson, a man who, even without an arm, can still tickle them (and MacHugh, too, who admits that "the onehandled adulterer," as Stephen refers to Nelson, "tickles me") and whose reputation remained unharmed even though, as an adulterer, he committed the act that later ruined the Irish Parnell.[2] The story's plumstones evoke the name Plumtree, the company whose ad for potted meat remains in Leopold Bloom's mind all day (*U* 5:144–47), and like the potted meat they serve as a marker of sexual frustration and satisfaction. Finally, as Stanley Sultan notes, Stephen's story ironically inverts and refutes Taylor's Romantic identification of the "youthful Moses" and the "youth of Ireland" (*U* 7:833, 829) and can inspire such postcolonial readings as those by Enda Duffy, who points out that in various ways, including Stephen's parable, "a gendered division of labor in the colony is implicitly posited early in the novel," and by Patrick McGee, who notes that Stephen has identified with "the woman who labors" and thereby "has aligned himself with the figure of the subaltern, the bondwoman."[3]

Third, the bold interpolations in the passage—critics variously describe them as newspaper headlines, subheads, captions, crossheads, or simply heads—break up any traditional narrative momentum. These interruptions include a sensationalistic restatement of the women's actions ("DAMES DONATE DUBLIN'S CITS"), a colloquial phone call seeking help for the tram system ("HELLO THERE, CENTRAL!"), and alliterative descriptions of Nelson ("DIMINISHED DIGITS") and the old women ("FRISKY FRUMPS").

Readers might understandably think that responding to the words in the printed *Ulysses* is a sufficiently large task. They might be forgiven for not knowing that when Joyce first considered "Aeolus" finished and sent it to his typist and then to the printer of *The Little Review* (the New York magazine that was serializing *Ulysses*), no newspaper heads or trams were in the episode, Stephen's name for his narrative was simply "*A Pisgah Sight of Palestine*," and the last words were slightly fewer. (Here is how it happened: Joyce added the heads to the first set of placards, although the first one in our passage contained only its first line, and in the last one "ANNE WIMBLES" was "ANNE SIGHS." On the same proof page on which he wrote "HELLO THERE, CENTRAL!" he also added the paragraph about the short-circuited tramcars, but the destinations were slightly shorter and in a different order. In the list of moving non-electric vehicles he first wrote "delivery cars" before changing "cars" to "waggons." Another addition makes Myles Crawford refer not to simply "the truth" but to "the God Almighty's truth." On the second set of placards Joyce corrected several printing mistakes, especially but not only in the names of the tramcar destinations, expanded "Sandymount" to "Sandymount green and Sandymount tower," and then made an addition to an addition when he inserted "Ringsend" after "green." He also added the second title for Stephen's narrative, "The Parable of The Plums," and in the final head changed "ANNE SIGHS" to "ANNE WIMBLES"—using as a verb an archaic word for a tool used to bore holes. On the first set of page proofs he added the first head's second line, "SPEEDPILLS VELOCITOUS AEROLITHS, BELIEF," capitalized the "g" in "green," and reinserted a question mark after "THEM" at the end of the final head that the printer neglected to include. All his other activities on the three sets of page proofs for this passage involved correcting printer's errors.)[4]

Readers might also be unaware that "Sandymount Tower" was "Sandymount tower" in the printed editions until 1932 and that in all the printed editions from 1922 through 1968, Professor MacHugh said "Onehandled adulterer" only "grimly." Not until Hans Walter Gabler's edition in 1984 did he speak "smiling grimly." (The details: Joyce wrote "tower" on the second placards and never changed it, but the word appeared as "Tower" in the 1932 Odyssey Press edition, the version corrected by Stuart Gilbert by comparing the proofs with the earlier printed texts and by occasionally consulting with Joyce. For the earlier appearance of "Sandymount Tower" at U 7:6, Joyce wrote an uppercase "T" on the third placards, and it was printed that way in all editions.[5] Joyce wrote "smiling grimly" on the Rosenbach Manuscript, but the typist—who probably worked from another, now lost, handwritten manuscript from which both the typescript and the extant Rosenbach Manuscript derived—did not include "smiling" on the typescript, and the word never appeared on any proofs or in print until Gabler included it in his edition.)[6]

Ulysses alone does not account for readers' indifference to Joyce's revisions or to variations among the printed versions. Textual critics, who study such matters (textual criticism investigates how texts are produced and transmitted and applies that investigation to scholarly editing), have long bemoaned the tendency of other critics to ignore textual matters completely. But faced with remarks like one from Fredson Bowers in 1959—"Every practising critic, for the humility of his [sic] soul, ought to study the transmission of some appropriate text"—who wouldn't stay away? (Bowers also noted that "many a literary critic has investigated the past ownership and mechanical condition of his secondhand automobile, or the pedigree and training of his dog, more thoroughly than he has looked into the qualifications of the text on which his critical theories rest.")[7] Furthermore, the dominant critical attitudes during most of the twentieth century restricted attention to the final printed text. In their influential *Theory of Literature* from 1948, René Wellek and Austin Warren argued for an "intrinsic study of literature," an approach in which textual study and establishing accurate editions are "preliminary to the ultimate task of scholarship," and drafts and other evidence of a work's development are "not, finally, necessary to an understanding of the finished work or to a judgement upon it. Their interest is that of any alternative, i.e. they may set into relief the qualities of the final text."[8]

Critical assumptions based upon statements like these were ubiquitous, even in specific considerations of drafts. In a 1948 essay called "Genesis, or The Poet as Maker," for example, Donald A. Stauffer asked, "What light . . . does the composition of a poem throw upon its meaning and its beauty? What difficulties in a finished poem may be explained, what pointless ambiguities dispelled, what purposeful ambiguities sharpened, by references found in its earlier states?"[9] The situation did not change as New Criticism (of which Wellek and Warren are prime theorists) faded and was supplanted by deconstruction and poststructuralism, whose practitioners emphasized the indeterminacies and instabilities of texts but only in relation to meaning and interpretation and not to the state of the texts themselves. (See G. Thomas Tanselle's "Textual Criticism and Deconstruction" for an analysis of the uses of the word "text" in the essays by Harold Bloom, Paul de Man, Jacques Derrida, Geoffrey Hartman, and J. Hillis Miller in *Deconstruction and Criticism*. See also Jerome McGann's discussion of how, in seeking to demonstrate that "textual indeterminacy is a function of the 'reader' rather than of the 'text,'" Stanley Fish in his reader-response criticism "wants to take the text as physical object at face value.")[10]

And yet, fifty years after Bowers, Wellek and Warren, and Stauffer, in a complete turnaround, Jean-Michel Rabaté called for an "ideal genetic reader" of Joyce.[11] How did such a reversal come about?

•

Despite claims like Wellek and Warren's, interest in how Joyce wrote *Ulysses* is as old as the work itself. Even before *Ulysses* was published in 1922, Valery Larbaud described "abbreviated phrases underlined in various-coloured pencil" on Joyce's working papers, and other observers referred to the unusual appearance of Joyce's notes and drafts.[12] The most prominent and fullest description came from Frank Budgen, who described Joyce's working documents in his 1934 book, *James Joyce and the Making of "Ulysses"*:

> In one of the richest pages of *Ulysses* Stephen on the sea shore, communing with himself and tentatively building with words, calls for his tablets. These should have been library slips, acquired by the impecunious and ingenious poet from the library counter. On that occasion he had forgotten to provide himself with this convenient writing material, and was forced to use the fag-end of Mr. Deasy's letter. As far as concerns the need for tablets, the self-portrait was still like, only in Zürich Joyce was never without them. And they were not library slips, but little writing blocks especially made for the waistcoat pocket. At intervals, alone or in conversation, seated or walking, one of these tablets was produced, and a word or two scribbled on it at lightning speed as ear or memory served his turn. No one knew how all this material was given place in the completed pattern of his work, but from time to time in Joyce's flat one caught glimpses of a few of those big orange-coloured envelopes that are one of the glories of Switzerland, and these I always took to be storehouses of building material. The method of making a multitude of criss-cross notes in pencil was a strange one for a man whose sight was never good. A necessary adjunct to the method was a huge oblong magnifying glass.[13]

Joyce referred to the physical appearance of his papers in *Finnegans Wake* when he describes the manuscript of Anna Livia Plurabelle's "untitled mamafesta" as "writing thithaways end to end and turning, turning and end to end hithaways writing and with lines of litters slittering up and louds of latters slettering down" (*FW* 104:4, 114:16–18), as "not a miseffectual whyacinthinous riot of blots and blurs and bars and balls and hoops and wriggles and juxtaposed jottings linked by spurts of speed: it only looks as like it as damn it" (*FW* 118:28–31), and as "engraved and retouched and edgewiped and puddenpadded . . . all those red raddled obeli cayennepeppercast over the text, calling unnecessary attention to errors, omissions, repetitions and misalignments . . . flinging phrases here, there, or returns inhibited, with some half-halted suggestion, Ŀ, dragging its shoestring'" (*FW* 120:10–16, 121:6–8 [my ellipses]). The *Wake* narrator recommends that the manuscript's students "see all there may remain to be seen" (*FW* 113:32–33).

Scholars predictably tried to "see all," looking more systematically at the documents that Larbaud, Budgen, and others described anecdotally. Early academic work on the *Ulysses* manuscripts focused on Joyce's writing of specific episodes or on particular stages in the book's development, such as the proofs. A pioneering study was A. Walton Litz's 1961 *The Art of James Joyce*, which studied the *Ulysses* notesheets and proofs and demonstrated how Joyce's notesheets led to his revisions of his novel. Litz also sketched out the process by which Joyce moved from a concept of revision as compression to one of revision as expansion. My book *"Ulysses" in Progress* (1977) built on previous work, including Litz's, and established two important aspects of Joyce's writing. First, it worked out a stemma, or family tree, of the *Ulysses* manuscripts, placing the documents in relation to each other. Second, it showed that Joyce's conception of *Ulysses* evolved as he moved from an "early stage" (the first nine episodes) to a "middle stage" ("Wandering Rocks" through "Oxen of the Sun") and then to a "last stage" ("Circe" to the end), with each stage featuring writing styles and techniques that seemed to come into being only as he worked. Joyce left traces of his early ideas and plans as he moved beyond them rather than eradicating them.[14] "Aeolus" was my main example of Joyce revising at this late stage: the newspaper heads were grafted onto an existing text, but that existing text was basically like the episodes that precede it. (I discuss Joyce's work on "Aeolus" more fully in chapter 8.) In presenting *Ulysses* as a "palimpsest involving all three stages," Joyce made it possible to read any passage in his book vertically—as the result of an elaborate composition process and a series of choices—as well as horizontally—as part of an unfolding text in the published novel.[15]

These early manuscript studies shared certain features. For one thing, they took it for granted that the study of manuscripts and the writing process made sense only in relation to the published work. As I wrote in *"Ulysses" in Progress*, "Once [Joyce] finished the book . . . the tasks of interpreting and assessing the complete work necessarily take precedence over any questions about the methods of composition."[16] Second, these studies looked at the manuscripts in order to interpret the works rather than to establish accurate texts of them. Third, the manuscript studies operated pragmatically and untheoretically: the scholar saw a specific problem and looked to the documents for possible answers. Like many other manuscript critics, Litz once hoped, as he says in *The Art of James Joyce*, that the manuscripts "would ultimately provide me with a thread for the labyrinth," but, he goes on to admit, "somehow the controlling design that I sought eluded me, and I have long since relinquished the comforting belief that access to an author's workshop provides insights of greater authority than those provided by other kinds of criticism." (Elsewhere, Litz suggests that every scholar approaching Joyce's manuscripts should be forced to read "The Figure in the Carpet," Henry James's marvelous short story about an obsessive and ultimately doomed quest for an authorially sanctioned key to a writer's works.)[17] Manuscript scholars now are more likely to share the assumption of Luca Crispi and Sam Slote, who, in their introduction to *How Joyce Wrote "Finnegans Wake,"* remark that genetic criticism cannot provide an answer or a key to the works but "should help make the questions more interesting."[18]

I am focusing mostly on *Ulysses* here, but I want to briefly consider *Finnegans Wake*. Litz studied the manuscripts for the *Wake* as well as for *Ulysses* in *The Art of James Joyce*, and at about the same time, other scholars produced editions of the manuscripts for individual *Wake* chapters and notebooks. In 1958 David Hayman published "From *Finnegans Wake*: A Sentence in Progress," a full-length article on the thirteen composition stages of one *Wake* sentence, and in 1963 he produced *A First-Draft Version of "Finnegans Wake,"* an edition containing the earliest available state of each passage in the *Wake*. The *Finnegans Wake* materials occupy thirty-six of the sixty-three volumes in *The James Joyce Archive*, and the *Archive* has inspired a great deal of scholarship primarily focused, it has turned out, much more on the notebooks than on the drafts. This work has culminated in the *"Finnegans Wake" Notebooks at Buffalo* project, an enormously ambitious edition of the forty-nine notebooks, including photoreproductions and transcriptions of each notebook page along with an identification of every note's source that the editors are able to identify and indications of Joyce's use of each note that found its way into a draft or into the published text of the *Wake*; twelve volumes have appeared so far.

Even though manuscripts were used by critics more than by textual editors, scholarly editions were produced. William York Tindall edited the poems in *Chamber Music* in 1954, and in the 1960s Robert Scholes edited *Dubliners* and Chester Anderson *A Portrait of the Artist as a Young Man*. Then, in 1984, Hans Walter Gabler, with Wolfhard Steppe and Claus Melchior, published his *Critical and Synoptic Edition* of *Ulysses* in three volumes (a one-volume reading text appeared in 1986), and this was followed in the 1990s by Gabler's editions, with Walter Hettche, of *Dubliners* and *Portrait*. In March 2010 the first edited edition of *Finnegans Wake*, edited by Danis Rose and John O'Hanlon, was published. No editions of *Exiles* have appeared, although in 1979 John MacNicholas produced a "textual companion" to *Exiles* that shows how to mark up an existing text to produce a more accurate one.

Two important developments occurred in the 1970s and 1980s to change the picture. First, the attention Gabler's edition of *Ulysses* received on its release and the "Joyce Wars" it provoked a few years later made all Joyce's readers, critics, and scholars, and even the general reading public, aware of textual matters. (See chapter 5 for a more extensive discussion of Gabler's edition and its aftermath.) Second, during the age of theory, manuscript study and other kinds of archival work remained a fringe activity in North America, but in France, where much of the structuralism and poststructuralism imported into English-speaking countries originated, scholars thoroughly conversant with the theoretical texts, in several cases students of the writers themselves, formalized manuscript study and even institutionalized it as *critique génétique*, or genetic criticism. We continue to work in exciting ways with the consequences of these two events.

■

Early American and English manuscript studies—concerned more with studying the documents as evidence of writing processes than with establishing accurate texts; operating pragmatically, looking at the papers to see what they could find without any overriding plan or theoretical perspective; and viewing the study as valuable only if it shed light on the final, published works—based themselves on powerful models. If you consider the finished work to be an organism or an icon or a monument, then anything that did not end up in the work will be secondary, a discard, a reject, or (in film terminology) an outtake. In Wellek and Warren's conception, it will be "extrinsic" to the "actual work."[19] The metaphors Henry James used in his 1907–1909 prefaces to the New York Edition of his novels all assume the works to be organic wholes: he "remount[ed] the stream of composition"; he sought the "germ" of a story, by which he meant the "virus of suggestion" or the "prick of inoculation" that instigated a work; and he followed "the growth of the 'great oak' from the little acorn."[20]

At the same time as the age of theory ended the dominance of New Criticism and its view of a literary work as an organism or icon, a new kind of criticism and scholarship centered around manuscripts began to develop in France, especially at the Institut des Textes et Manuscrits Modernes (ITEM), part of the Centre National de la Recherche Scientifique in Paris.[21] Earlier French manuscript scholars shared many of the assumptions of their English-language counterparts, but in the late 1960s and early 1970s this new scholarship began to look at manuscripts in relation to the final work in two different ways. One was the traditional teleological view, in which the drafts and other documents are seen as leading to the final work. The other was an opposite view in which every moment in the writing process that can be documented in surviving manuscripts reveals a series of possibilities, dilemmas, and choices, and these options—seen more as a series of variant possibilities than as rejects—are fascinating in their own right. (The English term "genetic criticism" is not as new as it might seem. Donald Stauffer used it, for example, in his 1948 essay in *Poets at Work*, a set of four essays based on and introducing the new collection of manuscripts, called "worksheets" for want of a better name, in the University of Buffalo's Poetry Collection.)[22] Almuth Grésillon speaks of metaphors of "the road . . . : travelling, course, path, way, march, route, tracks, trails, progression, movement," as well as "forks . . . , junctions, losing one's way, clearing the way, diversion, detours, short cuts, retracing one's steps, dead ends, accidents, false starts, taking a wrong turn," and she suggests balancing metaphors "borrowed from organicism" with "those borrowed from constructivism." She cites the conclusion of Charles Baudelaire's introduction to his translation of Edgar Allan Poe's 1846 essay "The Philosophy of Composition" (a seminal text for genetic critics, which Baudelaire translated under the title "Genèse du poème," or "Genesis of a Poem"): "We shall now see *behind the scenes*, the *workshop*, the *laboratory*, the *inner workings*."[23] (Conveniently and probably not coincidentally, these two views of literary creation—James's stream and Grésillon's road—parallel the dualism often evoked in the digital age of the line and the network.)

To genetic critics, the final work does not appear as the result of pruning the work-in-progress to let the rejected dead leaves fall away and the beautiful great oak, the final work, remain as one possibility chosen and singled out among many others. Rather, as Pierre-Marc de Biasi claims, the drafts reveal "a mobile image, far more hypothetical and often richer than the one the published text will eventually give us to be read as its *truth* after many reworkings"—the work, once seen as a monument, has evolved into a mobile. As the editors of *Drafts*, an issue of *Yale French Studies*, put it, "Whatever autonomy and internal logic formal analysis may reveal in a work of art, the actual work is only one among its multiple possibilities. . . . [T]he work now stands out against a background, and a series, of potentialities. Genetic criticism . . . attempts to reinscribe the work in the series of its variations, in the space of its possibilities." Louis Hay provocatively argues that "perhaps we should consider the text as a *necessary possibility*, as one manifestation of a process which is always virtually present in the background, a kind of third dimension of the written work."[24] Readers of *Ulysses* will probably find the thrust of these arguments familiar, because Stephen Dedalus considers them in a very different context in the "Nestor" episode:

> Had Pyrrhus not fallen by a beldam's hand in Argos or Julius Caesar not been knifed to death. They are not to be thought away. Time has branded them and fettered they are lodged in the room of the infinite possibilities they have ousted. But can those have been possible seeing that they never were? Or was that only possible which came to pass? . . . It must be a movement then, an actuality of the possible as possible. (U 2:48–52, 2:67 [my ellipsis])

In *"Ulysses" in Progress* I claimed that Joyce "presented *Ulysses* as a palimpsest of his development from 1914 to 1922," and if this statement is even partially true, then *Ulysses* is an example of those works that the editors of *Drafts* describe as having "managed to retain something of the aura of their potentialities."[25] In such works, the various relationships between the text's past and present—the ways in which the process leads to the text and the ways in which the text affects our sense of the process—are visible or at least implicit in the text itself.

As I suggested in this book's introduction, Paul Valéry goes further than Stephen or the genetic critics I've quoted, writing in one of his notebooks that "nothing is finer than a fine manuscript draft. . . . A complete poem would be the poem *of* that poem beginning with the fertilized embryo—

and the successive states, the unexpected interpolations, the approximations. That's the real Genesis." And even further when in another notebook Valéry expresses a desire "to transfer the artistry which is placed in a work to its process of production," and he fully subordinates product to process: "Creating a poem is itself a poem"; "*The making*, as the main thing, and whatever product is constructed as *accessory*, that's my idea"; "To consider composition itself as the principal factor," and, adding motion to this last desire, "or treat it as a work, as a dance, as fencing, as the construction of acts and expectations."[26]

Genetic critics tend to see the two poles inherent in all manuscript studies—the process by which the work came into being and the product that resulted—in oscillation with, not in opposition to, each other. The term "avant-texte," the central concept of French genetic criticism, stresses a continuity between the manuscripts and the final text. "Avant-texte" designates all the documents that come before a work when it is considered as a text and when those documents and the text are considered as part of a system. Built into the conception of the avant-texte is the assumption that the material of textual genetics is not a given but rather a critical construction—not all documents that survive are part of the avant-texte for a work—elaborated in relation to a postulated terminal state of the work.

As a result, whereas time for traditional manuscript critics involves looking back to see how the present work came into being, time becomes a fascinating multifaceted factor for genetic critics. According to Jean Bellemin-Noël, "We must never forget this paradox: what was written *before* and had, at first, no *after*, we meet only *after*, and this tempts us to supply a *before* in the sense of a priority, cause, or origin."[27] For Daniel Ferrer, genetic critics cannot renounce teleology, which "is inherent in the genetic mechanisms," no matter how much they might want to, but teleology is ultimately double-edged. "Once the text is declared as such . . . nothing prevents it from retrospectively engendering its *avant-texte*," he claims, and also, "Each genetic state not only depends on all the previous states but also alters their status in a kind of retrospective teleology. Each stage . . . identifies the relevant documents in the preexisting archive and turns them into the *avant-texte* leading toward that stage." We can read the manuscripts as evidence of works-in-progress, even if we remain aware of the end result (like reading a novel for a second time), or from the perspective of the final text. In either case, the genetic materials reveal a richer, fuller set of possibilities than the final text alone can provide; as Ferrer puts it, "If the study of manuscripts is necessary, it is indeed because the final text *does not contain* the whole of its genesis."[28]

If earlier manuscript studies follow the implications of Archibald MacLeish's poem "Ars Poetica"—"A poem should not mean / But be"—genetic critics endorse Frank Paul Bowman's description of the text as "becoming, not being."[29] The writer stopped writing for all kinds of reasons (he or she considered the work to be finished, got tired of working on it, died; an arbitrary deadline arrived; the publisher snatched the work away), but, set among the rich array of its possibilities, the work no longer appears as a complete, self-contained, finished entity. This concept, too, is built into *Ulysses*. When Leopold Bloom recalls lying with Molly on Howth Hill eighteen years previously and then thinks, "Me. And me now" (*U* 8:917), and when Stephen summarizes the changes in his body over time with the phrase "I, I and I. I," (*U* 9:212), they are imagining their minds and bodies, and their lives, as something like a text as genetic critics see it.

When studied genetically, even the most monumental works start to move. In "**Still** *Lost Time*: **Already** the Text of the *Recherche*," for example, Grésillon studies a draft of what became the opening of *À la recherche du temps perdu* and concentrates on Proust's use of the terms *encore* and *dejá* ("still" and "already"). Declaring that she "knew nothing of [the draft's] date or its eventual fate," she sees Proust's struggles with temporal markers as an instance of a writer coming to grips linguistically with a crucial problem in an evolving text. Focusing on a conclusion rather than a beginning, Raymonde Debray Genette in "Flaubert's 'A Simple Heart,' or How to Make an Ending" looks at Flaubert's tortuous path toward the last words of his story. "He goes from expansion to blockages and from blockages to displacements," she concludes, revealing a writer struggling to delay the ending as much as to reach it.[30]

Finally, and more directly relevant to this chapter, in "Paragraphs in Expansion (James Joyce)" Ferrer and Rabaté study Joyce's uses of paragraphs in his writing. "Do they belong to the text or to its layout?" they ask about paragraphs, formulating a version of the distinction between McGann's linguistic and bibliographical codes.[31] For Joyce, paragraphs are internal borders. Rather than dividing the inside of the text from the outside, they separate units of prose from each other, and once Joyce created paragraph divisions, he tended to retain them no matter how much a paragraph grew. Joyce's addition of the heads in his late work on "Aeolus" does not disrupt the paragraph divisions, because, with only one exception, he inserted the heads into already established paragraph breaks. And so his startling overhaul of the appearance of "Aeolus" maintains the paragraph structure intact. Ferrer and Rabaté conclude that paragraphs "play the role of mediation between the book, understood as a formal organization, and the proliferating letter of which they are . . . the very vessels of expansion."[32]

More recently, Rabaté has argued that Joyce's works—he speaks directly of *Finnegans Wake*, but his claim applies in many ways to *Ulysses* as well—call for an "ideal genetic reader," a "genetic reader," or a "genreader" (he uses all three terms): "a reader who has to approach the difficult and opaque language less with glosses and annotations than through the material evidence of the notebooks, drafts, corrected proofs reproduced by the *James Joyce Archive*." This genetic reader "confronts a new type of materiality and temporality"—a text, like Bloom, is "Me. And me now" (or, depending on the perspective, "Me. And me then"). Joyce's avant-textes reveal a series of possibilities, many of which Joyce never implemented, as well as his tendency to work with and build on whatever happened, correctly or erroneously, as he wrote, and just as Bloom connects time's passage with his human limitations and fallibility, so the archive teaches a reader to live amid error. The genetic reader "will have the choice between varieties of error," because, confronting *Ulysses* and the *Wake*, "we keep misreading, missing meanings, producing forced interpretations, seeing things which are not there." What Ferrer revealed as the avant-texte's fullness ("the final text *does not contain* the whole of its genesis") is for Rabaté an excess that will always overwhelm any single interpretation: "Facing an expanding archive, the 'genreader' progresses through an excess of intentions and meanings that never adequately match each other."[33] The genetic reader, like genetic critics studying the avant-texte, faces a "Pisgah sight" of *Ulysses*.

■

And what about Stephen Dedalus, the men who listen to his parable, his two old ladies at the top of Nelson's Pillar, and the stalled tramcars? We left them many pages ago in a tableau that contrasted with the bustle and noise of the preceding pages of "Aeolus." The trams won't move again, and the women will remain atop the monument: they are suspended in time. When we look at the passage from the perspective of Joyce's writing of it, however, all is mobile.

The ending of Joyce's first, provisionally finished version of "Aeolus" contained Stephen, his parable, and his listeners, but when Joyce inserted the trams at the beginning and end, he turned the mechanized Dublin—already important because of the machines in the newspaper office—into a frame for "Aeolus." With the trams cut off from their origins and destinations, the new words at the end emphasize the breakdown of the mechanized city. When the trams were absent from the episode, they presumably went on their journeys without any interruptions, but after Joyce added them, naming their origins and destinations but declaring them "becalmed in short circuit," they become simultaneously present and paralyzed, even if paralyzed in calmness. In the trams' oscillation between absence and presence, their stillness and stasis reveal a text perpetually in motion.

The newspaper heads—those artificial, stunning, and visually loud intrusions, usually considered as breaking the narrative's flow or interrupting the text's movement—are aswirl in motion, and Joyce's revisions after he first inserted them increase the activity. The first head in our excerpt originally described only the two ladies' "donation" of the plumstones before Joyce added a line emphasizing the falling objects' speed ("SPEEDPILLS VELOCITOUS AEROLITHS, BELIEF"). The second head—"HELLO THERE, CENTRAL!"—suggests a frantic emergency phone call. The final one is full of motion, with its "TITILLATING" missing fingers and its "FRISKY" women who "WIMBLE" and "WANGLE" (whatever "WIMBLES" might mean, it certainly suggests more motion, although less sadness, than "SIGHS," the word it replaced). Even the often absent word "smiling" in the last section—as I noted earlier, MacHugh speaks "grimly" or "smiling grimly" depending on the version of *Ulysses*—appears and disappears like *Alice in Wonderland*'s Cheshire Cat's grin.

In adding the trams and heads (as well as many allusions to wind elsewhere in the episode), Joyce revised "Aeolus" to conform with the kind of writing he had moved into in "Eumaeus," "Ithaca," and "Penelope." No longer writing stream-of-consciousness interior monologues, he was constructing more abstract structures for each episode, and his interpolation of newspaper heads into an episode located in a newspaper office is consistent with this late practice. As critics from as far back as Stuart Gilbert in 1930 have pointed out, the heads themselves progress historically; formal and static at the start, they become loud and colloquial at the end.[34] These intrusions make their presence known visually, but they also move in time.

Crucially, *Ulysses* itself is reinscribed back into time. A genetic view reveals that *Ulysses* as a text has its own history, one that became obscured by the book's publication but is far removed from Stephen's "nightmare from which I am trying to awake" (*U* 2:377). This history is also far from Joseph Frank's influential early approach to *Ulysses* as "spatial form": literary works are "apprehend[ed] . . . spatially, in a moment of time, rather than as a sequence," with their elements "juxtaposed in space rather than unrolling in time." "Past and present," Frank argues, are "locked in a timeless unity."[35] A critic writing in 1945 might understandably want to make the Dedalian move of eradicating time and awakening from the nightmare of history, but time has been restored to *Ulysses* in many different ways since Frank wrote, most prominently in the view that *Ulysses* has changed over the years as readers have approached it in their various ways. In that view, *Ulysses* has changed continuously starting from the moment of its publication, but reinserting *Ulysses* into the history of its writing gives it an altered past as well. The published text becomes a still point between the teeming histories of its production and reception. Everything suspended at Nelson's Pillar begins to move again as the monument becomes a mobile.

4

When First I Saw, Part 2

Discovering Joyce's Manuscripts

Looking back now at my first encounter with *Ulysses* in 1966, I can easily view it as a point of origin. Much of what has happened in my life since then stems from it, and I can draw a straight line from it through many subsequent events, including the writing of this book. But Jean Bellemin-Noël's statement about the temporal paradox involved in genetic criticism—"We must never forget this paradox: what was written *before* and had, at first, no *after*, we meet only *after*, and this tempts us to supply a *before* in the sense of a priority, cause, or origin"—gives me pause.[1] As an origin, my first response itself had many causes, only some of which can be grasped in retrospect. And while it may have set a certain set of events in motion, it was only the first of several discoveries, the first in a sequence of drafts.

A second encounter, a second draft, dates from the summer of 1972 while I was in graduate school at Princeton University. Like my first reading of *Ulysses*, in some ways even more so, this event can stand at the start of what Daniel Ferrer calls "a kind of retrospective teleology."[2] The pattern seems clear when viewed from the perspective of the later events, the now, even if it seemed far from clear while the events were transpiring. If, as Ferrer claims, the "the final text [of a work] *does not contain* the whole of its genesis," neither does the present moment of a life: the product at any particular moment can be seen in relation to a much more complex process.[3] Perhaps Stephen's "I, I and I. I" (*U* 9:212) expresses this better than Bloom's similar but not quite identical "Me. And me now" (*U* 8:917). The product and the process oscillate with earlier states, the monument of a life becoming a mobile.

■

After I read *Ulysses* in Peter Bien's course at Dartmouth, I threw myself into my new career as an English major and, unusually for someone who has often second-guessed what he has done, never looked back on the discarded draft of life as a mathematician, the possibility that never came to pass. When Richard Cross offered a specialized seminar on Joyce's works during my junior year, I eagerly enrolled in it and found reading *Ulysses* a second time to be as enjoyable and rewarding as before, even more so. During my senior year I decided to go to graduate school, and I applied only to departments that included Joyce scholars. Princeton, which satisfied my requirement as well as any department could, accepted me, and in my first term there I took a course with A. Walton Litz.

I enjoyed being a graduate student, although for the first time I didn't do particularly well in my classes. Despite this, Litz offered to supervise my dissertation, and I looked forward to eventually working with him. When the time came at the start of my third year, I decided to write a thesis on Joyce's influence on subsequent novelists (as we formulated such a topic then), especially William Faulkner, Virginia Woolf, and Samuel Beckett, and began reading through their novels and some of the secondary materials on them. Halfway through the year, in January 1973, Joyce's world came to life for me as I visited Dublin for the first time. Back in Princeton after that, I started writing the Faulkner chapter, which refused to come out. Every sentence, every word, was a struggle. In late May I finally finished a fifty-page chapter and gave it to Walt. About a week later, he asked me to stop by his office to talk with him about it.

When I arrived, he was gathering up his books and briefcase in order to catch a plane later that day for England, where he would be spending the summer. He bypassed almost all his usual small talk to get quickly to my chapter. About twenty pages in it were good, he assured me, perhaps with some reworking even publishable, but the rest were weak. The evidence was often trivial; the paragraphs didn't flow smoothly; the chapter lacked a convincing overview. He pointed to one paragraph, and I could see how my struggle with the material showed through on every line: opening sentence; then "But" and second sentence; next, "However" and the third sentence; finally, "And yet" and the last. The chapter obviously needed to be redone, Walt said, but he didn't really think that was worth doing. He couldn't see a successful thesis in it, and he recommended that I find a new topic. As I sat silently, he seemed about to leave, but then he stopped and mentioned that many new Joyce documents had become available since he had written his well-known book on the manuscripts, *The Art of James Joyce*. The University at Buffalo and Cornell University possessed big new collections, with published catalogs available for both, and Joyce's notesheets at the British Library (then the British Museum) had just been edited. Maybe I could look at manuscripts he hadn't seen and at Joyce's notes, he suggested, and augment or update his work. Let me know what you come up with when I get back in September, he said as he closed the conversation and guided me out of his office. I doubt that he expected to find me anywhere near the campus when he returned.

I spent about a month after that meeting lying in bed or sitting in a chair staring at a wall, but after that I decided to investigate Walt's idea. (Later, when I could look at the Joyce-Faulkner chapter from some distance, I extracted the successful pages that Walt had singled out into my first published article.) Peter Spielberg's catalog revealed that Buffalo's Poetry Collection included many early drafts of individual *Ulysses* episodes. I was pleased that, unbeknownst to me while I was living there, these documents were in my hometown, only a few blocks away from the house I had lived in as a teenager and in the university library in which I sometimes studied while I was in high school. But I was also a little concerned: was I never going to be able to escape Buffalo?

Microfilm copies of all the Poetry Collection's manuscripts were available for scholars to borrow. I ordered two reels containing *Ulysses* drafts, and while waiting for them to arrive I looked at Philip Herring's edition of the British Library notesheets for *Ulysses*, at that time less than a year old. I read through the notes with a sinking feeling, unable to discern any possible project that could develop from them. I became intrigued, though, whenever I saw a note containing words that I remembered from *Ulysses*. One, for instance, read "Inisfail the fair," part of a sentence from early in the "Cyclops" episode: "In Inisfail the fair there lies a land, the land of holy Michan."[4] Another was "Jew: love his country when sure which it is (SD. P. M'H)"; the initials at the end puzzled me, but the rest echoed a vicious anti-Semitic exchange in "Cyclops": "—And after all, says John Wyse, why can't a jew love his country like the next fellow? /—Why not? says J. J., when he's quite sure which country it is."[5] I also registered Herring's puzzlement over

Joyce's use of colored crayons. Joyce crossed out many of the notes with a red, blue, or green crayon, and Herring had compared these notes with the text of the published *Ulysses*. He found some of them in *Ulysses*, including "Inisfail" and "love his country." But he couldn't find many other intriguing "Cyclops" notes—for instance, "LB made up to mother-in-law" (a reference to Molly's mother?? Molly says in "Penelope" that she doesn't know who her mother was)[6] or a primitive four-line poem about Ireland—and no pattern at all emerged.

When the Buffalo microfilms arrived, I sat at the dark, cumbersome reader and glanced at the page images, marveling at Joyce's handwriting—there, in front of me!—and at the visually stunning pages. Sometimes Joyce wrote in ink, sometimes in pencil, in handwriting that was small and often very difficult to read. When he used a copybook, he began writing on the rectos (the right-hand pages), with a margin at the left that tended to widen as he moved down the page. To revise, he crossed out words and wrote new ones above or below them or nearby in the left, top, or bottom margin, often with a line connecting the body of the text to the marginal words. He added words, phrases, or longer passages above or below the line, in the margins (connected by a line or signaled by a superscript *F* or another letter), or on the facing verso page. Long additions are almost always on the versos, and sometimes they run over onto another verso page, even occasionally moving in the reverse direction as Joyce wrote from the back toward the front of the copybook. It is not always visually clear where a bit of marginal text fits into the main text, and sometimes the pages become so cluttered that following the lines connecting words in the body of the text with those in the margins is difficult or even impossible. Joyce obviously knew how all the elements fit together and did not need a precise visual indicator, but it astonished me that anyone could have known how the various bits of text on a page related to each other.[7] Colored lines and *X*'s often cover full pages or sections of pages. In the black-and-white microfilms I was looking at, the writing and markings all appeared as black and different shades of gray. Later, my first look at the original documents when I visited Buffalo's Poetry Collection resembled the sudden shift from black-and-white to color in the film of *The Wizard of Oz*: the pages were tan, not white; Joyce wrote in various shades of ink and pencil; and the diagonal lines, *X*'s, and other markings appeared in Technicolor.

The British Library notesheets cover only the last seven episodes of *Ulys-*

ses, starting with "Cyclops," so I began my reading with that episode's two drafts. In his catalog Spielberg designated one of the "Cyclops" documents—two reasonably clearly written large, loose sheets containing four scenes and a fragment of a fifth—as the earlier of the drafts, and I started with that one. Deciphering some of Joyce's handwriting was extremely difficult, but I slowly became acclimated to his formation of letters, and aided by the published *Ulysses* I was able to make out many, though hardly all, of the words.

Early versions of scenes that differed greatly from their published forms were fascinating, as were extended passages that Joyce had apparently discarded entirely as he developed the episode. One very different scene was a discussion of Ireland and Jews. Stephen Dedalus, entirely absent from the published episode, not only hobnobs here with the bigoted men in the pub but also offers the anti-Semitic answer to the question about a Jew loving his country, with J. J. O'Molloy, who answers "when he's quite sure which country it is" in the published version, now asking the question.[8] How could Joyce have included Stephen here, not only in a scene containing the most virulently anti-Semitic words spoken to or about Leopold Bloom, the man who will rescue him a few hours later, during the day but even speaking them himself? Also here is Professor MacHugh, who like Stephen appears earlier in "Aeolus," and so the initials "SD. P. M'H" in Joyce's note referred to these two characters. In a scene that explained one of the puzzling notes but which Joyce discarded, the men gossip about Bloom and Molly, mentioning rumors that they are going to be divorced and that, to win Molly, Bloom "^<made> sucked^ up to his mother-in-law."[9] Surprisingly, many of the characters are unnamed, with much of the dialogue attributed to a speaker identified only by a dash or an *X* (reversing the pattern, though, the published version's Citizen is named Cusack here); the hilariously vitriolic unnamed first-person narrator is largely undeveloped; and some of the writing is quite unformed compared to the published text, as in "Then did you speak, noble Cusack, lifting up your voice, and all men hearkened."[10]

The draft was gripping, but staring for hours into the dark microfilm reader and hearing the screechy grinding of the handcrank that I needed to turn in order to move the film forward and backward were giving me a backache and a headache. Near the end of the day, however, all physical discomfort evaporated as I unexpectedly experienced the first of two "Eureka!" moments regarding the "Cyclops" drafts. Following one of the scenes, Joyce wrote a little poem:

O Ireland! Our sireland!
Once fireland! Now mireland!
No liar land shall buy our land!
A higher land is Ireland!¹¹

This wasn't exactly Keats or Yeats, but it fascinated me because I remembered reading a similar quatrain a few days earlier in Herring's edition of the British Library notesheets. I rushed to find the book, and found the poem, only slightly different, on one of the "Cyclops" notesheets. Not only was it there, but Joyce had crossed it out in red.¹² *Ulysses* does not include the poem, and I wondered if Joyce had used other crossed-out notes in the drafts in passages that he discarded before he finished the episode. I found some others in the draft but not enough to establish a pattern.

After a few days with this draft, I turned to the other "Cyclops" manuscript, a twenty-four-page copybook containing the four scenes from the large pages as well as four other ones. Spielberg described this copybook as a later document than the loose sheets and gave it a higher number. The copybook is much more exciting to look at than the loose pages but also harder to read: the handwriting is messier, and the additions sprawl all over many pages. The first four scenes here are not in the other draft. Besides the unnamed characters (more than in the loose pages) and the barely developed narrator, these scenes surprised me in two ways. First, the copybook starts with an opening for the episode but not with the distinctive first-person narrative voice familiar from the published "Cyclops": "I was just passing the time of day with old Troy of the D.M.P. at the corner of Arbour hill there and be damned but a bloody sweep came along and he near drove his gear into my eye" (*U* 12:1–3). Instead, the draft's first words are an early version of a parody passage: "In ^<green Erin of the west> Inisfail the fair^ there lies a land, the land of holy Michan,"¹³ words that don't appear in the published episode until most of the way down the second page (*U* 12:68). The narrator is missing entirely from the first scene. Where was he? Equally surprising, on the back of the draft's first page appear several passages of interior monologue relating to Bloom walking along the street between the Ormond Hotel of "Sirens" and Barney Kiernan's pub in "Cyclops," a transition included in the published text only indirectly when the narrator tells Joe Hynes that he saw Bloom "sloping around by Pill lane and Greek street with his cod's eye counting up all the guts of the fish" (*U* 12:213–14). In his early work on "Cyclops," did Joyce consider using interior monologue for the episode? Maybe he did.

But the "Eureka!" moment for this copybook came with the final four scenes, the ones repeated from the loose pages. There again, on one of the copybook's more visually striking pages, were Stephen Dedalus's snide words about a Jew loving his country.[14] Surprisingly, I realized as I read, these scenes constituted not a later version of the loose pages but rather an earlier one. Joyce had apparently rewritten the last four scenes of this copybook onto the large pages, revising somewhat as he copied. Spielberg had misnumbered the two "Cyclops" documents and described them incorrectly, obscuring the relationship between them, something no one had mentioned in print in the nearly twenty years that Buffalo had owned the documents or in the more than ten years since Spielberg had published his catalog.[15] (I learned a little later that I wasn't the only graduate student who had noticed Spielberg's misnumbering and incorrect description at this time. After I revised my chapter on the "Cyclops" manuscripts into an article and submitted it to the *James Joyce Quarterly*, the *JJQ*'s editor, Thomas Staley, wrote me that, along with mine, he had almost simultaneously received another article about the documents. The journal published both Myron Schwartzman's and my articles in the same issue.) More important, it meant that this copybook was a very early draft, Joyce's first attempt to write the episode or close to it, and that questions about whether he had begun writing "Cyclops" with the narrator or with the parody passages and about whether he had once considered including Bloom's interior monologue in the episode pertained to his very early work on the episode. It also meant that any possible pattern involving his color cross-outs would probably show up in this copybook. One did. Many notes that Joyce crossed out in red—including, among many others, "Inisfail the fair" (apparently a trigger for his replacement of "green Erin of the west" in the draft's opening words) and the remarks about a Jew loving his country and Bloom making up to his mother-in-law (both of which Joyce first used in this copybook)—appeared here, enough to establish that he crossed out notes simply to indicate that he had used them rather than to signify some kind of thematic connection among the notes or grouping of them.

As I figured all this out and wrote a chapter on Joyce's writing of "Cyclops," I had a new thesis topic.

I turned to the "Aeolus" episode for a second chapter because in *The Art of*

James Joyce Litz had compared Joyce's revision of *Ulysses* with Henry James's rewriting of his novels for the New York Edition, describing Joyce's addition of the headlines to the episode at a late stage in its development as "the great revision."[16] I wanted to look at the revision more closely than Walt had been able to do, and as I read the proofs for "Aeolus" I saw that Joyce had added the heads in stages, not all at once, and had revised many of them after he first put them in. (Chapters 3 and 8 present details of Joyce's revision of the heads.) I went on to study his last years of effort on *Ulysses* to see if he worked in a similar way there, and when I saw that he did, I postulated that the "great revision," not just to "Aeolus" but to all of *Ulysses*, was less a sudden overhaul than an evolutionary development, and argued that *Ulysses* moved through three stages as Joyce worked on the novel, not as part of any preestablished plan. This argument about the early, middle, and last stages became the basis for my dissertation and then the revised version that became *"Ulysses" in Progress*.

■

I was so relieved that the thesis and the book worked out as well as they did that I didn't really stop to think about why the influence project had proceeded so badly and the manuscript one so well. The influence fiasco doesn't surprise me in the least now. At that time I knew very little about how literary language worked and even less about how human beings, and authors in particular, might relate to each other, and I had no concept of intertextuality or how, in any other formulation, texts might relate to other texts. I didn't feel very comfortable or competent doing criticism or interpretation, even though, of course, it is almost impossible to do any scholarly work on literature without engaging in those activities. The influence project seemed like a good one for someone to do (and it was: in 1977, Robert Martin Adams published *Afterjoyce: Studies in Fiction after "Ulysses,"* the writing of which would have overlapped with mine on my original dissertation had I continued with it), but genetic critic Almuth Grésillon's argument that the metaphor of the road for the progress from a work's conception to the denouement of its publication needs to be contrasted with "more indirect paths, . . . *dead ends, accidents, false starts, taking a wrong turn*" describes my first dissertation project very well.[17]

While I was working on my dissertation, I had completely forgotten that as a boy of seven or eight, in summer when the weather was warm and dry

I often passed much of the day outside on our house's front porch. Two or three times during the summer I pulled out a large bucket full of bottle caps that I had been collecting, mostly from sidewalks and picnic grounds in nearby parks. I distributed the caps according to brand and tabulated how many of each kind there were. At the same time, local radio station WKBW blared on my tinny transistor radio as I ignored my parents' repeated demands that I turn off the radio or at least turn it down. Nothing stopped me from listening, especially to KB's weekly countdown of the Top 30 songs. I kept statistics on how many weeks a song had been number one, how many weeks it had been on the chart, how many songs on each label were on the list, how many vocal songs were there and how many instrumentals, how many sung by men and by women, by individuals and by groups, and on and on. I always had hopes as to which song would be number one the next week. Sometimes things worked out mostly the way I wanted, but since I had wretched taste, more often they didn't. As I counted my bottle caps, I regarded the census almost like a track meet or horse race: would last time's winner Sceptre-Budweiser ("King of Beers") repeat, or would local brand Throwaway-Genesee Beer come out on top in a surprise? Whatever the result, I could satisfy myself that my lists and statistics reflected an underlying order, one I could rely on until the next bottle-cap count or Top 30 list.

Thinking back to those days on the porch, I can understand how the manuscript project let me put some quirky skills and interests that had been there all along to good use, and I can see the young boy who could spend hours counting bottle caps or itemizing the details in Top 30 lists in the scholar who could patiently read through nearly illegible manuscripts and remember tiny details to find relationships among the documents and coherent patterns in them. Like Leopold Bloom remembering his first sight of Molly, I wonder if it was fate or coincidence or fortuitous circumstance that brought Joyce's manuscripts and me together. Did Walt know or sense that I'd be good at this kind of work? Did he simply take a stab in the dark in an attempt to get me back on track? Did he try, after I had spent a year floundering around in a topic of my own, to direct me into the kind of project that he preferred and felt most comfortable with? (Many of the dissertations he directed involved manuscript work on such writers as Joyce, Ezra Pound, T. S. Eliot, William Butler Yeats, and William Carlos Williams.) More important than his motives is the fact that for the second time I was very fortunate in the teacher and mentor whom I found.

When I first worked on the manuscripts, I had no interest in using them to establish an accurate text of *Ulysses* (nor did Walt suggest this direction to me). Instead, I wanted to look only at how Joyce constructed his book and how it grew. In one sense this choice isn't surprising, since I had never been exposed to textual criticism and didn't know what it was. I'm not sure how I would have responded had I learned about editing beforehand or then. Bibliography or scholarly editing might have instantly satisfied the bottle-cap collector, census taker, and list compiler in me. But observing *Ulysses* come into being, I now think, satisfied other, perhaps more crucial, needs.

In chapter 2 I talked about my mother's habit of cutting off all ties with other people and suggested that I paid a huge price for turning myself into a person my mother would never stop talking to. That cost was my imagination. I wasn't interested in being exposed to other lives that perhaps seemed more alluring than my own because it was too dangerous to do that. In allowing me no access to anything going on inside his head, my father became a cipher. My mother constructed an alternative reality—everyone in our family was happy and loved each other, no one got sick, everything was pleasant—and any creative energy I had got sucked into maintaining that illusion and covering over the disconnect between it and her severed relationships.

But then there was *Ulysses*. I already knew, and marveled at, the way Leopold Bloom's personality gets built up as we experience the minutiae and fragments of his mind and his life. And now I was observing how minute textual fragments—"O Ireland! Our sireland!," a sentence of inchoate interior monologue, an early version of an over-the-top parodic description of Little Britain Street and Barney Kiernan's pub—grew in front of my eyes into the massive collection of small details that make up Leopold Bloom and the full world of the novel that so intoxicated me. In the process I was also constructing a picture of a human being, something I hadn't been able to do before, as I watched Joyce engage in his work. Textual critics and manuscript scholars, even when we give ourselves the fancier name of genetic critics, often get mocked for the attention we pay to tiny details—commas, individual letters—or criticized for rifling through private, unpublished papers or pitied for the dry-as-dust lot in life that we've chosen for ourselves. For me, however, those tiny details and left-behind papers offered access to the interior of a pulsating, juicy human novel and to the brilliant but fallible and very human person writing it.

I need to say a little more about this person writing *Ulysses*. I've mentioned that one of the aspects of the book that amazed me when I first read it was the extent to which the deepest feelings of characters are conveyed, all their thoughts are exposed, without anyone getting hurt or punished for anything they think or feel. This isn't quite true. Leopold Bloom tolerates a great deal—he accepts Molly's adultery as "less reprehensible than theft, highway robbery, cruelty to children and animals," and a host of other crimes (*U* 17:2182–83), and he thinks of the Citizen that "Perhaps not to hurt he meant" (*U* 13:1220)—but it's not the case that no one gets punished in *Ulysses*. Richard Best gets punished, and so do John Eglinton, Reuben J. Dodd, Horace Rumbold, Henry Carr, and other people who made the mistake of crossing James Joyce in ways he never forgot. I love reading Joyce's revenge on these people, even though at times I've wondered what it was like for Richard Best—who was director of the National Library of Ireland in the late 1920s and 1930s and who lived until 1959—to live on through all those years with the unflattering portrait Joyce froze him into. Richard Ellmann's biography shows us that if Joyce couldn't settle his scores in his fiction, he sometimes stopped talking to people. I've often noticed that, whereas I can read *Ulysses* over and over again, I've been able to get completely through Ellmann's biography only once. Then, much more recently than I'd like to admit, I had one of those "Duh!" moments when I realized that of course I'd have trouble reading about Joyce's treatment of his friend Ottocaro Weiss, whom he stopped talking to when he suspected, with no real grounds at all, that Weiss had helped to convince Edith Rockefeller McCormick to end her monthly subsidy to him,[18] or about his treatment of Sylvia Beach or Harriet Weaver. I've already lived with that person in the form of my mother; I'd like to limit the time I spend with him.

But Joyce the writer—now that's a different story. If, as John Eglinton claims and Stephen repeats during the discussion of *Hamlet* with Best and the other men in the National Library of Ireland, Shakespeare was "all in all" in his creations (*U* 9:1018–21), then it's no stretch of the imagination, for those people who have one, to see Joyce as both the righter of wrongs done to him and the creator of Leopold Bloom. This is the Joyce—the writer—that we Joyceans, and all readers of *Ulysses*, get to see. It is the best of James Joyce, and genetic critics have the privilege of seeing him at work.

In stumbling into this kind of scholarship almost thirty-five years ago after facing a false start, wrong turn, and dead end, I was able, I think, to exploit some of my talents, advance our knowledge of *Ulysses* and of Joyce a little, and—surely personally most important, even if I recognized it only much later—start to fill in some huge holes in the life I had been living up to then. The dry manuscript details let the parched riverbed that my imagination had become when I let it get diverted into supporting my mother's fiction of a perfectly happy family refill itself to some extent, drop by drop and textual detail by textual detail. Through the manuscripts, I was even able to eventually get part of my imagination back, like a blind person regaining partial sight. A partially blind man gave us both *Ulysses* and many, many manuscript pages for it, and using those manuscript pages to recover the writing processes that led to *Ulysses*, however incomplete and imperfect the results are and probably always will be, is intimately connected for me with that recovery of my imagination, however incomplete and imperfect but ultimately satisfying that might be. Drafts of a work, drafts of a life: they situate themselves on a line that leads to an end result, but they are fascinating in and of themselves, perhaps no more so than in their moving twists and turns, their forks, and their detours.

5

The James Joyce Archive and Hans Walter Gabler's Edition of *Ulysses*

A Personal History

Was any other novel's introduction into the reading world quite like that of *Ulysses*? The February 1921 New York court decision that declared the book obscene while Joyce was still writing it led to its publication in France as a collector's item, a cult object. Joyce wanted *Ulysses* published in English-speaking countries, both as a recognition of its respectability and as a response to the pirated editions that appeared in the United States in the late 1920s, and one of his ways of aiding the process was to encourage friends and interested critics to write extended, learned studies of it. By the time Judge John M. Woolsey nullified the ban in late 1933 and *Ulysses* appeared legally in the United States the next year, several articles and at least three books had been written about it. Just two weeks after Random House published *Ulysses*, it ran a two-page ad in the *Saturday Review of Literature* headed "How to Enjoy James Joyce's Great Novel *Ulysses*," urging potential readers to ignore the mass of criticism that had already built up around the book. A few months later, *Vanity Fair* published a parody—not of the book itself but of *Ulysses* criticism.[1] For better or worse, *Ulysses* has never been available in English-speaking countries without an accompanying factory of critics, a labor force eventually dubbed the "Joyce industry."

The first Ph.D. dissertation to focus exclusively on Joyce, according to Tetsumaro Hayashi's census, appeared only three years after Joyce's death: Joseph Prescott's "James Joyce's *Ulysses* as Work in Progress," completed at Harvard University in 1944 and based largely on the proofs for *Ulysses* that Harvard had acquired in the 1930s.[2] In the same year the first posthumous publication of any Joyce work appeared, Theodore Spencer's edition of the abandoned and fragmentary early version of *A Portrait of the Artist as a Young Man* that Joyce called *Stephen Hero* (a manuscript also at Harvard). Spencer and Prescott probably spent a great deal of time in close proximity in Harvard's library in 1942 and 1943, and they must have conferred with Harvard professor Harry Levin, whose book *James Joyce: A Critical Introduction*, published in the year of Joyce's death, was the first major book-length study of Joyce's works to be written by someone outside his circle of acquaintances.

Aside from this temporary location of Harvard as the Joyce industry headquarters in the first few years after the author's death, it is noteworthy that two of these three books were old-fashioned projects involving editing and manuscripts. (Thirty years later, Levin, too, became associated with Joyce's manuscripts when he wrote an introduction to the facsimile edition of the Rosenbach Manuscript.) If, as Peter Shillingsburg claims, the process of scholarly editing produces texts that "preserve or rescue a work of artistic, social, intellectual, or historical importance as an artifact," then by the time Joyce died, his novels had already entered the canon of works seen as worth such efforts.[3] In a way, it didn't even take Joyce's death for *Ulysses* to achieve this status. Morris Ernst and Alexander Lindey, who argued the case for Joyce's novel before Judge Woolsey in 1933 and wanted it to be judged according to the special criteria reserved for classic works, proclaimed *Ulysses*—"in essence, an eleven-year-old text, never published in a trade edition," Kevin Dettmar reminds us as he quotes Ernst and Lindey—a "modern classic" or even simply a "classic" that had "stood the test of time."[4]

Manuscript study thus constituted a major aspect of Joyce scholarship from the start. There are several obvious reasons for this. For one thing, many of the manuscripts became available for scholarly research quite quickly. Also, scholars gravitated toward any approach that might make *Ulysses* or *Finnegans Wake* more comprehensible, and manuscript study seemed like a promising possibility. And tantalizing glimpses of them came from some of Joyce's acquaintances who had seen his papers, most prominently Frank Budgen, who described Joyce pulling out "little writing blocks especially made for the waistcoat pocket" and jotting down "a word or two . . . at lightning speed as ear or memory served his turn." Budgen noted that this "method of making a multitude of criss-cross notes in pencil was a strange one for a man whose sight was never good. A necessary adjunct to the method was a huge oblong magnifying glass."[5] (Chapter 3 contains a fuller quotation from Budgen.)

I didn't plan to be a manuscript scholar, but, as I recount in the previous chapter, once I started working with documents like the ones Budgen described, I eagerly joined this branch of Joyce scholarship. After I finished my dissertation and then revised it into *"Ulysses" in Progress*, I became involved in the late 1970s and 1980s with two major projects that focused on Joyce's manuscripts, *The James Joyce Archive* and Hans Walter Gabler's edition of *Ulysses*. Here I offer a history of these two projects from the perspective on my own work on them.

■

Joyce manuscripts found their way into research libraries very soon after his death, and by 1960 four major collections were established. One is at the British Library, which possesses materials that Joyce gave to Harriet Shaw Weaver, who supported him financially with monthly payments for years. These documents include the *Ulysses* notesheets and the bulk of the drafts, manuscripts, typescripts, and proofs for *Finnegans Wake*. A second, huge gathering is at the Poetry Collection at the University at Buffalo (formerly called the University of Buffalo), which purchased a vast collection of documents that Joyce left behind in Paris, many of them saved from his apartment during World War II by his friend Paul Léon and brother-in-law Alexander Ponizowski (both of whom were killed by the Nazis during World War II) and then exhibited in 1949 at the Librairie La Hune, and subsequently purchased additional materials from *Ulysses* publisher Sylvia Beach and was given others by publisher B. W. Huebsch.[6] These papers include all the notebooks for *Finnegans Wake* and, for *Ulysses*, many early drafts, typescripts, and proofs. Third, Cornell University obtained the manuscripts and letters that Joyce left behind in Trieste and that were kept by his brother Stanislaus, including many of Joyce's newspaper articles and critical essays and other documents from the 1900s and 1910s.[7] Fourth, Yale University possesses a wide range of documents from a collection that John J. Slocum assembled in the 1940s and 1950s as he prepared his 1953 bibliography of Joyce's works with Herbert Cahoon. In addition, other institutions with large and small collections of materials include the Harry Ransom Center at the University of Texas at Austin; the Croessmann Collection at Southern Illinois University; Harvard University; Princeton University; the Rosenbach Museum and

Library in Philadelphia; the Henry E. Huntington Library in San Marino, California; the University of Wisconsin at Milwaukee; the New York Public Library; the University of Tulsa; University College Dublin—and this list doesn't cover every collection. The National Library of Ireland now belongs in the group of major collections. Before its 2002 acquisition it possessed a few but nonetheless significant Joyce holdings, the most important of which is the manuscript of *A Portrait of the Artist as a Young Man*.

This large number of libraries means that the surviving documents for any of Joyce's works are widely scattered. In the case of *Ulysses*, for instance, the notesheets are in London at the British Library; other notes and also early drafts are at Buffalo and now also in Dublin at the National Library of Ireland; the holograph, or handwritten, manuscript is in Philadelphia at the Rosenbach Museum and Library; the typescripts are at Buffalo; the first placards with Joyce's corrections and additions are in Cambridge, Massachusetts, at Harvard; later placards and the first sets of page proofs are at Buffalo (with unmarked duplicates of the proofs at Buffalo and Princeton); and the final page proofs are in Austin at the University of Texas's Ransom Center. This list does not include individual documents or sometimes single pages that are in other collections. Comparing any two documents was extremely difficult: some libraries loaned out microfilms, as did Buffalo when I worked on my dissertation (only two at a time, though), whereas other documents, such as the Rosenbach Manuscript, were not available in reproduction at all but only in the library itself. To work with more than one of these documents, a scholar had to carefully transcribe the text of one of them and indicate any important markings, such as differences between pencil and pen inscriptions, changes in paper, and so forth, and use those notes when it became possible to see another in microfilm or on a visit to the original. Needless to say, under these conditions it was a great deal easier to see the trees than the forest, and not surprisingly much early manuscript research on *Ulysses* dealt with specific issues or problems rather than with large questions regarding Joyce's writing of the book.

The conditions for working with Joyce manuscripts up until the mid-1970s being what they were, it would seem likely that *The James Joyce Archive*—a sixty-three-volume photoreprint edition of almost all the then-extant and available notes, drafts, manuscripts, typescripts, and proofs, released by Garland Publishing between 1977 and 1979—came into being because scholars wanted to make the manuscripts more accessible. But this is not the way it happened. The idea for the series, the first of its kind for any modern author, was Gavin Borden's, Garland's founder and co-owner. In the early 1970s, Garland was a fledgling for-profit company that had produced some author bibliographies (a couple of them of dubious reputation) and several series of photographic reprints of out-of-print books, especially the kinds of eighteenth- and nineteenth-century books that only established and large research libraries were likely to have in their collections and that new or newly expanded university libraries were eager to acquire. Borden had studied Joyce's works as a Harvard undergraduate with Harry Levin, and he remembered Levin saying something about the Joyce manuscripts being interesting. Without knowing anything specifically about what scholars were doing with the manuscripts or what frustrations they were encountering, he was convinced both that a series of manuscript facsimiles would be a fascinating project to undertake and that Garland could make a profit producing it. He traveled to Oxford University to discuss a possible series with Richard Ellmann, who suggested that he visit the University of Tulsa to talk with Thomas Staley, founder and editor of the *James Joyce Quarterly*. Staley, in turn, pointed him to A. Walton Litz in Princeton, a short train ride from Garland's New York offices, and when in early 1974 Borden asked to meet Litz for lunch to talk about his idea, Litz asked if I, then finishing my Ph.D. dissertation under his supervision, could come along.

Borden's idea was intriguing and tantalizing, but it also sounded wild, both because he seemed only partly to grasp or even to care about the scope of what he was proposing (he barely knew anything about *Finnegans Wake* and the immense number of surviving documents for that book alone) and because so many libraries needed to agree to participate for the project even to begin. Neither Walt Litz nor I thought it would ever be realized. Nevertheless, I agreed to provide Borden with a list of the major library collections and their holdings, and I created that census. Quite a while later, six months or a year, after the project seemed nearly dead several different times, Litz and I were startled when Borden called back and invited us to New York for drinks at his club. (I had never before socialized with my thesis supervisor in this way, and it must have made me extremely nervous, because, when Walt and I arrived at Pennsylvania Station to catch the train back to Princeton after our drinks and a dinner at the Oyster Bar in Grand Central Station, I discovered that I had spent the evening shredding the return ticket beyond usability in my pocket.)

In New York, Gavin told Walt and me that he had secured the permission for the project from the Society of Authors, which represented the Estate of James Joyce at that time (Giorgio and Lucia Joyce were the beneficiaries); as I learned only much later, when I consulted the Garland Publishing papers at Princeton, the Society of Authors charged Garland a total fee of one thousand dollars, 5 percent of the net receipts, and two copies of the series.[8] In addition, Gavin said that he had worked out agreements with many of the collections (several of which set their own additional fees), including the British Library, Buffalo, Cornell, the National Library of Ireland, Texas, and Yale—and that, with those agreements in place, the smaller ones would follow. Soon after this meeting, he asked Walt to be the general editor of the series, and when Walt said that he'd be happy to be involved in the effort but declined the invitation to run it, Gavin offered the position to me. Garland's main market was university and academic libraries, but Garland was completely outside the academic publishing world, so Gavin had no idea how bizarre it was for him to turn to a new Ph.D., twenty-eight years old, whose book hadn't yet been accepted by a publisher, to head a project of this kind. I was too young and inexperienced to know, either, and I gladly accepted the offer.

To start the project, with Walt's help I enlisted Hans Walter Gabler, Clive Hart, David Hayman, and Walt himself to be associate editors, with Litz working on the poetry and *Exiles*; Gabler on *Dubliners* and *A Portrait of the Artist as a Young Man*, the essays, and the miscellaneous writings; me on *Ulysses*; and Hart and Hayman on *Finnegans Wake*. Not very far into our initial planning, Hart took on administrative duties at the University of Essex and felt that he wouldn't be able to devote the necessary time to the *Archive*. He withdrew and suggested Danis Rose as a replacement, and so Rose, assisted by his brother John O'Hanlon, joined Hayman as the *Wake* editors.[9] In September 1975 I moved from Princeton to London, Ontario, to join the English Department at the University of Western Ontario, and I organized and supervised all the editorial work from there.

Despite Walt's and my initial impressions, Gavin (who, very sadly, died in the early 1990s at the age of fifty-two) turned out to be a real visionary regarding this project and many others. He was correct in assuming both that he could convince the major libraries to agree to the plan and that, with those libraries on board, the smaller collections would follow, even if reluctantly in some cases. (Not surprisingly, there was resistance to a proposal of this kind from a for-profit publisher.) When we first planned the series, we didn't know that the Rosenbach Library was working on its own color facsimile of its manuscript of *Ulysses*, but when we saw it after it was published in 1975 we concluded that we would be fine if we did everything else, since the two publications together would make every extant and available document relating to Joyce's works—nearly the entire workshop—available in published photoreprint editions.

As I think back on the *Archive* decades later, I'm amazed that we put together so much in a little over two years. The cooperation between the editors and the editorial and production staff at Garland, and especially Gavin Borden's personal involvement throughout, resulted in an incredibly smooth production on what was new territory for everyone involved. Even when crises developed, as they inevitably did with some regularity, the editorial and production staff, led by Elspeth Hart (unrelated to Clive Hart), or the technical staff, run by William Ludwig, somehow solved them. Or when they could not, Gavin would step in and perform what seemed like some kind of wizardry. Most of the libraries, especially the British Library with its huge collection, supplied microfilms of their holdings. Bill Ludwig himself photographed the Yale, Buffalo, and Cornell collections, and Bill or one of the editors checked those photographs against the originals. This tedious work had its oddly humorous moments. At Buffalo, the Poetry Collection's curator at the time, Karl Gay, adamantly opposed the library's participation in the project but was powerless to stop it. For our first meeting at the university to plan the photography schedule, he took Gavin and me to lunch and over cocktails declared me a "traitor to literature." While we were in the Poetry Collection photographing the materials, he refused to speak to any of us directly, instead yelling messages for us to his assistant, Walter, who then dutifully came out and relayed the communication that we had already easily overheard. A rotating team—sometimes Bill Ludwig and I, sometimes Ludwig and Hayman, sometimes the three of us—spent a couple of months during two visits in my hometown of Buffalo. We occasionally met Walter for a drink after the library closed, but he was so nervous about being seen by anyone from the library that we had to travel miles away from the campus, making the after-work unwinding over drinks seem like a clandestine affair.

The photographed documents were all gathered and assembled at Garland's New York offices, where I gladly spent all my breaks from teaching in

1976, 1977, and 1978. Ludwig did the technical work of processing the microfilm through a Xerox copyflo machine (which produced copies on a large roll of paper) at Garland's Connecticut offices, and the printer then rephotographed the copyflo rolls for offset reproduction. The five editors wrote prefaces, and the first two volumes—containing the manuscript of *A Portrait of the Artist as a Young Man* from the National Library of Ireland—were rushed out in order to be on display at the Sixth International James Joyce Symposium in Dublin in June 1977. The hurry produced the first of what would be several embarrassments for the project: we discovered only when we saw the printed books that the lefthand pages dutifully but unnecessarily reproduced all the backs of the manuscript's leaves, most of which are completely blank except for numbers indicating pages in chapter 4 and the beginning of chapter 5.

After the two *Portrait* volumes, the other sixty-one books came out in a steady stream later in 1977 and then in 1978 and 1979. Most of them reproduced the documents as the libraries and, where they exist, their published catalogs provided the arrangements. But we were able to manipulate photoreprints in a way that is impossible with the originals, and so we could reunite documents whose pages ended up scattered in different libraries, such as the part of the "Nausicaa" draft that is at Buffalo and the part at Cornell. We were also able to restore the sequence in which Joyce created and used the documents. The major innovation came in the *Wake* volumes. For the drafts, manuscripts, typescripts, and proofs (most from the British Library), Rose revised Hayman's arrangement in *A First-Draft Version of "Finnegans Wake,"* and the give-and-take between Hayman and Rose produced a new and updated conjecture of how all the *Wake* documents relate to one another. For the *Wake* notebooks (all at Buffalo), we realized that using filters on the camera caused some of Joyce's colored markings, especially the blue ones, to disappear, so we reproduced some pages twice, once with all the markings on display and a second time with some of them gone, thus making Joyce's words underneath them easier to read. The reproduction method was very primitive by today's standards, or even by the standards of a few years afterward, as became clear when Garland began to produce multi-volume reproductions of other authors' manuscripts as a result of the *Archive*'s success and used much better techniques for those series than were possible for the *Archive*. But now a scholar could undertake at least preliminary research on any of Joyce's prepublication materials in one place.

The seat-of-the-pants way in which the project was accomplished resulted in various oddities and embarrassments in addition to the blank *Portrait* pages. Garland wanted to release volumes as they were completed in order to recoup some of its expenses along the way, but the books were produced and released as the photocopies became available rather than in sequence. This meant that several of the early volumes were published before we knew exactly how the sixty-three volumes would be allocated. As a result, the books were released without volume numbers, to the immediate and continuing inconvenience of everyone who refers to them. (The sixty-three volumes do have numbers. I listed them in *James Joyce's Manuscripts: An Index*—the book-length index to the *Archive*—and the *James Joyce Quarterly* includes them in its guidelines for citing Joyce's works. But like the Homeric titles that almost everyone, including Joyce, uses to refer to the episodes of *Ulysses*, even though they do not appear in the book itself, the volume numbers remain extratextual.) We settled on sixty-three volumes as a result of a page count I compiled very early on, but as we assembled some of the later *Wake* volumes I realized that I had counted a large group of pages (a full volume's worth) twice. And so two *Wake* volumes are unusually thin in order for the series to fill the sixty-three volumes that had already been registered with the Library of Congress and *Books in Print*. Again because we needed to finish volumes as photocopies became available, we divided the *Ulysses* materials into three sections—notes and drafts, placards, and page proofs—rather than printing all stages for each chapter together. This has resulted in a most unwieldy organization; even after putting the reproductions together, I can't find specific passages in them without consulting Ian Gunn and Alistair McCleery's lists in their invaluable *"Ulysses" Pagefinder* and downloadable *"Archive" Tables*. And then there is "Oxen in the Sun": only when the bound copies of the volume of page proofs for "Cyclops," "Nausicaa," and "Oxen of the Sun" arrived at Garland's offices in New York did someone there notice that the huge display type on the title page read "Oxen in the Sun," not "of." This error had passed under at least a dozen pairs of eyes along the way, including mine two or three times. Garland created a new title page and tipped it in to replace the faulty one. I have what I think is the only surviving copy of the faulty original book.

Gavin Borden was correct that Garland could make a profit on reproducing Joyce's manuscripts. Only 250 copies of the series were produced for sale, and the price was a staggering five thousand dollars (1977 dollars). The volumes of the documents for the poetry, criticism, *Dubliners*, *Portrait*, and *Ulysses* sold out after a few years, and more than 200 copies of the *Wake* volumes were purchased fairly quickly and the rest as the years went by. Even after royalties and fees were paid to the James Joyce Estate and the libraries, Garland did quite well. The associate editors and I had no share in the profits, but each of us received a set of the books, something none of us could have afforded to acquire in any other way.

Everyone involved with *The James Joyce Archive* thought that Joyce studies would change immediately and profoundly as a result of the series. Phillip Herring's editions of Joyce's *Ulysses* notesheets and selected documents from the Buffalo collection were published in 1972 and 1977; my *"Ulysses" in Progress* appeared in 1977; Gabler was beginning to work on his scholarly edition of *Ulysses*; and the *Archive* made it possible for every critic and scholar with access to a library that had purchased the volumes to look at the manuscripts, at least in reproduction. We didn't pay much attention to Herring's observation in his 1981 *James Joyce Quarterly* review that "these volumes have yet to make the impact on Joyce criticism that manuscript scholars had hoped and expected." Herring also predicted that "[d]espite the riches" in the *Archive*, "it seems unlikely that there will be a gold-rush to the new territory any time soon."[10] As it turned out, his skepticism was justified: for *Dubliners*, *Portrait*, and *Ulysses* at least, people dipped into the books occasionally, but except for Gabler's edition and a few other studies, there were few systematic studies of the documents in the years that followed the *Archive*'s publication. (*Finnegans Wake* was another matter, as scholars quickly started publishing varied studies of small details and large patterns based on the reproductions in the *Archive*.) The *Archive* appeared just as European-based theory began to dominate North American English departments, and a general shift away from precise text-based studies took hold. The series remained relatively unused and undiscussed until Gabler's edition of *Ulysses* appeared in 1984.

In the late 1980s, the 1990s, and the first decade of the twenty-first century, this situation changed considerably, especially as the Institut des Textes et Manuscrits Modernes (ITEM) in Paris began developing *critique génétique*, and a fresh generation of young scholars turned to the manuscripts, beginning even before the new Joyce manuscripts came to light in the early 2000s but especially since then. Herring predicted in his review that "it may take another generation before [the *Archive*] is sufficiently used," and the subsequent years proved him correct.[11]

Writing in the famous eleventh edition of the *Encyclopædia Britannica*, J. P. Postgate concludes his entry on textual criticism with incredibly naive optimism: "As time goes on, textual criticism will have less and less to do. . . . In the newer texts . . . , it will have from the outset but a very contracted field."[12] Almost as if in response, Sylvia Beach included a stunningly direct note in the first edition of *Ulysses*, printed over her initials but actually written by Joyce himself and another aspect of the unique introduction of *Ulysses* to the world: "The publisher asks the reader's indulgence for typographical errors unavoidable in the exceptional circumstances."[13] In his letters Joyce noted the errors and hoped they would be corrected (*L* 1:176, 1:180, 3:86). For many years, however, *Ulysses* was considered uneditable: the existing texts seemed too corrupt, and the manuscript record too uncertain, to make an edition possible.

The James Joyce Archive's most direct and visible scholarly offspring was Gabler's 1984 edition of *Ulysses*. In one sense, the *Archive* led directly to the edition, in that the existence of the photoreproductions encouraged Gabler to think that the once seemingly impossible task of editing *Ulysses* was now feasible. When I first met Hans Gabler in 1974, while I was still a graduate student, he was a textual scholar specializing in the works of Shakespeare and other Renaissance and seventeenth-century authors, but he had recently begun to study the text of *A Portrait of the Artist as a Young Man*. He saw *Ulysses* as a chance to test theories of editing on a uniquely problematic twentieth-century work. Because I could bring detailed knowledge of the *Ulysses* manuscripts to the project, Hans and I initially planned to edit *Ulysses* together. I realized fairly early on, however, that despite my tolerance for transcribing nearly illegible manuscripts (and for censuses of bottle caps and statistics regarding Top 30 lists), I didn't particularly like the unique daily work that is part of an editing project (nor did I have any training for the job or, despite my experience with the manuscripts, know much about textual editing), and it was also clear that Gabler's early investigations into the manuscripts and other documents had made him just as knowledgeable about the genesis of *Ulysses* as I was. And so, with my agreement, he proceeded to edit *Ulysses* on his own, and Walt Litz and I became informal advisers to him. (The layout of the title page of the three-volume Garland edition, *Ulysses: A Critical and Synoptic Edition*, suggests that Litz and I were advisers to the

Academic Advisory Committee that the James Joyce Estate set up, but our relationship throughout was directly with Gabler and not with the committee.)

Gabler's editing of *Ulysses* was unique in several ways. First, he attempted to merge established Anglo-American and German genetic methods of editing. Traditional Anglo-American editors create a new version of a work by choosing one extant text as copytext and emending the copytext with readings from other surviving documents, thus producing an "eclectic text" (it combines readings from more than one extant text) in order to reflect what Fredson Bowers called the "final authorial intention." German genetic editing, in contrast, is more concerned with documenting the stages through which the work passed during its composition.[14] Second, Gabler used computers to transcribe the many different documents and to collate them, producing instantly readable printouts of all differences between any two or three selected documents for a particular section. Working with his staff in Munich, he produced a prototype of the "Lestrygonians" episode, which was distributed at the Seventh International James Joyce Symposium in Zurich in 1979. On the basis of this prototype, the James Joyce Estate (as at the time of the *Archive*, administered by the Society of Authors, with Peter du Sautoy of Faber and Faber and Joyce scholar and original *Archive* associate editor Clive Hart as trustees) gave Gabler its approval for the full edition. It set up an Academic Advisory Committee consisting of Richard Ellmann, Philip Gaskell, and Hart to advise it and, indirectly, Gabler.

The main impediment to editing *Ulysses* involved the existing states of the text: none seemed adequate as a copytext.[15] The Rosenbach Manuscript offers a handwritten beginning-to-end version of the text (almost: the last "sentence" of "Penelope" is in a separate document at Buffalo), but because Joyce revised the text so heavily on the typescript and proofs, it sometimes represents only about two-thirds of an episode's text. The first edition contains the full text, but its many errors seemed to rule it out as a copytext. Gabler reasoned, however, that in theory the Rosenbach Manuscript plus all Joyce's additions on the many sets of typescripts and proofs should add up to the full *Ulysses* and that this text, which he would have to assemble as part of the editing process and which he called a "continuous manuscript text," could serve as the edition's copytext. In reality, things were much more complicated, since sometimes we can't know what Joyce wrote because documents are missing, and sometimes the printers set a different word from the one Joyce wrote and he then changed it to something else. The most complicated uncertainty involves the Rosenbach Manuscript, because only about half of it was the document the typist used to create the typescript from which the proofs and so the first edition were set, and in several places it contains words, phrases, and even sentences that were never typed or printed. For the rest of it, Gabler speculated that Joyce sent a manuscript to the typist and later recopied the text to provide a more attractive manuscript to send to John Quinn, the New York lawyer and collector who purchased the manuscript-in-progress while Joyce was writing it. In several places the text of the surviving Rosenbach Manuscript is fuller than the version that was typed, set by the printer, and published, containing words, phrases, and even full sentences that were never typed or printed.

To construct the continuous manuscript text, Gabler used German genetic practices to assemble a "virtual" text (it never existed as a single text before) that could serve as a copytext in Anglo-American practice. Once this copytext was assembled, he compared it to the extant states of the text and emended it whenever that seemed appropriate. His goal, as he explained it, was to produce "*Ulysses* as Joyce wrote it," which signaled a substantial break with the Anglo-American goal of reproducing the "final authorial intention."[16] The edition is authorial—it privileges Joyce's writing over the contributions of everyone else connected with the publication—but it reflects what Joyce did (activities for which we have evidence) rather than what he might have intended.

Gabler worked with two guiding principles. First, he accepted Joyce's written words rather than those of the typist's or printer's transcriptions unless the evidence convinced him to do the opposite, and he argued that all Joyce's words, even if he wrote them onto a document that the typist and printer wouldn't see, were part of his revision process. Second, he followed what he called the "rule of the invariant context": if Joyce later worked on the text surrounding the problematic words, Gabler accepted the typed and printed version without the manuscript's words, but if the context was untouched, he admitted the manuscript's words into the text. This is how the edition's most famous "new" passage—Stephen Dedalus's thought as he expounds his theory of Shakespeare in the National Library of Ireland, "Love, yes. Word known to all men" (*U* 9:429–30)—entered the text. (I discuss this passage in more detail in chapter 1.)

For the *Critical and Synoptic Edition*, which Garland published in three volumes in 1984, the left-hand pages provide a so-called synoptic text, a coded version of the text that indicates the composition stage at which Joyce entered each word or phrase and also Joyce's revisions and deletions—what Gabler in the afterword to the 1986 one-volume version called "a text as it constituted itself in the process of writing," a presentation that both "records the documentary evidence and explains and justifies all editorial decisions"—and the right-hand pages offer a clear reading text, which is the left-hand page without the codes and the words that Joyce either changed or deleted as he wrote and revised.[17] The synoptic text is not a complete genetic edition but rather a visualization of how the continuous manuscript text came into being. (This is different from a visualization of how *Ulysses* itself came into being.) In 1986 the commercial publishers—Random House and its Vintage paperback imprint in the United States and Bodley Head and its licensee Penguin in England and the rest of the world—released a one-volume version of the reading text alone, at first called *Ulysses: The Corrected Text* and later *Ulysses: The Gabler Edition*.

Parts of Gabler's procedure were unfamiliar to editors in the Anglo-American tradition, and they provoked some disagreement and debate while the edition was in progress. But most literary critics and scholars have little knowledge of textual matters, and so Gabler's progress was followed with interest and curiosity but not much attention. A dispute with the Academic Advisory Committee erupted in 1983, near the end of Gabler's work, when the committee objected to some of his procedures—all based on his acceptance of passages from the Rosenbach Manuscript and all from the "Lestrygonians" episode—and Gabler balked at changing any of his readings, arguing that he had made the procedures and examples cited by the committee public in the 1979 "Lestrygonians" prototype and that they had provoked no objections then. The advisers resigned briefly, but they returned with an understanding that they would explore their disagreements with Gabler's procedures in a publication of their own, which appeared in 1989 as Gaskell and Hart's *Ulysses: A Review of Three Texts*.

Apart from reviewing printouts of various stages of the editing as Gabler sent them to me, my most direct involvement in the preparation of the edition followed from this dispute with the committee. In order to try to ensure that Gabler's uses of previously unpublished passages from the Rosenbach Manuscript were justified on textual grounds, he and I traveled to Princeton in the fall of 1983 and spent a weekend in Walt Litz's office discussing, one at a time, each Rosenbach passage that Gabler either strongly or tentatively planned to admit into the text. The weekend ended with Hans deciding to admit only about half the passages on his original list into the text, and this decision helped to bring the advisers back on board. Echoing the original publication of *Ulysses*—which Joyce determined would occur on his fortieth birthday, February 2, 1922—the new edition had a pre-set publication date. Gabler and Garland decided to publish it on Bloomsday 1984 and to present the first copy on that day to Joyce's grandson, Stephen James Joyce, at the Ninth International James Joyce Symposium in Frankfurt. (Stephen Joyce accepted the first copy of the edition at a public ceremony and then in his remarks attacked Richard Ellmann for publishing Joyce's erotic 1909 letters to Nora in the 1975 *Selected Letters*.) The text, both synoptic and reading versions, was finished months before the publication date, but the need to meet the deadline did affect Gabler's afterword, which would have benefited from more stylistic editing and revision than time allowed.

The edition was published to great fanfare, including a front-page article in the *New York Times* and many local newspaper articles and television reports that followed from the attention the *Times* gave to it. As one of only two North American scholars on the title page, I found myself talking to a *New York Times* reporter and interviewed on the Canadian Broadcasting Corporation's national radio news show *As It Happens*. The heady response, and the nearly universal praise, made it easy for those of us involved with the edition to overlook some potentially troublesome ways in which it was being promoted and described: Garland and the journalists called it "definitive"; the journalists focused on the correction of errors rather than, as Gabler had in his work, establishing a new text from the ground up (the *Times* article was titled "New Edition Fixes 5,000 Errors in *Ulysses*," whereas Hans tried to describe the edition, more accurately but less quotably, as a "non-corrupted counterpart to the first edition of 1922"); and two years later the commercial publishers subtitled the paperback "The Corrected Text"—this was the publishers' title and not Gabler's, just as the inane stars at the beginning of each chapter were the publishers' intrusions, but the subtitle nonetheless went out over Gabler's name.[18]

During the course of Gabler's work on the edition, I published two articles explaining and attempting to create an audience for it, both of which I wrote after I was invited to lecture on it. The first, "Editing Joyce's *Ulysses*: An International Effort," was initially a talk I gave at the June 1980 conference of the Society for Scholarly Publishing in Minneapolis; it very much described a work-in-progress. I lectured on the edition a second time at the California Institute of Technology in March 1984, as Gabler's work neared its end, and I reworked that talk into an article whose title exploited one of the words that was appearing in the book for the first time: "Foostering over Those Changes: The New *Ulysses*" (cf. *U* 5:118). I offered the article, unsolicited, to Thomas Staley at the *James Joyce Quarterly*. Staley had announced in the most recent issue of the *JJQ* that the next one would contain a review of Gabler's edition, but he liked my account, which acknowledged my involvement in the edition at the start and disclaimed any pretensions to be an objective review. So he ran my piece as an article in the next issue and, for better or worse, never did review the edition.

■

In his foreword to the three-volume edition, Gabler states that the "main editorial achievement, centered on the establishment of the text and the analysis of its evolution in the synoptic display of the edition's left-hand pages, is submitted to the scrutiny of every critical reader and adventurous explorer of the novel," and in a review Jerome McGann noted that the *Critical and Synoptic Edition* should "be a required object of study for every scholar working in English literature" because it "raises all the central questions that have brought such a fruitful crisis to literary work in the postmodern period."[19] Things progressed differently, however, and for several years Gabler's *Ulysses* became known for the controversy it provoked almost as much as an edition. Following my attempts to explain the edition, I became more directly involved in defending it than I was in its production.

I didn't fully realize that it was happening at the time, but the so-called Joyce Wars, which erupted in 1988, began in April 1985, when John Kidd delivered a talk at the Society for Textual Scholarship conference in New York and Gabler responded on the same panel. In what was to become a regular pattern, Kidd found a journalist willing to promote his talk before he gave it, but an article that appeared in the *Washington Post* and the text of Kidd's talk (which I saw before he delivered it) seemed to me to contain more bluster than substance. Hans's response (which I also read beforehand in order to make what turned out to be only minor suggestions for revisions) seemed forceful and on the mark.[20] As Kidd and then Gabler presented their papers, I listened with shock as I discovered how wrong both of my impressions were: Kidd managed to deliver his talk with David-meets-Goliath innocence that I had failed to read out of the printed text, and Gabler's response came across as heavy-handed, to say the least, as he seemed to imply in his tone and manner that he was beyond criticism from upstarts. (Reading it again afterward, I couldn't believe I didn't see and flag those implications in my earlier perusal.) The encounter was unfortunate at best, a disaster at worst, but nothing seemed to follow from it, and I didn't pay much attention to it as time passed. (Both talks were published in 1990 in Charles Rossman's special issue of *Studies in the Novel* on editing *Ulysses*.)

The Joyce Wars began in earnest in June 1988. Fritz Senn set up a panel on Gabler's edition at that month's Eleventh International James Joyce Symposium in Venice, and Senn wanted the panel to critique the edition and not just praise or describe it. He invited Gabler and Kidd, among other people, to join him, and as the conference approached there was a great deal of flurry about whether Gabler would appear on the panel with Kidd and whether Kidd would participate on the panel or attend the symposium at all. In the end Kidd didn't attend, and the panel went on with Gabler and others but without him. In a move that blindsided everyone involved with Gabler and his edition, as it surely was intended to do, Kidd's attack on the edition in the *New York Review of Books*, "The Scandal of *Ulysses*," was published in New York while we were in Venice, but copies of the issue—thousands and thousands of them, it seemed—were available in Venice, eagerly offered on street corners and in conference sessions as if they were perfume samples at Bloomingdale's. Thus, Kidd managed to dominate Senn's panel even though he wasn't present. (In what turned out to be a very unfortunate scheduling coincidence, at the same time as some of us were listening to this tense discussion of Gabler's edition, a now-famous panel on biography featuring Stephen James Joyce, Ezra Pound's daughter Mary de Rachewiltz, and William Butler Yeats's son Michael was proceeding in a room across the hall.)

None of us knew how to react to Kidd's article, and there was extreme pressure to respond. Kidd made a variety of charges: that Gabler misread the manuscripts, spelled the names of historical figures incorrectly, relied too heavily on facsimiles, and departed too often from the book as it was originally published. In focusing on the one-volume *Ulysses: The Corrected Text*, Kidd deflected attention away from the three-volume *Critical and Synoptic Edition*, with its synoptic presentation and apparatus that scholars assumed would be the focus of attention, and toward the one-volume reading text, which is isolated from the editorial principles and procedures that produced it. We had to read and digest the article while the conference was in session, and we didn't have access at the moment to any of the documents we might have consulted in order to counter the charges with specific details. I found myself called on to give an on-the-spot defense against specific charges that I didn't feel capable of providing. Hans at first felt that no response was the best one, but the next few months proved that approach to be impossible as it became clear that this time Kidd's charges were not going to disappear, and the result was an ugly exchange of letters in both the *New York Review of Books* and *TLS* throughout the summer and fall of 1988 and into early winter 1989 that turned the debate from an arcane dispute about textual editing into a kind of World Wrestling Federation sideshow for the intellectual crowd. My friends and colleagues would repeatedly tell me what a summer diversion the exchange was turning out to be, even though they sometimes thoughtfully added that it probably wasn't so much fun for the people involved.

I never felt that I or anyone else trying to defend Gabler's edition against the charges made by Kidd or his allies managed to state the case for the edition effectively or to gain even ground in the debate. Kidd seemed to me to possess a talent, a genius even, for self-promotion and for convincing journalists and other non-specialists to accept his charges, which were much simpler than Gabler's complex (sometimes turgid) explanations for what he had done and therefore more easily grasped by non-specialists. As I wrote letters and talked to people from newspapers and magazines, the journalists always seemed already to take Kidd's version as true, and Kidd always managed to be able to respond to the letters before they appeared and therefore to get the last word on the page. But, also, I lost sight of the fact that many of Gabler's procedures and also some of the new words and passages that he admitted into the text of *Ulysses* were indeed unsettling and that reasonable people could disagree with what he had done. It began to seem to me that anyone who didn't support Gabler publicly—and hardly anyone seemed to be doing that at the time—was on the other side. These misconceptions certainly hindered the effort to produce an effective response.

Another combatant entered the scene later in 1988 when Charles Rossman, after investigating the Richard Ellmann archive at the University of Tulsa, published his own article in the *New York Review of Books* that dealt, among other issues, with the 1983 dispute between Gabler and the advisers.

Rossman went on to write two other narrative accounts of the dispute and to edit a special issue of *Studies in the Novel* on the controversy. Rossman's intervention only increased my sense of frustration. Like so many other people who entered the debate on Kidd's side, he seemed to me to know little about how scholarly editors actually do their work and specifically about how Gabler did his, and he relied on Kidd's descriptions and statements, in the process accepting them as true. He appeared to me—although he would, and did, disagree strongly with me—more as an enthusiastic partisan than the objective reporter he pictured himself as being. His work seemed to confirm the pattern that every new account was providing further support for Kidd's attack.

The debate acquired a social dimension when the organizers of the annual Miami J'yce Birthday Conference at the University of Miami chose to devote the February 1989 meeting exclusively to it. All the combatants—Gabler, Kidd, Rossman, Gabler's associate editors Claus Melchior and Wolfhard Steppe, Advisory Committee members Hart and Gaskell, me—plus editors such as the *JJQ*'s Staley, interested commentators such as Arnold Goldman, and even a copyright lawyer—were invited to the conference, housed in the same hotel, and brought together for panel after panel to discuss the edition and the charges against it. Nothing was resolved, of course. Kidd repeated his charges, and in what I saw as an encouraging sign, Gabler delivered a response that acknowledged the need to address the issues and started to talk about them.[21] The weekend was both my first introduction to the glories of Miami and Coral Gables in February, a pleasure I was able to repeat several times at subsequent February Miami conferences, and the most uncomfortable scholarly meeting I have ever attended. The main consolation for me was that the Joyce community, while deeply concerned about Kidd's charges, did not seem as ready to turn away from Gabler's edition as I had feared.

Kidd had announced a forthcoming full presentation of his charges against Gabler in his *New York Review of Books* article, and he later promised it for the Miami conference. It wasn't ready for public viewing there, however, even though he flashed a large ring binder and pointed some of us to individual pages of what he said was the long article. "An Inquiry into *Ulysses: The Corrected Text*" finally appeared in the summer of 1989 in the *Papers of the Bibliographical Society of America*. I read its 174 pages and was surprised at how scattered the arguments seemed, how little they tried to confront what Gabler did on his own terms, and how often the argument proceeded from a diametrically opposite (and almost always unacknowledged) editorial starting point from Gabler's. The article concluded with page after page of lists, some made up of categories that seemed to have little relevance to Gabler's work, others that made sense from one starting point but not from Gabler's. The lists contained some legitimate errors, but even though Kidd claimed that Gabler's edition was a huge disaster, on closer inspection his lists seemed to me to reflect differences in editorial orientation and irrelevant categories. When time passed and neither Gabler nor anyone else seemed prepared to respond to the article, I wrote a substantial reply in which I suggested that two narratives regarding the achievement and reception of the Gabler edition had already been constructed—the initial flurry of glowing newspaper reports and supporting scholarly articles and then the attacks and defenses—and I hoped that a third narrative, one in which the edition would be studied and assessed in a scholarly manner, would begin.[22]

I wrote my response to Kidd's piece assuming that I would offer it to *PBSA*. However, when it was finished, I asked Robert Spoo, by then the editor of the *James Joyce Quarterly*, to read it over and make suggestions for improvements, and he asked if he could have it for the *JJQ*. He offered to publish it quickly, and I gave it to him. As a courtesy he sent the typescript to Kidd, who demanded and received space to reply in the same issue. And so my response to his "Inquiry" and his response to me appeared in the same 1990 issue of the *JJQ*. By then the momentum of the debate was waning, and perhaps people were numbed by the mass of detail that Kidd presented and that I included in my response. Whatever the reason, Kidd's *PBSA* article, my counterargument in the *JJQ*, and his rebuttal to me provoked no further discussion until Gabler published his own response, "What *Ulysses* Requires," which Joyce scholars barely seemed to notice when it appeared in *PBSA* in 1993.

Kidd's goal as he stated it in the *New York Review of Books* article was to convince Random House to stop distributing the Gabler edition and in its place to restore its 1961 version, which it had dropped in 1986. Random House formed a committee to look into the matter in 1988, and I certainly considered the 1984 edition's disappearance just a few years after its release to be a real possibility. Nothing much happened, though, as the debate wore on, and eventually Random House disbanded the committee before it ever reached any conclusions—or, apparently, ever met. In 1990 Random House reissued the 1961 version and started selling it along with the Gabler edition. Both sides could claim a victory of sorts: the Gabler opponents had an alternative, whereas the supporters were relieved that the edition remained available. In the world outside the United States, the Gabler edition didn't fare as well. In 1992 Penguin stopped publishing its paperback version of the edition and replaced it with a reprint of an earlier Bodley Head edition from 1960. Bodley Head, publishers of the hardcover edition, released a paperback in 1993, with a couple of corrections to the text and a new afterword that I wrote, but this version was expensive and nearly impossible to find. In the mid-1990s Random House quietly replaced its 1986 paperback, the one it called "The Corrected Text," with the 1993 Bodley Head version, now subtitled "The Gabler Edition" (and also including my afterword), and in 2008 Vintage in the UK re-released the 1993 Bodley Head printing and began to distribute it more widely.

In early summer 1991, I realized that Kidd's goal was more ambitious than just replacing Gabler's edition with an earlier one when W. W. Norton announced that it had given him a contract to edit all four of Joyce's prose works. (I first learned about this development directly from Norton, when they canceled a contract they had signed with me for a Norton Critical Edition of *A Portrait of the Artist as a Young Man* in order to free up Joyce's works for Kidd. This devastating cancellation, however, had an extremely positive effect on a different aspect of my life. I have it, and perhaps Kidd as well, to thank for bringing me back together with my high school girlfriend, Molly Peacock. Knowing that she was a New York poet who had significant experience with publishers, I telephoned her daily in June 1991 to ask for advice on how to deal with Norton. When the crisis was over and I resigned myself to the loss of the Norton contract, I invited her to London, Ontario, for a visit. By mid-July we were lovers once again, and in August 1992 we got married.) An anonymous article in *Lingua Franca* reported a huge advance— $350,000—for Kidd, but this was never confirmed, then or since, by Norton.[23] Kidd had now gone from being an attacker to an alternative editor.

I assumed that Kidd as editor would be textually oriented toward the published first edition rather than toward Joyce's original handwritten inscriptions, and along with other scholars who were following the debate, I waited for the kind of early explanations and statements of principles that Gabler had provided several times while he was doing his work. They never appeared. The most obvious opportunity, and the one where the expectations were highest, came at the Thirteenth International James Joyce Symposium in Dublin in June 1992, where Kidd was one of the keynote speakers. Instead of discussing what he would do as an editor, he delivered a ninety-minute talk consisting entirely of alternating quotations from Joyce's works and from critics. People began to walk out after about ten or fifteen minutes, but I thought that my leaving would be interpreted as a refusal by a Gabler supporter to hear what Kidd was saying. When the president of the International James Joyce Foundation walked out after about twenty minutes, though, I concluded that exiting would no longer look like a partisan act, and I left. In the lobby I saw that someone had taped a sheet of paper to a pillar near the lecture hall, and people were eagerly writing acerbic comments about the performance, including several sarcastic limericks, as they left the room. These impromptu creations mysteriously disappeared shortly after the lecture ended. I think it is fair to say that by then the Joyce Wars had entered their baroque phase. (Kidd never did produce his edition of *Ulysses*. In the early 2000s Norton gave me a new contract for a Norton Critical Edition of *A Portrait of the Artist as a Young Man*, along with one for *Dubliners*, but for reasons completely unrelated to this history I decided to pursue other projects and gave up both volumes.)

For several years, the debate precluded almost all discussion about the conceptual, theoretical, and practical significance of this particular edition of this work and about what the edition might say about works in general. Even now, such discussions among Joyce scholars remain relatively few, but they do exist, and their number now seems to be increasing. In "Intentional Error: The Paradox of Editing Joyce's *Ulysses*," written in the midst of the debate, Vicki Mahaffey highlights the paradox between textual editing, which strives to "eliminate error," and the much more tolerant attitude toward error that *Ulysses* exhibits. Leopold Bloom, for example, notices and then toys with Martha Clifford's two typos in her letter to him—"I called you naughty boy because I do not like that other world" and "So now you know what I will do to you, you naughty boy, if you do not wrote" (*U* 5:244–45, 252–53)—and even though he is "nettled not a little" by seeing his name misprinted in a newspaper account of Paddy Dignam's funeral as "L. Boom," he is also "tickled to death" at seeing the names of two absentees in the list of mourners (*U* 16:1260–63). For Mahaffey, "the difference between the tolerant, even opportunistic attitude the book encourages its readers to take toward the vagaries of print and the precise, scholarly attitude an editor must take to allow the narrative to convey the message is something that should be explicitly stated: the book's theory is necessarily and meaningfully at odds with editorial *and* critical practice." Mahaffey links this dichotomy to a more basic distinction between writing as process, which Gabler's theory and synoptic text largely promote, and as product, as in the reading text. (Using similar evidence from *Ulysses* but reaching a different conclusion, Sebastian Knowles argues in favor of reading unedited texts of *Ulysses* on the grounds that the book demonstrates that "errors are inevitable" and that "errors are not only forgivable but necessary.")[24]

In his early review, McGann claimed that Gabler's edition "should remove forever that illusion of fixity and permanence we normally take from literary works because they so often come to us wearing their masks of permanence."[25] Some later considerations of the edition followed up on this suggestion. Writing ten years after the controversy began, and noting that the debate "has been characterized by missed opportunities and missed understandings throughout," Robert Spoo argues that "for all our celebration of textual indeterminacy, . . . we Joyce critics have placed great importance on stable, reliable texts of our author's works" and as a result resist looking at the principles and theory that lie behind the "Gablerian indeterminacy" of the left-hand synoptic pages in favor of the "particularized instances (however numerous) of alleged textual misconduct" that Kidd deduced from the right-hand reading text and the paperback editions.[26] J. C. C. Mays, observing how few editors, much less general readers, have considered the implications of the left-hand synoptic text, remarks that "I find it eerie that the instability of texts is widely discussed and increasingly acknowledged, as is the fact that texts exist in multiple versions, and that at the same time texts continue to be presented as if they constituted univocal expression," especially since a choice regarding editions "situates a chooser in a different—I think looser— relation to any one of them. Absolute authority becomes relativised by the consideration of use: the version you call up is determined by why and how you want to read it."[27] And George Bornstein argues that Gabler's diacritical symbols in the synoptic presentation "signal that there is no 'the' text, but only a series of texts built up like a layered palimpsest over a variety of compositional stages; further, they signal that any text is always already a constructed object, and that other constructions would have been (and are) possible." As an indication of how far away Gabler's edition—both as a concept and as a presentation of a text—takes us from New Critical assumptions, Bornstein concludes that "the synoptic pages signal that far from being a well-wrought urn, the text itself contains gaps and fissures, opportunities for revealing differences as well as concealing it."[28]

More than twenty years after the Joyce Wars began, the Gabler edition remains in print, and it continues to be used by scholars and teachers and respected for its achievement. But I don't think that it has ever completely recovered from Kidd's attack on it. This is probably partly because of the inflated claims that were made for it when it was first released, which set up an impossibly high standard to measure it against (and which I along with Gabler and other members of his team accepted without qualifications for too long), and partly because the responses to the charges were not as effective as they might have been. But, also, Gabler had run up against a relentless, single-minded adversary, one with a genius for self-promotion. The attack went far beyond the normal give-and-take of scholarly debate, and well beyond the usual eccentricities of the scholarly life, especially when the media became involved. It was almost impossible to counter such an onslaught and still live a life; in some ways, it may be impossible to counter any such assault if the attacker is relentless and determined enough. I have always considered the edition to be an impressive, even brilliant, amalgamation of Anglo-American and German editorial theory and practice applied to an extremely complex text, but I am much more aware now that its theory and execution are alien and counterintuitive to many readers; that it is flawed both in theory and execution, although no more flawed than any human endeavor; and certainly that it is not the only way in which *Ulysses* might, and should, be edited. Some of its central principles, such as the emphasis on Joyce the isolated writer at the expense of the other participants in the publishing process, no longer seem as inevitable to me as they once did. The reputation of the edition will, I expect, remain basically as it is now until sometime in the future when it and the debate are studied by a scholar with no allegiances to any side in the dispute, one who can produce a more objective account and assessment for a new generation of readers, critics, and scholars.

6

Revisiting the "Cyclops" Manuscripts, Part 1

Wandering in the Avant-texte

"Ulysses" in Progress treats Joyce's novel as a monument. Not unusually for a manuscript study from 1977, my book was researched and written in ignorance of anything that might be called "theory," and its facts were gathered and presented as part of an argument that took for granted the unity of the published *Ulysses* and the secondary position of the prepublication documents in relation to the finished book. I didn't feel much need to pay attention to the interpretation I was putting on the facts that I was presenting. As I became aware of *critique génétique* in the decades following the writing of my book, I grew curious about how the facts offered there and the evidence mounted to present the argument might look in view of the new and increasingly sophisticated approaches to manuscripts that genetic criticism offered.

In arguing that Joyce wrote *Ulysses* in three stages—early, middle, and last—*"Ulysses" in Progress* adopted a resolutely teleological model of Joyce's writing. I subordinated Joyce's writing to the finished work and assumed that "once he finished the book . . . the tasks of interpreting and assessing the complete book necessarily take precedence over any questions about the methods of composition." I also argued, though, that "Joyce's book was composed in ways so idiosyncratic as to be interesting in themselves" and that "the processes by which he wrote the book cannot be separated from other aspects of its meaning."[1]

I took for granted that a literary work was characterized, even defined, by unity, even if *Ulysses* itself caused a lot of problems for this assumption, and

I glossed over the difficulties in bringing my three statements together into one argument. Instead, I argued that the radical dichotomies within *Ulysses* could be reclaimed for a unified concept of the book within such formulations as "a 'both/and' approach which seems to me the most fruitful critical one to *Ulysses*" and "the most valuable [responses to one-sided readings of *Ulysses*] have been attempts to incorporate both the human drama and the symbolic structure into a unified theory of the book." And I assumed that a history of Joyce's composition of the book would reveal the ultimate unity coming into being, even if unity meant "a multiple or ambiguous combination" of opposed tendencies. The suggestion of a middle stage of composition between the early and late ones was designed to show a gradual, evolutionary procedure rather than an abrupt, radical break, but my metaphors of palimpsest and superimposition were offered in the service of a view of the book as a unity, even if a complex one.[2]

Needless to say, conceptions of a literary work changed drastically around the time I wrote *"Ulysses" in Progress*. Roland Barthes, for one, traced a path "from work to text": "the work is a fragment of substance, it occupies a portion of the spaces of books (for example, in a library). The Text is a methodological field. . . . the work is held in the hand, the text is held in language. . . . *the Text is experienced only in an activity, in a production*."[3] Formulations such as Barthes's emphasize openness, splits, and fissures, anything but closure and unity. The text's methodological field, or "network," includes other texts, whether these are preexisting texts—"influences" or "sources" in other contexts but here called "intertexts"—or, specifically for the purposes of genetic criticism, the avant-texte, the text's own past.[4] The old terms "prepublication documents" and "finished work" are usefully superseded by "avant-texte" and "text," and the sense of a teleological movement from early stages to finished product can be replaced at least provisionally by one of a mobile textual field that extends backward and forward between avant-texte and text. Thus, for Hans Walter Gabler, genetic criticism is "concerned with the *différence* of all writing as it materializes in variants and in the advancing and receding of textual states."[5] Seen in this way the process need not be interpreted as heading toward "one great goal," as Garrett Deasy in "Nestor" claims all history tends to do (*U* 2:381), and the published text can be reconceived as a provisional central point, a "caesura" in the line of writing.[6]

■

The *Ulysses* avant-texte, and especially that of the "Cyclops" episode, offers a gold mine of material for these purposes. The avant-texte—notes (British Library notesheets, a notebook at Buffalo), lists (one at Buffalo, another at Cornell), drafts (one in two copybooks at Buffalo and the National Library of Ireland, a second one at Buffalo, plus short passages in three other Buffalo documents), manuscript (the Rosenbach Manuscript), typescript (at Buffalo), *Little Review* serialized version, and proofs (at Harvard, Buffalo, Texas, and Princeton)—can show *Ulysses* coming into being, as *"Ulysses" in Progress* attempted to do, but it can also tell other stories.[7] (Louis Hay notes in "Does 'Text' Exist?" that "in defining the pre-text as a constructed object, one must accept the existence of a variety of possible constructions.")[8] For one thing, the avant-texte shows that the text of *Ulysses* can indeed be seen as a caesura within the full "Cyclops" archive, since there is an aprés-texte of "Cyclops" in the various notebooks and other documents for *Finnegans Wake*. The avant-texte can also tell other stories involving the form and structure of *Ulysses*, concepts of characterization, and the role of the author in the text.

As almost everyone who has looked at the earlier of the two Buffalo "Cyclops" drafts, the first part of the earliest extant draft of the episode (from around June 1919), has noted, this copybook contains a draft that was written before Joyce's sense of the episode's structure had solidified.[9] The copybook contains eight scenes, all quite sketchy. The first four, drafted in ink, move from the beginning of the episode ("In ^<green Erin of the west> Inisfail the fair^ there lies a land, the land of holy Michan.") to the end ("And they beheld Him ^<in His Glory ascend to Him Who the Heaven in the direction of a beeline over Hogan's in Little Green Street.> amid Clouds of ><Glory> angels< ascend to the Glory of the Brightness at an angle of fortyfive degrees over ><Hogan's> Donohoe's< in Little Green Street like a shot off a shovel.^").[10] Scenes 5–8, written in pencil, add some sections for the middle of the episode. The copybook ends in the middle of scene 8, and a note on page 23r of the twenty-four-page book referring to page 28, plus the continuation of scene 8 in the next draft (onto which Joyce copied and somewhat revised scenes 5–8), indicates that there was at least a second document that continued on from the earlier draft, a manuscript that now exists. Frank Budgen reports that Joyce, as he was writing *Finnegans Wake*, said, "I feel like an engineer boring through a mountain from two sides. If my calculations are correct we shall meet in the middle. If not . . . ," and the copybook serves as an earlier instance of Joyce trying to meet in the middle.[11] But it can also show his willingness not to push too hard to meet. For someone as obsessed with form and structure as he was, the copybook is surprisingly unconcerned with form. Barthes describes "the classical sign" (or the "work") as "a sealed unit, whose closure arrests meaning, prevents it from trembling or becoming double, or wandering," and the draft is a wonderful example of wandering or motion—authorial, textual, or Odyssean—without too great a concern for the destination.[12] As a document, it can enjoyably be read in a spirit of wandering.

The third scene of the copybook consists of talk about the Keogh-Bennett fight and about Irish sports. It contains dialogue, a rudimentary narrative voice, and two passages of "gigantism" (Joyce's term for his technic in the episode in his 1921 schema):[13] the accounts of the fight and of the "most interesting discussion" of "the revival of ancient Gaelic sports." In *"Ulysses" in Progress* I discussed part of the scene in terms of Joyce's "problem of developing an alternative" to the interior-monologue technique that he was dropping from *Ulysses*.[14] Brief conversations come and go in the passage, jokes are uttered and ignored, questions get asked but not answered:

> —I wouldn't like to see that, — said. And those butting matches they have in California, going for each heads down like a bull at a gate.
> —And bullfighting, Mr B—, and cockfighting all those sports are terribly inhuman and hare hunting
> —Well, yes, of course . . .
> —What about bughunting, — asked with a grin.
> —Cimex lectularius, L— put in.
> —Isn't it what you call brain versus brawn

"Ay, that's a fact" serves as a transition from a speaker who would like to see Bloom "in the nine acres in a hurley scrap" to the question "How many feet could you put it?" but it seems to be responding to something reported only in the gigantism style:

> —He is that, — said sourly. He'd shove a soft hand under a hen. But I'd like to see him in the nine acres in a hurley scrap.
> He sang the Pæan of the Games of the Gael: he sang the Deeds of his Prowess. Youthful he drove the Wolf and the Boar: in the Chace he led the Knights of Uladh. From his godlike Shoulder sped the Stone: terrible, swift as the Glance of Balor.

—Ay, that's a fact, — bore out. ^He was.^ How many feet could you put it?¹⁵

The conversations themselves are aimless, and they come from speakers whose names and individual identities don't seem to matter. Like several other parts of the copybook, the passage uses dashes in place of characters' names. (As the copybook moves along in its eight scenes, names become more prominent. Even in scene 2, though, Alf Bergan, Ned Lambert, Bob Doran, and John Wyse Nolan are named.) Only "B—" and "L—" emerge here from the indistinguishable dashes: "B—" expands once to "Bloom," and the reader probably fills in "L—" to "Lenehan" on the basis of scene 5 in the copybook and later documents from the avant-texte and the text.

In *"Ulysses" in Progress* I discussed these details as evidence of Joyce's struggle with the details of characterization, but the situation can also be read in terms of the words in the conversations, as they are reported in this written text, taking precedence over the identity of the particular speakers who utter them.¹⁶ The language predominates over any identifiable center of attribution. If in "The Dead" Gabriel Conroy's "identity was fading out into a grey impalpable world" (*D* 223), here voices predominate over identity, words are spoken in a convincing way from sources who can't be identified or who could be identified in one of several ways. The effect is like overhearing a conversation whose speakers can't be specified (as happens later at different points in "Circe" and especially in the last pages of "Oxen of the Sun"), but because of the dashes (and also, elsewhere in the draft, *X*'s) it isn't quite this. Rather, speech comes from figures whose identity has not yet emerged from the "grey impalpable world," from speakers whose identity perhaps cannot emerge in this way. It is tempting to supply the speakers' identities from the text of "Cyclops" and to read these fragmentary conversations with that awareness (thus supplying not only Bloom and Lenehan but also Bergan, Joe Hynes, and the Citizen), but if, as Gabler and others have argued, there is a "circularity" in the relationship between text and avant-texte, the text can just as validly be read with an awareness of the avant-texte in mind.¹⁷ Read this way, the "characters" of "Cyclops" oscillate with the identity-less speakers of the copybook, and it then seems as if little more than the presence of the characters' names turns the copybook speakers into the recognizable characters of the text. (As John Eglinton asks and Stephen Dedalus repeats twice in the "Scylla and Charybdis" episode, "What's in a name?" [*U* 9:901, 9:927, 9:986].)

The text's wandering involves not only the conversation and the characters, who in the copybook as well as in the text drift in and out of the barroom, but also the imagery. Animals of all kinds—bulls, cocks, hares, a hen, a wolf, a boar—move in and out of the dialogue with surprising speed. Mr B——/Bloom sets himself up to be the butt of a joke when he takes literally one speaker's simile involving a bull; in a context in which "that's a fact" is only a figure of speech, it's dangerous to treat any language as anything but figurative. In a quip that pleases its speaker, Bloom is called a bug (expanded by another speaker to bedbug, *Cimex lectularius*), and then he is considered "humane" because of his concern about animals. As the conversation turns to sports—almost suggesting that, when one speaker boasts, "That's what'll build up men Ireland a nation once again," the "men" are the last items on the list of animals—the contrast between the "soft" Bloom ("He'd shove a soft hand under a hen") and the "hard" Irish athletes ("From his godlike Shoulder sped the Stone") is far more obvious in this document than in the text of "Cyclops." By rearranging these details, the text presents the contrast less explicitly and less directly throughout the episode.

In *"Ulysses" in Progress*, looking for unity, I claimed that "only the combination of first-person narration and parodic exaggeration provides the double, two-eyed vision that is lacking in all the characters except Bloom."[18] Missing in this claim for "two-eyed vision" is the way in which the copybook scenes and the text itself work in terms of the relationship between the separate visions (or voices) rather than the ways in which the voices can be brought together. The passage in question, and much of the "Cyclops" copybook, illustrates very well M. M. Bakhtin's claim that novelistic language "is a *system* of languages that mutually and ideologically interanimate each other."[19] The bits of dialogue come from at least two recognizable positions, those of B——/Bloom and of the other Dubliners in the pub, and they contrast with the position represented by the passages of gigantism, identifiable in general terms within their own intertextual networks (the Butcher-and-Lang *Odyssey*, newspaper sports reporting, etc.) but not more specifically. Within these networks, the words that are used within the gigantism passages (like everything in "Oxen of the Sun") surely support Bakhtin's claim that words in a novel "have 'conditions attached to them,'" that each language system represents "a working hypothesis for comprehending and expressing reality."[20] Thus, whereas it is possible to see the copybook as revealing the different parts of "Cyclops" developing in the order in which Joyce refined them (in *"Ulysses" in Progress* I argued that the gigantism passages came first, then the dialogue, and finally the "I" narrator), it is also possible to see it as a Bakhtinian site in which the systems of language are privileged.[21] Only after these systems develop do names get attached to them and delimit them in terms of specific speakers and styles. Reading the avant-texte into the text allows the Bakhtinian nature of the dialogue, and the dialogism, of "Cyclops" to stand out from the details (names, etc.) that gained prominence in the episode after the copybook.

The copybook with its fragmentary dialogue and unattributed speakers is Bakhtinian in yet another way. For Bakhtin, "there is no unitary language or style in the novel. But at the same time there does exist a center of language (a verbal-ideological center) for the novel. The author (as creator of the novelistic whole) cannot be found at any one of the novel's language levels: he is to be found at the center of organization where all levels intersect."[22] Bakhtin's formulation is opposed to John Eglinton's statement in the "Scylla and Charybdis" episode that Shakespeare "is all in all" (*U* 9:1018–19); the author for Bakhtin is not incarnated in all or any of the characters. Nor should the author be configured, New Critical style, as either Wayne Booth's "implied author," posited between the historical writer and the fictional narrator, or as David Hayman's "arranger," located between the implied author and the narrator.[23] Bakhtin collapses the author/implied-author and author/arranger distinctions, but at the same time he avoids the assumptions of a unified authorial consciousness that underpin Booth's and Hayman's formulations. Bakhtin's author-as-organizational-center is a meeting place, a network hub ("Hello There, Central!" [*U* 7:1042]), anything but a unified whole. The voices without names and the gigantism passages without specific identifiable sources, and eventually the "Cyclops" episode's "I" narrator, come together in Bakhtin's terms only at the level of the author defined in this way.

The "Cyclops" copybook seems to accept, even to welcome, this formulation of the author and of authorial presence. For instance, in the scene in question there is at first a direct transition from the dialogue to a passage of gigantism that begins with "He sang the Pæan of the Games of the Gael." Except for B—/Bloom's words, all the dialogue is implicated in the demeaning barroom deflation of everything it mentions, whereas the "He sang" passage can do nothing but heroically inflate its subject. The neat, and obvious, dichotomy between these two dialogic systems is disrupted by the addition of a third one, the voice of a paragraph involving the hen Black Liz: "Gara, Klooklooklook. Black Liz is our hen. She lays eggs for us. When she lays her egg she is so glad. Gara Klooklooklook. Then comes good uncle Leo. She puts his hand under Black Liz and takes her fresh egg. Gara Klooklooklook." Also a voice of inflation, but less easily attributable than other gigantism passages to a generic source, the insert upsets the easy dualism that the passage had developed until now. Furthermore, as it exists on the page of the copybook, it visually disrupts any smooth movement. Joyce signaled the insert with a superscript *F* at the end of the sentence "But I'd like to see him in the nine acres in a hurley scrap" on page 12r of the copybook, and this refers the reader (including Joyce himself) to the verso of page 11 for the passage.[24] The *F* signaling the "Gara Klooklooklook" insertion, as has often been noted, is a very common feature of the documents of the Joycean avant-texte, and it helps to create another impression of textual instability, this time a visual one. In the Rosenbach Manuscript (more so in the middle thirty folios than in the first or last fifteen) and the typescript, and throughout the placards and page proofs, the document usually assumes the form of basic text plus extensive augmentation, with Joyce's ubiquitous *F*'s and his other letters (*H, M, S, T*, etc.) indicating an addition somewhere on the same page or a nearby one.

While *Ulysses* and *Finnegans Wake* were in progress, Joyce thought of his text as fluid and in motion; as he wrote to Frank Budgen when he sent him a manuscript version of the "Penelope" episode, "This is only the *draft* a great deal will be added or changed on 3 proofs" (*L* 1:171 [Joyce's italics and punctuation]), and *Finnegans Wake* notes "all those red raddled obeli cayennepeppercast over the text" in ALP's letter, "flinging phrases here, there, or returns inhibited, with some half-halted suggestion, E, dragging its shoestring" (*FW* 120:14–15, 121:6–8). Startling in their own right, these flung phrases can be seen not as insertions to be incorporated into the next transcription (typescript, proof, or published book) but rather as part of a multidirectional text moving out along innumerable lines from a physically centered but sometimes verbally dwarfed text. (There are proof pages on which the handwritten revisions overwhelm the printed text.) While he was writing "Ithaca" and "Penelope" at the same time as he was correcting and adding to the proofs for earlier parts of *Ulysses*, Joyce compared himself to "the man who used to play several instruments with different parts of his body" (*L* 1:179), and the avant-texte documents have the appearance of a textual body with appendages jutting out in many different directions. In a way, only an electronic medium can begin to match Joyce's presentation; traditional print media, with the possible exception of Gabler's synoptic text, can offer only pale, dull substitutes.

■

A second passage that can be looked at anew is the copybook draft's opening scene. I observed in *"Ulysses" in Progress* and earlier in this book that the draft begins not with the "I" narrator, dialogue, or interior monologue but rather with a gigantism passage:

> In ^<green Erin of the west> Inisfail the fair^ there lies a land, the land of holy Michan. There rises a watchtower beheld from afar. There sleep the dead as they ^<slept in life> in life slept^, warriors and princes of high renown. There wave the lofty trees of sycamore; the eucalyptus, giver of good shade, is not absent: and in their shadow sit the maidens of that land, the daughters of princes. They ^sing and^ sport with silvery fishes, caught in silken nets; their fair white fingers toss the gems of the ^fishful^ sea, ruby and purple of Tyre. And men come from afar, heroes, the sons of kings, to woo them for they are beautiful and all of noble stem.[25]

I assessed the opening as revealing "an easy mock-heroic attitude toward the events to follow" and noted the technical advance that Joyce accomplished after he developed the "I" narrator.[26] The copybook opening can, however, be analyzed in other ways.

Three different voices coexist in Bakhtinian dialogue in the opening: first, the narrator of the gigantism passages, as in the paragraph just quoted; second, the narrator accompanying Bloom's interior-monologue passages: "Bloom went by Mary's Lane and saw the sordid row of old clothes' shops, the old hucksterwomen seated by [the] baskets of battered hats, amid the dangling legs of ^<?> legless^ trousers, ^<culprits limp> limp^ coats [hung by the neck.] [manless]";[27] and third, Bloom's interior-monologue voice:

> Like culprits. Be taken to the prison from whence you came and there be hanged by the neck till you are ^<bought> sold^ and may the Lord. ^Emmet. Martyrs they want to be. My life for Ireland. Romance.

Girl in a window watching. Wipe away a tear. ?Hung up for scarecrows. Quite the ?contrary effect. Of course— where was it battle of Fontenoy they charged. Remember Limerick.^ Hard times those were in Holles street when Molly tried that game. Nothing in it: blind ?rut. Chiefly women, of course. Devils to please. Come back tomorrow Ta, ta.[28]

In *"Ulysses" in Progress* I talked about this section of the "Cyclops" copybook, with its few examples of Bloom's monologue that soon disappeared, as "the precise chronological point at which [Joyce] stopped writing one kind of book, basically concerned with Stephen and Bloom, and began to write another, in which a succession of parody styles, and eventually a group of schematic correspondences, began to take over."[29] I emphasized the relative obviousness and awkwardness of the gigantism passages as a sign of Joyce's uncertainty as he made the transition, but the passages can be seen in other ways as well. The copybook's second scene introduces the "I" narrator— "Little Alf Bergan popped in and hid behind Barney's snug, squeezed up laughing. ^I didn't know what was up.^"[30]—and also the characters' dialogue, so the first three copybook pages contain at least five systems of dialogic voices, without distinguishing among the different speakers in the pub or the different gigantism narrators. This group of voices represents as complex a situation as Joyce had created up to this point in *Ulysses*, and even though most readers would not want to sacrifice the increased subtlety of the three systems that he retained—"I" narrator, gigantism narrators, spoken dialogue—the subtlety does come at the expense of the elaborate network that Joyce briefly worked with in the first pages of the "Cyclops" copybook.

If the athletics passage is dominated by animal imagery, this one features slaughter of various kinds, from the fish and meat in the market to the old clothes that, hung as they are in windows, remind Bloom of hanged men:

><O'Bloom went ^<by> on^> Who comes< through Inn's quay ward, the parish of saint Michan.> ^<He moved>^ [^the son of Rudolph^] It is O'Bloom, the son of Rudolph <the son of Leopold Peter, son of Peter Rudolph> he of the <<intrepid heart> heart impervious to all fear> ^moving,^< a noble hero, eastward towards Pill Lane, among the squatted ^stench of^ fishgills, and by the gutboards where lay heaps of red and purple fishguts ^of gurnard, pollock, plaice and halibut^ He went by the city market, [O'Bloom ^a man^ of the intrepid heart.] >Gurnard & plaice those are. Speckled backs. One after another hook

in their gills. Can't be hunger drives them. Probably curiosity. Curiosity killed the fish<[31]

The sequence of paragraphs in the second passage—gigantism-narrator's description of the heroes' objects ("And on the dexter hand in solemn array are set forth the accoutrements of noble heroes: there hangs the breastplate of Brian, by whose might the Vikings were brought to nought: there, the helm of Oscar, son of Finn: there the bardic cloak of Ossian, the sightless seer, wanderer to many shores");[32] Bloom-narrator's description of presumably the same objects, now "brought to nought" like the Vikings; Bloom's thoughts inspired by the clothes—offers three takes on the same scene. Like much of the copybook, this passage presents the gigantism version first as the "ground," then offers a "translation" (here into the Bloom-narrator) before presenting the more obviously subjective account in Bloom's mind. Later, after Joyce developed the "I" narrator, that narrator's version tends to appear first, so that the gigantism passages appear as "translations" of the narrator's account. "Translation" needs to be kept in quotation marks, because these passages are excellent examples of Bakhtin's argument that a novel is "a dialogue between points of view, each with its own concrete language that cannot be translated into the other."[33] The opening copybook paragraphs contain no realistic ground against which other elements might be measured, and in this way they resemble the kind of radical disruption introduced by the opening fragments of the "Sirens" episode and later in the avant-texte by the first newspaper head in the "Aeolus" episode. (Joyce added the newspaper heads to "Aeolus" on the first proofs for that episode two years after he wrote the "Cyclops" copybook.)

Many of the details from the first paragraphs of the "Cyclops" copybook remain in the text, but they appear in altered, sometimes greatly changed, contexts. The gigantism passages of the first and third paragraphs remain relatively intact (*U* 12:68–117), but they are delayed to follow the introduction of the "I" narrator and Joe Hynes and then the Moses Herzog contract (which, rather than one of the "heroic" translations of mundane action, becomes the first passage of gigantism). The two paragraphs are split into three (fish, fruits and vegetables, meat and dairy products), and all are expanded. The first paragraph, with its "fishful streams," "lofty trees," and "lovely maidens," acquires some of the details about fish from the abandoned paragraph describing Bloom's walk through the market, and it also, in subsequent revisions, gains adjectives ("wafty sycamore," "eugenic eucalyptus"), items for lists ("the gibbed haddock, the grilse, the dab, the brill," "creels of fingerlings"), and long, encyclopedic passages, as the "heroes" eventually come "from Eblana to Slievemargy, the peerless princes of unfettered Munster and of Connacht the just and of smooth sleek Leinster and of Cruachan's land and of Armagh the splendid and of the noble district of Boyle." Also, by the time of the Rosenbach Manuscript the paragraph has acquired its tendency to self-destruct, as the "maidens" who are now "lovely," sit by "lovely trees," sing "lovely songs," and play with "lovely objects," all of which are introduced in a list that begins "as for example."

Second, the fruits-and-vegetables passage, smoothly written out in the "Cyclops" copybook, remains remarkably intact throughout the avant-texte and into the text, with the predictable exception of additions to the lists of examples at all stages of the manuscript, typescript, and proofs. Third, the paragraph of meat and dairy products, separated from the description of fruits and divided from it by the plumber Geraghty's cry against Moses Herzog—"*I dare him*, says he, *and I doubledare him*" (*U* 12:100 [Joyce's italics])—gains many new details in its lists of examples.

The Bloom passages, with their inchoate interior monologues, differ the most from later documents in the avant-texte and from the text. Bloom's walk toward Pill Lane, partially retained in the text in a gigantism passage, is first mentioned by the "I" narrator, who says that "I saw him . . . sloping around by Pill lane and Greek street with his cod's eye counting up all the guts of the fish" (*U* 12:213–17 [my ellipsis]; "and Greek street" is an addition). The walk by the clothes shops disappears as a separate unit, but the "noble heroes" Oscar, Finn, and Ossian are all part of the list of "the twelve tribes of Iar" enumerated in a gigantism passage (*U* 12:1127–29). The references to Fontenoy and Limerick become part of a patriotic remark uttered by John Wyse Nolan while Bloom tries unsuccessfully to join the conversation (*U* 12:1380–82). Bloom's monologue thoughts about Robert Emmet and martyrs, here inspired by the appearance of the clothes, relate to and seem to be a continuation of his sight of Emmet's last words in a window at the end of "Sirens" (*U* 11:1284–93), and his thought, "Martyrs they want to be," is similar to his reactions to the Ormond bar scene during Ben Dollard's singing of "The Croppy Boy" (as at *U* 11:1101–2).

Has part of the text of "Sirens" wandered into the opening pages of the "Cyclops" copybook? (Daniel Ferrer has detected "the seed of 'Cyclops'" in an early draft of "Sirens" that the National Library of Ireland acquired in 2002.)[34] Gabler talks about Joyce's use of "pre-text from within the *oeuvre*," by which he means that the intertextual network connects to a bit of text not from another author but from Joyce himself, even from *Ulysses* itself; Gabler thus talks of "the *oeuvre*'s intratextuality."[35] This process is most evident in "Circe," in which the text regularly seems to be quoting itself. In *"Ulysses" in Progress* I claimed that "*Ulysses* itself becomes one great 'character': like strands of thought in Bloom's and Stephen's minds, any themes or correspondences in *Ulysses* become usable sources of new juxtapositions or cross-references," but it isn't necessary to anthropomorphize the text in this way.[36] For Gabler, for instance, the text of *Ulysses* becomes "increasingly capable of oscillating between text and pre-text functions."[37] The "Emmet" passage shows this beginning to happen. If it somehow wandered from "Sirens" into "Cyclops," it eventually moved back to "Sirens," since various parts of the "Emmet" sentence here became a typescript addition to that episode: "To wipe away a tear for martyrs that want to, dying to, die" (*U* 11:1101–2).[38]

The most elaborate reuse of material involves the sentence "Hard times those were in Holles street when Molly tried that game." Molly's attempt to sell old clothes in Holles Street after the "hard times" when Bloom lost his job at Wisdom Helys was already mentioned in "Sirens," when Ben Dollard talked about borrowing clothes and Simon Dedalus quipped that "Mrs Marion Bloom has left off clothes of all descriptions" (*U* 11:496–97), and *Ulysses* goes on to include in the Holles Street scene the selling not only of old clothes but also of Molly's hair combings, Bloom's suggestion that she pose for nude photographs, and his washing and (in a "Circe" passage) wearing of Molly's underwear (*U* 15:2986–88; also 13:840–41, 16:716–17, 18:560–62). Given the extensive connections regarding both the martyrs and the clothes to other parts of *Ulysses*, it is possible that, like the Emmet passage, this one may not be part of "Cyclops" at all; it may just be visiting or have wandered in. Once it joins the copybook context, though, it takes on the atmosphere of male nastiness, bigotry, and violence that pervades so much else of the copybook and of "Cyclops."

Does it matter whether this passage was ever intended for "Cyclops"? For certain genetic histories of *Ulysses*, surely it does; it is important to document and understand the genesis of the book to the extent that documentation and understanding are possible. But Louis Hay cautions that "even the most detailed and well-conserved documentation reveals but a fraction of the complicated mental processes to which it bears witness. The ink on the page is not the writing itself."³⁹ If this is always the case, Joyce is a particularly acute reminder of it. Much of his creative efforts were not written down; he seems to have turned to paper only when the "writing" had advanced to a certain stage. He occasionally indicated this explicitly. Because of his eye problems, he had to dictate the last third of the fair copy (the Rosenbach Manuscript) of "Wandering Rocks" to Frank Budgen, and he appended a note saying that he had dictated "from notes," which suggests that he did not have a fully written-out draft preceding the fair copy. And regarding "Sirens," he told Harriet Shaw Weaver that "the elements needed will only fuse after a prolonged existence together," echoing an earlier remark to Ezra Pound that "the ingredients will not fuse until they have reached a certain temperature." This fusion presumably happened in his head. Gabler notes "the importance which the pre-writing processes had for Joyce's writing" and calls the written documents Joyce's "secondary *loci* of writing."⁴⁰

It is tempting to see this process as a further way that Joyce found to confound his critics and ensure immortality (according to Richard Ellmann, Joyce told Jacques Benoît-Méchin that "I've put in so many enigmas and puzzles that it will keep the professors busy for centuries arguing over what I meant, and that's the only way of insuring one's immortality"), but it also ensures that the origin of the text—whether it be the original idea for *Ulysses* as a whole or for "Cyclops" or the author's interpretation of the relationship between the *Odyssey* and *Ulysses*—remains private, inaccessible to the most scrupulous and diligent genetic critic.⁴¹ This inevitable gap can throw us back to conceptions of the author as the genius at the heart of the mystery, but it can also lead to a willingness to live with and enjoy wandering through the evidence that does survive, looking not at Joyce the genius but at Joyce the author who functions at the Bakhtinian center of various systems of discourse in dialogue with one another, the author in motion as "the man who used to play several instruments with different parts of his body."

The drafts can, finally, open up at least one other kind of possibility. Gabler refers to "the interdependence of text and pre-text" and to "the ultimate circularity of their relationship."⁴² If it is possible to read the avant-texte into the text of *Ulysses* as well as reading the text back into the avant-texte, then another "text" is created that is neither *Ulysses* itself nor any of its earlier documents. With its nascent Bloomian monologue, its gigantism opening, and its interchangeable characters, "Cyclops" is an excellent test case of Hay's suggestion that "perhaps we should consider the text as *a necessary possibility*, as one manifestation of a process which is always virtually present in the background, a kind of third dimension of the written work" and also Jerome McGann's argument that we probably "read" the earlier, longer version of Marianne Moore's "Poetry" even when we see in front of us the three-line poem she published in her *Complete Poems*.[43] So is Stephen Dedalus's presence in two of the copybook's scenes and the attribution to Stephen of the words "when he is quite sure which country it is" in answer to the question of why a Jew can't love his country,[44] both of which open up the possibility of the reader oscillating between recalling Stephen in the deep background of the episode and accepting his absence from the text of *Ulysses* between "Wandering Rocks" and "Oxen of the Sun." Instead of revealing "false starts and uncertainties" or "unclear" plans,[45] the copybook and the other documents from the avant-texte can reveal alternate states, ones that became superseded but that, once encountered, are never entirely canceled. The text's network thus extends not only out in many directions in space but also back and forth in time to reveal the rich possibilities in the avant-texte.

7

Revisiting the "Cyclops" Manuscripts, Part 2
The National Library of Ireland Draft and Its Contexts

Revisiting the "Cyclops" manuscripts in the light of new theories and models, wandering in them and setting them in motion, is one thing. But, as I've suggested several times in this book, revisiting the manuscripts acquired a new urgency and excitement in 2002 when the National Library of Ireland announced its acquisition of previously unavailable documents, including an early draft of part of "Cyclops" as well as several new gatherings of notes for the episode. How, I wondered, would the picture I presented in *"Ulysses" in Progress* change based on not only new theoretical models and methods of procedure but also new documents? My initial exploration of the new "Cyclops" materials at the National Library not only filled in more parts of the picture of Joyce's early writing of the episode than had been possible before but also led me to ask some questions that I hadn't thought of until then.

Before the National Library acquired its manuscripts, notes for *Ulysses* were extant mainly in the notesheets at the British Library and in two notebooks at Buffalo, as well as in a few other documents. To these gatherings can be added four more notebooks.[1] The first of these is earlier than the other three. Joyce labeled its pages by topic—Simon, Leopold, Stephen, Jesus, Theosophy, Irish, Jews, Weininger, Words, and others—rather than by *Ulysses* episode, as was his practice in the other three and also the British Library notesheets and a Buffalo notebook from late in his work on *Ulysses*.

As with the previously extant collections, Joyce seems to have used the National Library notes more for revisions and additions to existing drafts than for new writing or for general conceptualizing. (This statement, however, needs to be made with some hesitation, because he rarely discussed his general thinking about *Ulysses*, and, as is also the case with the Buffalo "Cyclops" draft, it can be unclear whether a surviving document is a first inscription or one copied from previous writing.) In the British Library notesheets there are some general notes for "Cyclops," such as a cluster on "Cyclops" notesheet 5 that includes "Cycl. Exaggeration of things previously given: Superlatives," "Style. Longwinded simile," "Technique: Sudden vituperation follows depression," and a note that reprises phrases from "Nestor": "It seems history is to blame, nightmare, God noise in street, never let jews in."[2] In one of the National Library notebooks, a page of notes, in German and taken from Otto Weininger's *Über die letzten Dinge* (*On Last Things*), includes some ideas that might have fed into "Cyclops," such as (in translation) "people who are in a space together always form a community against newcomers."[3] It is hard to know how much weight to put on these general notes. If Rodney Wilson Owen is correct, Joyce had settled on a core element of what became "Cyclops"—a cuckolded Jewish man facing a group of hostile men in a pub after he claims that he is Irish—when he thought of a "Ulysses" story for *Dubliners* in 1907, and the general notes might have served primarily to reinforce or extend ideas he already had.[4] (Owen's suggestion might seem like a wild conjecture, but the National Library documents have borne out several of the guesses and speculations Owen made in the early 1980s on the basis of scanty available evidence.) Significantly, the notes also point to the books, articles, and newspapers that Joyce read and found useful as he worked on *Ulysses*.

We are on more solid ground when we look at Joyce's notes in relation to his additions and revisions. In one reassuring way, the new notes follow and reconfirm the pattern regarding the dramatic color clusters on the notesheets and notebook and copybook pages that manuscript scholars recognized many years ago: the colors—red, blue, and green—represent Joyce's runs through the notes and nothing more elaborate or arcane than that.[5] In *"Ulysses" in Progress* I list twelve phrases Joyce added to the long "last farewell" passage in "Cyclops" that recounts the execution of an Irish revolutionary as if it were a society event (*U* 12:525–678) after it appeared in *The Little Review* in November 1919 and before he submitted the typescript for the book printing in late summer 1921. There were no notes in the British Library notesheets for any of these additions. The notes that led to such additions now exist: they appear in three of the National Library gatherings, and Joyce crossed them out in blue.[6] Falling in line as they do with the pattern of Joyce's writing as we have come to know it, the notes for these additions to the "last farewell" passage suggest that probably every revision and addition to the text—to one of the early drafts, the fair copy manuscript, the typescript, or the proofs—is signaled by a note, whether or not the note has survived.

The National Library "Cyclops" draft offers more immediate rewards. Two features of the early twenty-four-page "Cyclops" copybook at Buffalo made it clear that Joyce must have used at least one other copybook to complete his draft, and the National Library's document is that other copybook.[7] For one thing, the final scene in the Buffalo draft, which features the men in the pub talking about Sir Frederick Falconer and his leniency as a judge, ends in the middle of a sentence with the words "And there <dight in the garb of justice> he sat to," and the National Library manuscript completes the infinitive with the word "administer" and then continues the sentence and the scene.[8] Second, Joyce wrote a note on page [22r] (his 23r) of the Buffalo copybook, near a passage in which the characters gossip about Molly (*U* 12:1003–8), directing himself to page 28,[9] and page 4r of the National Library draft (which would be the twenty-eighth leaf overall) includes an addition to the passage. The Buffalo and National Library "Cyclops" documents are also physically similar: both are blue-covered copybooks with dimensions of 21.6 × 17.5 centimeters and twenty-four leaves (forty-eight pages) of graph paper.

If the National Library's "Cyclops" draft is interesting at first simply because it is the long-missing continuation of the Buffalo copybook, it ultimately proves to be more exciting than that. Joyce followed the continuation of the Buffalo copybook's final scene (which he numbered as 8) with drafts of two more passages of gigantism (he did not number any of the scenes in the National Library copybook). But then, starting on page 7r, a new passage appears, an early version of what became the episode's opening: "I was just passing the time of day with old Troy of the D. M. P. at the corner of Arbour hill there" (*U* 12:1–2). In other words, after drafting ten scenes, including an opening (in Buffalo's scene 1) and the ending (in its scene 4), Joyce wrote a new beginning. This draft of the beginning contains many *currente calamo* revisions, but except for a few minor details, this beginning is the book version, containing both the "I"-narrator and the initial passage of gigantism, the legal brief concerning the dispute between Moses Herzog and Michael E. Geraghty (*U* 12:33–51).

We have something very surprising here: the episode segues into a more advanced state in front of our eyes, like a blurry image coming into focus. (As Daniel Ferrer has demonstrated, an early "Sirens" draft at the National Library divides in two, with Bloom completely missing from the first half but present in the second as both a character and as a point of view on the events. In a way that parallels the National Library "Cyclops" draft, "Sirens" evolved into something more advanced as Joyce wrote.)[10] The narrator that Frank Budgen depicts as a "snarling Thersites" appears, and the characters become more developed: they go from unnamed (X, Y, — , etc.) to named (by page 11r of the National Library copybook, for example, the narrator is calling the figure who earlier was Cusack "the citizen").[11] The scenes too develop from a primitive state to something more tightly structured and plotted, even if no shape for the episode is clear by the end of the National Library draft. In fact, the development of the episode's opening nearly concludes Joyce's work in the copybook: after the opening, there is only a draft of the "last farewell" scene, also fairly advanced (pp. 12r–15r). The rest of the document is blank except for a list of scenes on the last page.[12] Apart from a next draft of scenes 5–8 of the Buffalo copybook (also at Buffalo) and the last scene's continuation in the National Library draft, as well as a few individual and self-contained pages, no documents exist between the stage represented by the Buffalo and National Library drafts and the Rosenbach Manuscript fair copy.[13]

It has usually been assumed that intermediate documents are missing,[14] but perhaps the extant manuscripts are all that Joyce needed to put the episode into shape. He may have done most of the intervening work in his head, with a large degree of fluidity and motion in his writing as he worked on his drafts. He has frequently been described as a mosaic worker, an artist filling in details into a predetermined plan,[15] and his notes—often precise words or phrases destined for an apparently predetermined place in the text—seem to support this picture, as do Joyce's two schemas, with their columns of times, locations, colors, symbols, technics, body organs, and correspondences for each episode.[16] But the schemas are products of Joyce's late work on *Ulysses*, and the early versions of the episodes suggest something more nuanced, a writer working with much less certainty who composed short scenes that lack narrative sequence and sometimes serve as little more than placeholders for more-developed writing to follow. Joyce seems to have known that, once he put something down on paper, he could revise his words into what he needed and wanted: Phillip Herring has written that Joyce took notes "trusting to genius for transforming trivia into the sublime," and he appears to have done much of the writing on his early drafts with the same kind of confidence.[17] His efforts to accomplish the transformation might very well have taken place in his head more than on paper, and so they cannot be found on documents, even though much more written evidence—more than most scholars probably ever expected—is now extant to show the complex ways in which he worked and to point to his even more complex mental processes.

Finally, the National Library "Cyclops" draft is fascinating in ways that point beyond this one episode, and it provokes some tantalizing broader questions. It is not alone among the *Ulysses* manuscripts in containing two draft stages in one document: the early "Sirens" draft similarly consists of different stages of that episode, and the document uniquely contains drafts of two different episodes, with "Proteus" preceding "Sirens."[18] In *"Ulysses" in Progress* and in several places in this book I note some intriguing connections between the Buffalo "Cyclops" draft and "Aeolus," especially the presence of Stephen Dedalus and Professor MacHugh in both episodes, along with many other characters from "Aeolus" who remain in "Cyclops," such as Lenehan, J. J. O'Molloy, and O'Madden Burke.[19] There is no new "Cyclops" evidence in the National Library manuscripts, but the existence of "Proteus" and "Sirens" in one draft and of a primitive "Ithaca" draft, where the episode is in a question-and-answer format but lacks shape or any main narrative developments (the order of events and the kinds of questions seem random, and some of the questions and also some answers are a kind of interior monologue in disguise), provokes some new questions about Joyce's plans for the book and the sequence of his draftings.[20] For example, we have tended to assume that he drafted the episodes in order, but were some of the episodes that the drafts bring together, such as "Aeolus" and "Cyclops" or "Proteus" and "Sirens," drafted closer in time to each other than we have thought? Also, did Joyce first conceive of "Sirens" as an early Bloom episode rather than as one for the middle of the book (Owen offers various kinds of evidence to argue for Joyce's early work on at least part of the episode)?[21] Third, Herring has noted that some notes related to Stephen migrated from the "Cyclops" notesheets to those for "Eumaeus," presumably after Joyce decided to remove Stephen from "Cyclops."[22] The newly available manuscripts can guide us not only toward a more refined sense of Joyce's work on individual episodes but also toward a greater awareness of how the episodes relate to each other and the movements among them as Joyce worked on them.

■

Joyce did not write "Cyclops" or *Ulysses* in isolation. Like all manuscripts, the newly available National Library "Cyclops" draft gives scholars access to what genetic critics might formulate as "an immaterial object (a process) through the concrete analysis of the material traces left by that process."[23] The manuscripts serve as the most important evidence of a process that nevertheless remains largely inaccessible, and they are not and cannot be the whole story in other ways. Joyce's writing took place within a context of personal, social, cultural, and national and international political events. Ford Madox Ford's biographer notes that "The simultaneous processes of living and writing shape each other in complex and often surprising ways," and an investigation of Joyce's work on "Cyclops" and of *Ulysses* should take the various kinds of events in his life into account and place the writing as shown in the notes and drafts in relation to these events.[24]

Stephen Greenblatt has speculated about ways in which William Shakespeare brought his "passionate life—his access through personal experience and observation to the intense emotions he represents"—into his plays. (Greenblatt also singles out Stephen's discussion of Shakespeare in "Scylla and Charybdis" as preeminent among "the most compelling reflections on the presence of Shakespeare's emotional life in his plays.")[25] He makes a case for a connection between Shakespeare's emotional reactions, both immediate and delayed, to the death of the playwright's son Hamnet in 1596 and his ability four years later in *Hamlet* to represent thinking in a soliloquy. Without any surviving letters, working notes, diaries, or manuscripts to use as concrete evidence, Greenblatt can only speculate on this connection. The extant Joyce archive shows, however, that even a vast array of surviving documents can leave connections between the author's personal life and the writing almost as problematic as with Shakespeare.

Joyce spoke to his friends, wrote letters, and published fiction about many aspects of his life; no novel presents a closer use of an author's personal life and at the same time more difficulties in separating the character's life from the author's than does *A Portrait of the Artist as a Young Man*. But he also withheld many important aspects of his life, and of his life as a writer, from his conversations, letters, manuscripts, and published works. He discussed his intentions regarding *Ulysses*, for example, only in the most general terms, declaring, according to Budgen, that Odysseus was his example of a "complete all-round character" and that Bloom was "a good man" who was "not 'gut' but 'gutmütig,'" that is, not good but decent, or writing that the style of "Nausicaa" was "namby-pamby jammy marmalady drawersy (alto là!).".[26] A great deal of scholarly work has naturally focused on Joyce's uses of his early Dublin experiences in *Ulysses* and on some aspects of his emotional life—such as his general sense that the people closest to him would betray him or his jealousy in 1909 after Vincent Cosgrave told him that Nora had gone out walking with him in June 1904 on the nights she was not with Joyce.[27] Beyond this, though, it is difficult to specify how he incorporated much of his ongoing emotional life, both what he experienced and what he observed, into *Ulysses* as he worked on it.

Joyce has often been presented as a writer fixated on his earlier life in Dublin to the exclusion of anything going on around him as he wrote, and the problem of looking into the contexts of his writing is the opposite of what might be expected, since the main difficulty is trying to discern how his ongoing life and events affected him and his work on *Ulysses*. "Joyce's existence ran parallel with the Great War," Herbert Gorman writes in his biography, "in a city that was fearfully like a boiling cauldron and with the *brouhaha* of mad days about him but walking through it with his mind intent upon an olive-faced man whom he had created and set peregrinating through the streets of the Dublin of 1904." For Brenda Maddox, *Ulysses* "was more than a book; it was a whole private world into which Joyce had withdrawn."[28] There will always be a gap between the writer and the living person, one that can never be closed completely even if the writer wants to do that. Joyce, hardly atypically, did little to close the gap, and so, except for providing evidence of his reading, his surviving manuscripts tend not to take us far into the life he was living as he was writing.

If Joyce did withdraw into his book, he nevertheless reacted to events around him as possible material for it. Budgen writes that Joyce once asked him, "When you get an idea, have you ever noticed what I can make of it?" and Richard Ellmann recounts some of Joyce's conversations with friends—sometimes, it seems, staged ones—that he subsequently worked into *Ulysses*. In a fascinating and detailed account, John McCourt has demonstrated how Joyce blended aspects of the lives and personalities of several Jewish men he knew in Trieste to create Leopold Bloom.[29]

Joyce drafted "Cyclops" near the end of his four-year stay in Zurich, the city to which he had moved in June 1915 after Italy's entrance into the war made it impossible for a British subject to continue living in Austrian Trieste. He was working on the episode by mid-June 1919, since on June 19 he mentioned it in a letter to Budgen:

> The chapter of the *Cyclops* is being lovingly moulded in the way you know. The Fenian is accompanied by a wolfhound who speaks (or curses) in Irish. He unburdens his soul about the Saxo-Angles in the best Fenian style and with colossal vituperativeness alluding to their standard industry. The epic proceeds explanatorily "He spoke of the English, a noble race, rulers of the waves, who sit on thrones of alabaster, silent as the deathless gods." (L 1:126 [Joyce's italics]; with some variations in wording, Joyce refers to the end of scene 2 of Buffalo's copybook, revised to 12:1212–14)

He mailed the finished episode to Ezra Pound a few days before he left Zurich for Trieste on October 16 so that Pound could send it on to *The Little Review* (L 2:455).[30] The magazine published the episode quickly, running it in four issues starting in November 1919.

Joyce's last several months in Zurich were eventful both personally and politically. I will consider seven aspects of his life there and offer some preliminary observations on each. (I have not dealt with other important topics, such as the possible impact of contemporary art movements and individual artists, of intellectual influences on Joyce, or of ongoing responses to his work.[31] Many of his notes for *Ulysses* point to his reading, and scholars have also determined much of his reading from the published text alone. In an appendix to *Inverted Volumes Improperly Arranged: James Joyce and His Trieste Library*, Michael Patrick Gillespie attempts to isolate the books Joyce owned in Zurich. Important as Joyce's reading is, I have passed over the topic here, including ways in which his reading is reflected in the contents of the notes he took.)[32] When Robert Darnton outlines the six players in the "communications circuit" that make up the life of a book (authors, publishers, printers, shippers, booksellers, and readers), he suggests that "however [book historians] define their subject, they will not draw out its full significance unless they relate it to all the elements that worked together."[33] This claim applies equally to Joyce's writing of *Ulysses*: the seven aspects I discuss here need to be seen in relation to one another even if one or another dominates at individual moments. It is also important to keep in mind Ronald Bush's argument that Joyce's mind—intellectual, emotional, and artistic—was hardly "independent of connections with literature and history, whether mediated through cultural pressures or through the power of the unconscious" and that "Joyce's cultural practices" had "historically contingent dimensions." Bush cites Arnold Goldman's claims that we have access only to "versions of Joyce, filtered . . . through text and letter, diary and memoir, interview and conversation" and that any picture of Joyce will be one of "discontinuity" and "discrepancy."[34] Probing into the details of even a few months of Joyce's life reveals just how contingent and discontinuous a picture of Joyce writing *Ulysses* has to be.

The War in Europe

The armistice ending the Great War was signed on November 11, 1918. Zurich was in turmoil then, however: the European influenza epidemic spread there, and so did the German revolution, causing a general strike.[35] Farther away, the civil war following the 1917 Russian Revolution continued, and in January 1919 the Anglo-Irish guerrilla war began.

Joyce said and wrote little or nothing about the world war or about any other political events after he moved to Zurich in 1915. Several personal accounts from people who knew him speak of his involvement with political matters—Italo Svevo remarks that Joyce took part in Irish struggles "from afar," for example, and Silvio Benco writes that Joyce "brought with him from Ireland a passionate interest" in politics—but almost all descriptions like these come from his earlier Trieste years. Also, only in those earlier years did he lecture and write newspaper articles about politics, especially Irish politics.[36]

In contrast to Svevo and Benco, Budgen says that in Zurich Joyce was "on one subject . . . more uncommunicative than any man I know: the subject of politics," and writer after writer describes his near-total silence on political matters there. Budgen also writes that "as I knew him in Zurich he was the Mr. Dooley, 'the coolest card our country ever knew,' who had turned his back alike upon Marx and Engels and upon 'Jingo Jesus.'"[37] Mr. Dooley comes from Joyce's 1916 poem "Dooleysprudence" (which remained unpublished until the 1959 *Critical Writings* and Ellmann biography but presumably circulated around Zurich), whose neutral hero is "the man when all the gallant nations run to war / Goes home to have his dinner by the very first cablecar" (*CW* 246). Remarks attributed to Joyce—such as his statement to

Oscar Schwarz, "Oh yes, I was told that there was a war going on in Europe," or his question to Budgen after the conflict was over, "Who won this war?"—reinforce the image of someone completely indifferent to the war going on around him, as does Gorman's picture of a man whose devotion to his art eradicates any concern for politics: "What was the war to him? . . . He was marching into a new terrain of literature where no man had ever marched before." For Ellmann, Joyce was "supremely indifferent to the result" of the war "and, so long as gunfire could not be heard, to the conflict itself."[38] All these pictures lie behind the Joyce whom Tom Stoppard creates in his play *Travesties*, a man who can answer Henry Carr's question "And what did you do in the Great War?" with the response, "I wrote *Ulysses*. What did you do?"[39]

Even in his letters, Joyce's few references to the war are limited to such general phrases as "these dangerous days" (*L* 1:122). Joyce could, however, use much more specific terminology when it suited him. In his April 28, 1919, "Statement" regarding his treatment by the English authorities in the English Players affair, which he circulated widely, he referred to himself as "a prisoner of war liberated on parole to Switzerland in July 1915 by the Austrian Government in consideration of my health" (*L* 2:439). It would be interesting to know how Stanislaus Joyce, recently released from his four-year internment in a detention camp, reacted to his brother's description of himself as a prisoner.

Joyce had reasons to remain silent. In order to obtain a visa in 1915 allowing him and his family to leave Trieste for neutral Switzerland, according to Gorman, he had to give his word to the Austrian officials who controlled Trieste that he would remain politically neutral. And in Zurich he saw himself in an ironically compromised political situation—as Benco puts it, "the official position of the Irishman at war with England was now that of a British citizen at war with Austria." Joyce opposed the war on pacifist grounds and also thought that neither side deserved to win it, but from his experiences in Trieste he had relatively good feelings toward the Austrian Empire, his official enemy, and general hostility toward Britain: "They called [Austria-Hungary] a ramshackle empire," he wrote to Mary Colum; "I wish to God there were more such empires."[40] He was opposed to nationalisms of any kind and, especially as nationalistic sentiments grew in Ireland, rejected any solution to the war based on nationalism.

Not all reports of Joyce's later attitudes toward politics suggest indifference. Eugene Jolas describes Joyce in Paris as "little interested in pure politics and economics, although he followed events faithfully." Joyce's Zurich friend Claud Sykes often saw him reading English newspapers, and according to Ellmann, at a particularly angry moment against the English, Joyce "changed his daily newspaper from the pro-Allied *Neue Zürcher Zeitung* to the pro-German *Zürcher Post*." Silence about the outcome or the large issues, or even disinterest in them, is hardly evidence of indifference to the war itself; as Vincent Sherry notes, "to be anti-nationalist . . . is not to be apolitical."[41] Some scholars, in fact, perceive Joyce's deep involvement with the war despite his silence: Declan Kiberd claims that "Joyce affected an unconcern for its battles, but it is clear that the war touched him to the quick"; Robert Spoo, focusing on "Nestor," argues that the episode "subtly register[s], under unlikely formal auspices, attitudes toward the situation of 1917"; and Peter Barham sweepingly calls *Ulysses* "a war novel *par excellence* that is permeated by the war without once mentioning it."[42]

Dominic Manganiello approaches the question of the war's effect on Joyce by suggesting that "Dooleysprudence," which depicts a man who "cries" to the English and the Germans, "The curse of Moses / On both your houses" (*CW* 247), "is in fact indicting both Church and governments as causes for the bloodshed." More specifically regarding *Ulysses*, Kiberd argues that, when Stephen talks to Garrett Deasy in "Nestor" about "those big words . . . which make us so unhappy" (*U* 2:264 [my ellipsis]), Joyce is responding to "the futility of war" and the causes he perceived—nations, governments, Church.[43] Spoo and James Fairhall have each shown how language used during the war permeated the text of *Ulysses*. Spoo argues that a source for Stephen's comment to Deasy that "history . . . is a nightmare from which I am trying to awake" (*U* 2:377 [my ellipsis]) was the war, "during which 'nightmare' was used widely as an expression of cultural malaise."[44] Fairhall considers Joyce's use of the word "casualties"—Tom Kernan thinks of the "thousand casualties" of the General Slocum disaster, an event from June 15, 1904 (*U* 10:726), and Bloom, reflecting in "Eumaeus" on the effects of political opinions like those of the Citizen in "Cyclops," is described as "only too conscious of the casualties invariably resulting from propaganda and displays of mutual animosity" (*U* 16:1599–1600)—and notes that the word "inevitably referred to or brought to mind the war." (Fairhall also argues that the often-quoted desire that Joyce expressed to Budgen, "to give a picture of Dublin so complete that if the city one day suddenly disappeared from the earth it could be reconstructed out of my book," might have come from a sense of fragility brought on by the Easter Rising, the Russian Revolution, and the death toll of the war.)[45] Joyce includes a direct prediction of the war in the "Cyclops" drafts, when O'Madden Burke tells Cusack, the early version of the Citizen, and the other men in the pub that "there's a war coming on for the English ["the Sassenachs" in the next draft] and the Germans will give them a hell of a gate of going. What they ["the imperial yeomanry" in the next draft] got from the Boers is only what you might call an hors d'oeuvre.... But this time, whether they win or lose, ... They'll be up against an army ["a conundrum" in the next draft] that'll kill a man for every man they kill. Wait till you see."[46] Joyce dropped Burke's prescient remark from the episode before he wrote out the Rosenbach Manuscript fair copy.

Joyce wrote "Cyclops," this most belligerent of episodes and one whose "art" Joyce listed on his schema, included in Gilbert's *James Joyce's "Ulysses,"* as "politics," while Zurich, like much of Europe, was settling into the return to peace and adjusting to the political and national realignments that followed the end of the war. He was also writing as the Anglo-Irish war was taking Ireland into yet more uncertain and dangerous times and as he faced a personally uncertain future due to his increasing impatience to leave Zurich.[47] As both the statements from people who knew him and also the quotations from *Ulysses* and its critics suggest, the ways in which the war permeated Joyce's consciousness and *Ulysses* are not easy to discern except very generally or very specifically, but that it did permeate seems clear and unavoidable. As Spoo concludes, "Joyce's texts frequently give the lie to his pose of indifference to any history or politics not directly concerned with his picture of the Dublin of his youth."[48]

The War in Ireland

After *Finnegans Wake* was published, Budgen "confess[ed] that I was once guilty of helping to create the impression that Joyce was nonpolitical" but said now that "no man can be nonpolitical who spends the greater part of his life in celebrating his native city."[49] Joyce's attitude toward Dublin was, of course, far more complex than mere celebration, but he never stopped writing about it. Asked in the late 1930s why he did not return to Ireland, he responded, "Have I ever left it?"; as Manganiello puts it, he "carried with him a consciousness of the political situation of his city and of his country" no matter where he was living.[50]

Turmoil raged in Ireland while Joyce was writing *Ulysses*, including the 1916 Easter Rising and the subsequent British executions of several of the Irish leaders, and then the Anglo-Irish war that began in 1919 in the wake of Sinn Fein's victory in the late 1918 election, the party members' refusal in January 1919 to go to England to sit in the Parliament, and the establishment instead of the Dáil Éireann in Dublin. Joyce professed hostility to the revolutionaries' aims: Gorman reports that, when asked whether he looked forward to an independent Ireland, Joyce answered, "So that I might declare myself its first enemy?"[51] He apparently followed the events in Ireland with keen interest, though, reading the *Times* of London instead of the less accessible *Irish Times* and also personal reports and newspaper clippings that friends and relatives in Ireland sent him.[52] (Joyce received clippings from Dublin newspapers, including a notice about the death of J. G. Lidwell, a man whom he had recently mentioned in "Sirens," which he mentions in an August 1919 letter [*L* 1:129].) As with the world war, he hardly ever mentioned any of the events in specific terms, referring in his letters only to "these evil days" or "these troubled days" (*L* 1:96, 1:124). These phrasings perhaps reflect his own uncertain attitudes toward the events; Emer Nolan has analyzed in detail what she describes as the "symptomatic ambiguity in [Joyce's] political thought," the "uncertain, divided consciousness of the colonial subject."[53]

Parallel to the claims about the war's indirect presence in *Ulysses*, G. J. Watson and Andrew Gibson both argue—albeit from somewhat different positions—that *Ulysses* is built on Joyce's knowledge of ongoing events in Ireland. For Watson, "the famous day in 1904 is seen by a consciousness saturated with [the] later knowledge" of what happened in Ireland during and after the Easter Rising. (F. L. Radford and Ellen Carol Jones also make cases for the impact of the Easter Rising on Joyce's writing of *Ulysses*, Radford linking it to the execution scenes in both "Cyclops" and "Circe" and Jones to "Circe.")[54] Watson is concerned with Joyce's response to the Romantic notions of nationalism—a cult of the peasant, hostility to city life, belief in "'true' Irishness" and in the power of myth and legend, and "an attitude to history which is simultaneously aesthetic and theatrical, teleological and even apocalyptic"—that became dominant in Ireland after the Easter Rising.[55] Gibson focuses on the Anglo-Irish components of Romantic Ireland and sees "Cyclops" in particular as Joyce's "assault on Anglo-Irish revivalism," which granted a privileged status to the Anglo-Irish within Irish culture, assumed that Anglo-Irish Ireland and Irish Ireland share much common ground in that culture, and believed that the goal of a unified Irish culture is "cultural fusion and regeneration."[56]

Watson sees *Ulysses* as a critique of Romantic Ireland that is "deeply scandalous . . . to a certain type of nationalist consciousness." The scandal includes Joyce's use of a Jewish man as his central character who nevertheless has to confront Irish anti-Semitism; Watson points to the "chosen-people strain in Irish cultural politics," which Joyce refers to in "Aeolus" when Professor MacHugh recites John F. Taylor's speech linking "the youth of Ireland" with "the youthful Moses" (*U* 7:829, 833). More generally, Watson argues that Joyce's "aesthetic of incompleteness" results from his "hostility to the teleological narrative of romanticized Irish history."[57] In this sense, *Ulysses* counters Deasy's position in "Nestor" that "all human history moves towards one great goal" by being itself a huge "shout in the street" (*U* 2:380–81, 2:386). That shout is nowhere louder than in "Cyclops," where many of the Romantic nationalist ideas are encapsulated in the loud and belligerent Citizen, a figure Sherry describes as the "caricature-in-voice" of Irish nationalism.[58]

Gibson also considers *Ulysses* as Joyce's response to ongoing events in Ireland and the cultural and intellectual ideas behind them. He believes that Joyce mocked the kind of Anglo-Irish revivalist discourse that "speciously presented itself as a form of historiography," especially targeting styles of revivalist poetry, translation, and historical writing, and that Joyce did this through parody in the passages of gigantism in "Cyclops" and also through "a stubbornly realist aesthetic that insists on the significance of almost numberless historical particulars." (Fairhall, in a somewhat parallel way, describes Joyce's concerns as local rather than global: Joyce "felt attachment to the 'knowable community' of a small city—that of a Dublin or a Trieste, as opposed to the imagined community of a nation.") The fact that Joyce began writing "Cyclops" with the parodies rather than with the first-person narrator suggests to Gibson that his imagination went to the assault on revivalist discourse before anything else in the episode.[59]

In Watson's and Gibson's accounts of *Ulysses* as at least partly a response to the Easter Rising and subsequent events in Ireland, both the "aesthetic of incompleteness" and Joyce's use of historical details are among Joyce's "weapons," in Gibson's words, against Romantic Ireland and Anglo-Irish revivalism.[60] Gibson's use of war imagery here is intriguing; in its light, Joyce's techniques in "Cyclops" look like one of the "only arms" that Stephen reserves for himself in *A Portrait of the Artist as a Young Man*: "silence, exile, and cunning" (*P* 247). If Radford is correct that "It is odd that Joyce should be criticized for not responding to the apocalyptic politics of his world, when he was actually creating the fictional equivalent of that world," then, combined with Joyce's silence about any Irish or international political issues while he was, as he felt, in exile in Zurich, his techniques indicate how much importance he placed on cunning as a strategy.[61] They also make Stoppard's imaginative creation of Joyce's assertion that during the Great War he wrote *Ulysses* sound less like the glib boast of an aloof and indifferent aesthete and more like someone fighting a battle in his own way and on his own terms.

Joyce's Eyesight

As we move more into Joyce's personal life while he was writing "Cyclops," it is amazing how many different events were going on when he was supposedly devoting himself single-mindedly to *Ulysses*. For one thing, his eyes were causing him a great deal of difficulty and pain. He suffered eye attacks as he moved from the early to the middle stages of *Ulysses*, with one of the serious ones forcing him to dictate the last section of the fair copy of "Wandering Rocks" to Budgen. Peter Hartshorn notes that "as [Joyce's] creative vision grew, his real vision—painfully— diminished in Zurich." After an operation for glaucoma in August 1917, his vision was permanently reduced,[62] and even after the operation the attacks continued. He experienced several major attacks of iritis (or uveitis) and glaucoma, especially in May–July 1918 and January–February 1919, with the two longest ones lasting nine and six weeks. His letters throughout the periods of these illnesses repeatedly attest to his difficulties in working because of the pain. As 1919 went on, however, he experienced some respite from the attacks: after the one in early 1919, the next serious incident did not come until November 1920.[63]

Joyce apparently suffered from iritis, an inflammation of the iris and other parts of the front of the eye that is often caused by an infection, or uveitis, an inflammation, not caused by an infection, of the uvea, a layer of the eye that includes the iris.[64] Someone with iritis or uveitis will experience both pain and blurred vision. Joyce's illnesses also included glaucoma, which damages the optic nerve at the back of the eye, though it is not clear which type he had. One type causes a loss of much peripheral vision and can result in tunnel vision; another produces severe pain and blurred vision. Joyce's vision must have been very blurred, and he might also have seen only in a narrow range, making things appear fragmented. An eye patch is a familiar image in the photographs of Joyce from this period: the impairment of his eyesight while his creative vision was expanding transformed him, in appearance at least, into a kind of Cyclops.

Joyce's eyesight affected not only his ability to work on *Ulysses* but also the form of the drafts. In *Joyce's Iritis and the Irritated Text: The Dis-lexic "Ulysses,"* Roy Gottfried, who calls *Ulysses* "the book of [Joyce's] impaired and compromised vision," notes that "at every stage in its long process, from conception through composition to completion, the making of *Ulysses* was clouded with episodes of eye attacks." Joyce's experiences with iritis, uveitis, and glaucoma affected the way he wrote *Ulysses*—including, according to Gottfried, his fragmented and abbreviated notes and the often discontinuous and broken text in his drafts—since he needed to "assemble small units that would be more easily recognizable by limited vision." Gottfried looks at several symptoms of Joyce's illness—"discontinuity, irritation, imprecision, deception, incompleteness," which are "equally the symptoms of his illness and the features attendant on the creation of his text" and also "the features of his or anyone's reading of it"—in terms of the words and even the individual letters Joyce saw as he was taking notes for, writing, and correcting the proofs for *Ulysses* and also of the finished book.[65] Intriguing as are these connections between Joyce's eyesight and *Ulysses*, I am more interested here in the genetic questions, especially the implications of what Joyce did and did not see for the evolving text and for the documents he produced and used.

At one point in *James Joyce and the Making of "Ulysses,"* Frank Budgen presents a scene of Joyce writing in Locarno. Joyce asked him to look at something he had written, but Budgen couldn't decipher it: "There are about a dozen words written in all directions, up, down and across," he reports telling Joyce. "I can't make out one complete word." Joyce gave him a magnifying glass and asked him to try again, saying that even a few letters would help him if Budgen couldn't make out a full word: "But the magnifying glass magnified also the pencil smudges and made the labyrinth of pencilled lines bigger but not clearer, so I had to give it up after sighting and reporting several foggy shapes of letters which, however, were sufficient to give him his bearings."[66]

Budgen's anecdote implies that Joyce saw both foggy letters and fragmented blocks and also that he laid out and designed his pages with just enough visual clarity to allow him to recall what he had already done and to plan what to do next. If he saw only small fragments, then a tiny bit of writing, even a few letters, could serve as a mnemonic for a larger body of text. Perhaps the fragments he wrote—the scenes in the Buffalo and National Library "Cyclops" drafts; the fragments in the National Library "Proteus" draft; the separate and often unconnected question-and-answer units in the National Library's "Ithaca" draft; and the lost "Scylla and Charybdis" draft, which apparently contained "fragmentary conversations, which appear altered in the final version"—were extensions of the fragmented words he saw.[67] His limited vision makes it even more understandable why he would do so much of his work in his head and why he could work with drafts on which he sometimes did not bother to indicate clearly where a revision or addition fit into the existing text. Unlike someone with clearer vision, Joyce apparently did not primarily find his bearings—or found them only partly—by seeing the words on the pages he wrote.

An intriguing aside: the two visual possibilities of blurriness and fragmentation have been replicated in recent catalogs for auctioned *Ulysses* manuscripts. When Christie's produced its catalog of the "Circe" draft that it auctioned in 2000—this is the draft Joyce sent to John Quinn in April 1921 as a "curiosity" along with the fair copy of the episode (*L* 3:40)—in order to avoid reproducing a manuscript page illegally without the permission of the copyright holder, it blurred the page images, thus providing an adequate sense of what the pages look like but making the text on them unreadable.[68] On the other hand, when Sotheby's produced its catalog of the "Eumaeus" draft in 2001, it printed clear reproductions of Joyce's writing but only in fragmented blocks of text. Individual letters and words remain clear, but a reader cannot see a whole page or even an entire sentence.[69] Unlike many other observers, Joyce probably could have "read" the reproductions in both catalogs.

As we try to reconstruct the process of Joyce's writing by accounting for the movement of words from his head to paper and then from draft to draft, we need to remain aware of his limited vision and the specific nature of the limitations. Not only the revisions and additions crowded all over the pages' margins and connected to the main text by lines and superscripts but also the fragmentary blocks of text and the fluid state of the writing are surely based on what Joyce saw and did not see as well as on what he thought and saw in his mind's eye. He would have included the metaphorically one-eyed

Citizen and the many references to eyes in the "Cyclops" episode based solely on his use of Odysseus's encounter with the one-eyed giants in the *Odyssey*, but these aspects of "Cyclops" certainly took on added importance because of his eye troubles.

Theater and the English Players

Joyce was also greatly preoccupied at this time with the English Players, the English-language theater company he had founded with Claud Sykes in early 1918, and especially with the fallout from the Players' first endeavor, its successful April 1918 production of Oscar Wilde's *The Importance of Being Earnest*. The nonprofessional actor who played Algernon Moncrieff, Henry Carr, complained both about the low fee Joyce paid him and about Joyce's refusal to reimburse him for the clothes he had purchased to wear in the performance. Joyce in turn claimed that Carr insulted him and, in Gorman's account, "threatened to 'wring his bloody neck and chuck him down the stairs.'"[70] The incident led to a protracted lawsuit. First, on October 15, 1918, Joyce won a judgment against Carr, but a new hearing was held on December 7, 1918, and a new trial on February 11, 1919—that is, at or near the end of Joyce's serious January–February eye attack. This time the judge ruled against Joyce (according to a court document reproduced by California Appeals Court justice Conrad Rushing, Joyce moved to dismiss the case before a trial began),[71] and working out the arrangements for the financial settlement ran on into May and June. In December 1918 Joyce withdrew from the activities of the English Players, largely because of his ongoing conflict with the British consul, Percy Bennett, over the Carr incident.[72]

Joyce was concerned to the point of obsession with the legal complications involving this incident, as his letters and the biographies make abundantly clear.[73] Perhaps it is not surprising that one of the books he owned in Zurich was called *Every Man's Own Lawyer*.[74] In April 1919 he wrote a lengthy "Statement" and distributed it to anyone who might help publicize his plight (*L* 2:438–40). He lost in court but, as with Richard Best and the other members of the 1904 Dublin literary world, got the final word in his writing. He composed four private satirical poems inspired by the event, two short ones about Horace Rumbold, the British Minister to Switzerland who declined to intervene in the case, and two about Bennett. Rushing notes the similarity between the words "We're going to wring your bloody necks" in the longest of these poems (called both "New Tipperary" and "The C. G. is Not Literary") and Gorman's account of Carr's threat, an account that Joyce presumably supplied to him.[75]

Joyce's fullest revenge came in *Ulysses*. He worked Rumbold into "Cyclops" as the hangman whose illiterate job application letter is read aloud in the pub and who hangs the Irish revolutionary in the long execution scene (*U* 12:415–31, 12:592–625), with an even more ghastly reprise in "Circe" as the "Demon Barber" who hangs the Croppy Boy and then "plunges his head into the gaping belly of the hanged and draws out his head again clotted with coiled and smoking entrails" (*U* 15:4531–58). Two consulate employees, Gann and Smith, whom Joyce included on his witness list but who apparently perjured themselves at a hearing and denied seeing Carr's threat, show up as murderers named by Rumbold in his application letter (*U* 12:420, 12:425). British Consul General Percy Bennett (the "C. G." of Joyce's poem) provides the name of the English fighter who is heroically defeated by "Dublin's pet lamb," Myler Keogh (*U* 12:939–87; "Ole Pfotts Wettstein," named as Bennett's second in "Cyclops" account of the fight [*U* 12:984], acquires his surname from the Norwegian Vice-Consul in Zurich who served as Carr's attorney), and also the surname for a "sergeantmajor," not present in *Ulysses* but called a "whitearsed bugger" in "Circe" (*U* 15:625, 15:4796–97). Finally, Henry Carr gives his name to the private who, following through on the threat that Joyce claimed the historical Carr made against him, knocks Stephen down at the end of "Circe" because "I'll wring the neck of any fucking bastard says a word against my bleeding fucking king" (*U* 15:4644–45). As Rushing concludes, "Joyce needed a scenario where he would still lose but in a way that would be bearable," and if life couldn't provide that scenario, then *Ulysses* could.[76]

Two other theater incidents from this time are relevant. First, on August 7, 1919, in Munich, the inaugural production of *Exiles* was staged. Joyce was unable to obtain a visa and could not attend. The production was not a success; according to Gorman, Joyce consoled himself by blaming a bad German translation.[77] Second, Stanislaus Joyce wrote in a letter that the idea for the first-person "Cyclops" narrator came to Joyce during a Zurich performance of a German translation of Shakespeare's *Troilus and Cressida*. One of the characters in this play is Ulysses, and another is "Thersites, a deformed and scurrilous Greek." (Ellmann also describes a Zurich production of *Troilus* that Joyce saw with Claud Sykes; he might have seen two productions, but maybe this is the same one that Stanislaus mentions.)[78] The possibility that a specific incident from this period inspired Joyce to create the narrator is especially interesting in the light of his sudden introduction of the figure in the National Library's draft. If Joyce developed the narrator with Shakespeare's character in mind, he probably also supplied Budgen with "snarling Thersites" as a descriptive term for the figure.

Joyce and Women

As Joyce was suffering from his eye problems and preoccupied with the litigation over the English Players, his relationships with women also became more complicated. In late November or early December 1918 he became infatuated with a young woman who lived in a building opposite his when he looked out a rear window and observed her in her bathroom pulling a toilet chain. He saw her—Marthe Fleischmann—soon afterward on the street and noted that she walked with a slight limp and also reminded him of the girl he had seen in 1898 wading in the Irish Sea and had re-created in the figure at the end of chapter 4 of *A Portrait of the Artist as a Young Man* who helps lead Stephen Dedalus to the discovery of his vocation as an artist.[79] During December he sent her several letters, writing partly in German but mostly in French, asking her "why do you not want to write even one word to me—your name? And why do you always close your shutters? I want to see you. / I do not know what you think of me. . . . But yesterday evening you gave me a sign, and my heart leapt for joy" (*L* 2:433n [my ellipsis; cf. *L* 2:426–35 throughout]). He spent time alone with her in Budgen's studio on his thirty-seventh birthday, February 2, 1919, and told Budgen that he had "explored that evening the coldest and hottest parts of a woman's body."[80]

Several months later, on June 19, 1919, Joyce was confronted by Marthe's lover Rudolf Hiltpold (she referred to him as her "guardian"), who accused him of causing a nervous breakdown that she had recently suffered.[81] In a letter to Budgen from that day (this is the same letter in which he says that "Cyclops" "is being lovingly moulded in the way you know"), Joyce talks about assuaging Hiltpold in a "long interview wherein I displayed all that suave human diplomacy, that goodness of heart, that understanding of others, that timidity which yet is courage, those shining qualities of heart and head which have so often . . . Result, stasis: Waffenstillstand" (*SL* 239 [Joyce's ellipsis]). The last word in Joyce's letter means "armistice" and is yet another displacement of war terminology into his personal life, and the list of the qualities he displayed to Hiltpold echoes some of his parodically exaggerated lists in "Cyclops." The brief passage from "Cyclops" that he quotes in his letter—"The epic proceeds explanatorily 'He spoke of the English, a noble race, rulers of the waves, who sit on thrones of alabaster, silent as the deathless gods'" (*U* 12:1213–14)—suggests that his encounter with Hiltpold might have reminded him of the toilet chain that initially attracted him to Marthe and in that way inspired the "thrones of alabaster" he had just written into the episode.

It is worth recalling that the turmoil Joyce invited into his life when he became infatuated with Fleischmann came at a time when Zurich was struggling with the influenza epidemic and the general strike, both of which hit the city simultaneously with the signing of the armistice (Rushing also links the influenza epidemic with the English Players difficulties),[82] and that the serious eye attack he suffered erupted between his December letters to Fleischmann and the birthday tryst in Budgen's studio and lasted beyond the meeting. Also, intriguingly, the scene with Fleischmann in Budgen's studio that Joyce invites us to imagine echoes the one that Richard Rowan sets up involving his partner Bertha and his friend Robert Hand in Robert's room in *Exiles*. In both cases, what went on behind the closed doors remains a mystery. In *Exiles*, where the Joyce figure is the one left outside the closed door, the scene plays as anguished drama—"I have a deep, deep wound of doubt in my soul," Richard says at the end (*E* 146)—but when Joyce is the center of the intrigue, recounting the event to a male friend, he plays the scene as self-deprecating farce.

Ellmann attributes Gerty MacDowell's limp to Fleischmann, and he also notes that Joyce used Greek *e*'s rather than Roman ones in his letters to her, an orthographic feature of Bloom's letter to Martha Clifford,[83] but Martha Clifford was in *Ulysses* long before Joyce met Marthe Fleischmann, so the similarity of the names of the two letter writers and recipients is a coincidence. More generally, it is significant that, as Joyce was writing episodes that alternated between female- and male-dominated scenes ("Sirens," "Cyclops," "Nausicaa"), his own life shuttled between instances of "love" and "war" as he ricocheted among Fleischmann, Carr and the courts, and (soon) Harriet Shaw Weaver.

Joyce's Finances

Joyce's financial situation changed dramatically at this time. Since February 1918 he had been receiving a monthly check from Mrs. Edith Rockefeller McCormick, a stipend that lasted until just before he left Zurich in October 1919. More important, however, on May 14, 1919, he learned that he had been given an anonymous gift of the interest on a £5,000 war bond, an amount that would come to the significant sum of £250 per year. From a pronoun that the benefactor's solicitors used in one of their letters to him, Joyce figured out that his patron was a woman, and he convinced himself that she was Nancy Cunard before Weaver (the publisher of *A Portrait of the Artist as a Young Man* first in her magazine *The Egoist* and then as a book and also of a few episodes of *Ulysses* in *The Egoist*), who had already helped him out financially, identified herself to him on July 6, 1919.[84] According to Ellmann, Weaver's gift freed Joyce from any worries about how to pay the settlement in the English Players decision and, in general, "made it possible for him to be poor only through determined extravagance." Joyce seems to have functioned only when he had generated a high level of chaos and anxiety in his life, and perhaps some of his other activities during these months—including breaking with his friend Ottocaro Weiss when he convinced himself, with no real grounds at all, that Weiss had betrayed him by convincing McCormick to end her stipend to him—were a way of keeping the anxiety level high when people like Weaver were doing their best to lower it.[85]

Joyce and Nora

The biographies of Joyce present a man struggling heroically against eye troubles and legal and financial worries in order to continue his work on *Ulysses*, and this effort to write his novel in the face of great difficulties (even if some of them were of his own making) is real and even heroic. The biographies of the people around Joyce, however, paint a differently nuanced picture. Brenda Maddox, as I have already indicated, describes Joyce as withdrawing into the private world that was *Ulysses*, "taking his libido with him," she adds. According to Carol Loeb Shloss, *Ulysses* "took up more and more psychic and literal space" as the days in Zurich went on, and for Joyce's family it drew him "farther and farther into a realm where none of them could follow."[86]

To reach Joyce, Nora sometimes had to go to *Ulysses*. This could involve using the manuscripts for the book as psychological hostages or throwing Joyce's obsessions back at him. For instance, when she felt that Joyce was drinking too much, Nora announced that she had destroyed one of his manuscripts for *Ulysses*, and he remained sober until he determined that his work was safe. Or, in response to his attempts, according to Budgen, to set her up with other men so that he could gauge his reactions, she began a letter to him with "Dear Cuckold."[87] It could also involve treating the pages of Joyce's drafts almost like refrigerator sticky notes on which he and Nora could communicate with each other, and it shows how well she could play along with him and also twit him about his obsessions.

The National Library's "Cyclops" draft offers a wonderful example of this. At the bottom of the verso of the first page, Joyce wrote a note—it is not addressed to anyone, but it is clear a few pages later that he wrote it to Nora—that comically demands a loan of ten francs (revised to five) for liquor he has just "stood you."[88] Then, on page 4v, Nora responds with a mock-formal note regretting that she cannot lend him "the maximum sum" but offering to loan him fifteen francs (revised to five). Joyce responds in turn by adapting a phrase that appears as an addition on one of the pages of Buffalo's "Cyclops" copybook—"the curse of a lopsided God light sideways on the bloody thicklugged sons of whores' gets" (with "lopsided" revised to "goodfornothing," the phrase appears intact in the published *Ulysses*[89]—to make Nora the recipient of the curse. (Presumably he wrote his playful note to Nora after his addition to the draft, but it is possible that the note preceded and inspired the addition. In a parallel case, on one page of T. S. Eliot's manuscript of *The Waste Land*, Vivien Eliot wrote, "What you get married for if you dont want to have children," a phrase that Eliot incorporated into his poem.)[90] Finally, Nora ended the exchange by modifying a note that Joyce had written a year earlier when the British consul suggested to him that he enlist in the British army—"James Joyce presents his compliments to the B. M. Consul General and returns a document addressed to him in error," as quoted by Gorman—by replacing Joyce's name with that of his arch-enemy of the moment, Sir Horace Rumbold, as the presenter of the compliments. While Joyce was, as Ellmann puts it, "vent[ing] his tireless indignation" on the pages of the "Cyclops" drafts, Nora was there as the one person who could mock and puncture his obsessions, and she must have realized that the best place to do this was on the pages of the drafts of *Ulysses*.[91]

■

In the previous chapter I quoted Joyce's remarks to Ezra Pound and Harriet Weaver regarding elements of *Ulysses* fusing together: he told Pound early in his work that "the ingredients will not fuse until they have reached a certain temperature," and he wrote to Weaver about "Sirens" that "the elements needed will only fuse after a prolonged existence together."[92] Later on, though, Joyce talked about *Ulysses* in ways other than mixing by melting or blending. He spoke of molding (*L* 1:126), resolving into equivalents (*L* 1:159), spinning (*L* 3:48), putting in order (*L* 1:172), and, after he added the headlines to "Aeolus," recasting (*L* 1:172). Instead of letting elements fuse, Joyce did something more like welding them together or abutting them against each other, sometimes neatly, sometimes jarringly. (Joyce apparently thought of fusing in relation to his early efforts on his works. In October 1923, as he drafted the first sketches of *Finnegans Wake*, he wrote that "these are not fragments but active elements and when they are more and a little older they will begin to fuse of themselves" [*L* 1:205].)[93]

The different aspects of Joyce's life during the months he was writing the drafts of "Cyclops" don't fuse, either. The Buffalo and National Library of Ireland drafts permit us to watch the episode evolve from fragmentary and rudimentary parody passages surrounded by roughly written bits of dialogue into the beginnings of an episode narrated by the first-person "snarling Thersites," but as we place his writing in relation to his reactions to the recently ended world war and the ongoing Anglo-Irish war, his eyesight, the legal complications involving the English Players, his relationship with Marthe Fleischmann, his financial situation, and his communications with Nora, a seamless picture of Joyce at work refuses to emerge. "If the study of manuscripts is necessary," Daniel Ferrer has argued, "it is indeed because the final text *does not contain* the whole of its genesis," and likewise the manuscripts, the avant-texte, cannot contain the whole of the writing.[94] The excess, partly Joyce's mental labor, is also his ongoing life as he worked. The drafts and the contexts are fascinating, and even more so because they leave us finally with a tantalizingly fragmented picture that changes whenever we move our viewpoint.

8

Mobile Pages

Ulysses in Print and on a Screen

Leopold Bloom has just received a tantalizing letter from Martha Clifford, and you are looking at it along with him. You have read about fifteen sentences before you come to two—"Please write me a long letter and tell me more. Remember if you do not I"—one a complete sentence and one a fragment. If you have a paperback version of Hans Walter Gabler's edition of *Ulysses* in your hands, you will have to hold your breath and turn the page to learn that Martha has told Bloom that she "will punish" him (*U* 5:251–52). Martha typed her letter on one side of a sheet of paper, so Bloom was able to receive this pleasurable threat with less effort, but with less suspense. About half the printed editions of *Ulysses* will make you move to a new page at some point in Martha's letter, usually with a less dramatic break than in the Gabler edition. In the others, the vagaries of the font and page size permit the letter to fit on one page.

But what if you are reading *Ulysses* on a computer screen? The text might be presented in a way that retains printed page units, so you would see a replication of one of the printed editions, with the letter either intact or divided. Or the letter might be broken up into screen-sized units, maybe fifteen or twenty lines per screen. It might just fit onto one screen, but more likely it would be divided between two. As a third possibility, it might be part of a long scrolling text comprising all of "Lotus Eaters," the episode in which it appears, or even all of *Ulysses*, and it would fit on one screen or not depending on which line of the text you positioned at the top. As a fourth alternative, you might be able to change the size and maybe also the font to suit your preferences, so the letter would fit on one screen or not, depending on how big you decided the text should be.

In *Ulysses* Bloom holds a physical document that was typed in a particular font with determinable spacing and margins and on paper of a certain size and thickness. The novel doesn't specify any of these particulars, just the facts that Martha typed the envelope and the letter (*U* 5:61, 17:1841), pinned a flower to the paper—presumably in response to the name Henry Flower, Bloom's nom de plume in his letters to her (*U* 5:239)—and made several typos and grammatical mistakes that tickle Bloom, such as "I called you naughty boy because I do not like that other world," "you know what I will do to you, you naughty boy, if you do not wrote," and "do not deny my request before my patience are exhausted" (*U* 5:244–45, 5:252–53, 5:253–54). The letter's text has been transmitted through all the editions of *Ulysses* (sometimes imperfectly, as some editions, thinking that Martha's typos were Joyce's, corrected them) and will live on in future editions. But as a material object, a page, the letter will remain forever locked away in the drawer where Bloom stores it after he returns home (*U* 17:1840–42).

If the text of a printed book is presented on a computer screen or on a digital reading device, should the page units, like the sheet of paper of Martha's letter, simply disappear? Should they be retained, with scroll bars or some other device compensating for the smaller size of screens compared to pages, or with the original page breaks indicated by lines, bracketed numbers, or some other marker? Should the typography and other graphic features of a page be reproduced as a unit? Anyone engaged in a digital project that involves a text originally printed as a book needs to think about these issues, and such thoughts lead to intriguing questions about what pages mean and what the future of the page might be.

Pages are especially vulnerable and problematic for a presentation of *Ulysses* in a digital format. Each edition of *Ulysses* offers different page units and paginations—does that eliminate the page as a meaningful unit? If the pages should be preserved in some way in the electronic presentation, how should they be retained, since in all their forms they are bigger than a screen? What would the pages be preserved *as* in a medium lacking the tangibility of printed pages and also lacking anything that corresponds to a printed page's front and back?

In the next few pages I want to consider some issues regarding pages before I say a little about possible aspects of their future.

■

Joyce was acutely aware that the words he was writing as *Ulysses* would eventually be published as pages in a book. He serves as an excellent example of the statement from William Morris that Jerome McGann cites as the epigraph to *The Textual Condition*: "You can't have art without resistance in the material." Joyce worked both with and against his medium, exploiting the possibilities of printed words and pages as much as he could and extending those possibilities when the words and pages seemed unable to do what he wanted. For example, in "Proteus," Stephen Dedalus begins to formulate a poem, and phrases that come and go in his mind include "Mouth to her kiss," "Mouth to her mouth's kiss," and "mouth to her moomb" (*U* 3:399–402). Joyce labored to make the words appear on the page in a particular way. In the margin of an early draft of the episode he lists various possibilities for the last word, spelling it in several elaborate ways before settling on "moomb," a simpler option than any he listed in the draft. The possibilities all sound slightly different from each other, but more important, they *look* different. Presumably Joyce was trying to find the word that best provided a visual indication of his character's exploration of various sound possibilities.[1]

Stephen isn't really oriented toward printed words and pages, though. The result of his creative efforts appears in "Aeolus" (*U* 7:523–26), and it turns out to be a rather lame effort, a depersonalized and romanticized version of one of the poems that Douglas Hyde translated in *Love Songs of Connacht*.[2] The poem is Stephen's best written creation in *Ulysses*, but later in "Aeolus" he presents a much more effective effort, a cryptic spoken narrative that he apparently puts together on the spot as he walks to a pub with men from the newspaper office (*U* 7:917–1058; see chapter 3 for further discussion). Like his other major creation in *Ulysses*, the theory of *Hamlet* that Stephen expounds to skeptical listeners in "Scylla and Charybdis," his talents seem best suited to oral delivery.

Not so Leopold Bloom. Described by Patrick McCarthy as "predominantly a reader" in a "town of talkers,"[3] Bloom reads texts in all their richness, including a handwritten letter from his daughter Milly (*U* 4:397–414) and the typed one from Martha Clifford (*U* 5:241–59), a newspaper article about Paddy Dignam's funeral in which his surname is spelled without its "l" (*U* 16:1248–61), and another article about the Gold Cup race, whose results proved unfortunate for him earlier in the day (*U* 16:1274–89). He also reads visually. In order to distract himself from a boring conversation he cannot get out of, he scans a newspaper he is holding and notices the words in an advertisement:

> What is home without
> Plumtree's Potted Meat?
>   Incomplete.
> With it an abode of bliss. (U 5:144–47)

Later, he renders a judgment on both the ad's words and its placement on the page, faulting its location under the obituary notices (U 8:743–44). The ad sticks in his mind all day, though (see U 17:596–99), probably because he knows that his and Molly's ten years without sexual intercourse have made their home incomplete. In McGann's terms, Bloom is aware of both a text's linguistic code—the words—and also its bibliographical code—such features as the layout of the text on a page, the size of the margins, its illustrations, the dimensions and thickness of the paper, and, for a book, the kind of binding and covers.[4]

Bloom places ads in newspapers for clients, and in "Aeolus" he is at work. He describes a proposed ad for the tea and liquor distributor Alexander Keyes to the editor and the other men in the room. In it, a pair of crossed keys both puns on Keyes's name and visually suggests the House of Keys, the lower house of the parliament of the Isle of Man, which England allowed to function under a qualified form of home rule.[5] For Bloom, reading is contrapuntal (he is aware of the pun), visual (he is thinking about how the words and graphics will look), and rhetorical ("Catches the eye, you see," he tells the editor [U 7:151]). He reads this way throughout the episode and throughout *Ulysses*. As he describes Keyes's proposed ad, however, the text's puns and its visuality are highlighted in another way: a bold, uppercase tag preceding the section reads "HOUSE OF KEY(E)S" (U 7:141). Bloom does not respond to this visual pun because he is unaware that it is there. Part of the reader's page, not the character's, it and other tags like it are excellent examples of Joyce's involvement with his text's pages.

"Aeolus" is the seventh episode in *Ulysses*, and originally, lasting until late in Joyce's writing of the book, it matched the preceding six in combining a narrator who functions mainly to locate characters as they move around various spaces in Dublin, a report of Bloom's and Stephen's interior thoughts, and the characters' spoken conversations. After Joyce sent the episode's typescript to Maurice Darantiere, his French printer in Dijon, he received a set of placards. In form and content, the pages resemble the ones that precede them.[6]

Joyce returned the proofs with some corrections and a startling number of additions. Most dramatically, he added bits of text interrupting the narrative a few times on each page, which he did by inserting numbers into the main body of the text at the point of each insertion and including the new bits of writing in numbered lists at the top of the placard pages. As if that weren't enough, he also added a large chunk of new text for the beginning of the episode, indicating with a symbol that it should precede the printed text on the proof, so the number at the top of the printed text is "2," which is accompanied by a letter *M* signaling the addition. The number "1" comes at the beginning of the added text. (Sebastian Knowles justifiably calls the proofs for "Aeolus" a "visual event.")[7] Darantiere and his men set all the new text in print, with the inserts in uppercase bold type, understandably making a lot of mistakes along the way, and sent a new set of proofs to Joyce. He again made corrections and dramatic revisions to the proofs, both to the narrative and to the bold-type inserts. On the first page alone, along with adding new narrative text he added two new bold-type inserts, deleted one, replaced one with completely new words, and modified the first one. (Chapter 3 contains additional discussion of Joyce's revisions to "Aeolus.")

Critics have variously called these bold-type inserts newspaper headlines, heads, subheads, crossheads, or captions, and they have often explained them as Joyce's desire to make his episode, which is about a newspaper and is set in a newspaper office, look like a newspaper. The fragmented bits of narrative between the inserts resemble the sections of newspaper articles, which in the past routinely fell between subheads. Sometimes the relation between the head and the narrative that follows it is clear, at other times obscure. In no way does the episode read like the seamless narrative it was at first; rather, it announces itself dramatically as a text printed in a book. Significantly, Joyce's desire to make the pages look like a newspaper didn't extend beyond inserting the heads. There is only one column of text, and the heads are all printed in the same type. The episode appears not so much like a newspaper as like pages in a book trying to suggest a newspaper.

Joyce was under no obligation to explain why he made this dramatic change to the appearance of "Aeolus," and he never did, at least not directly. We do know that by August 1921, when he added the heads to the proofs, he had written all the episodes except for the last two, "Ithaca" and "Penelope" (which he was working on while he revised and augmented the first sixteen), so he had already created daring typographic experiments on pages in later parts of *Ulysses*. By adding the heads to "Aeolus" he transformed an early episode into one that in some ways resembles the later ones. Stuart Gilbert, who wrote his 1930 book *James Joyce's "Ulysses": A Study* with Joyce's help, might have been speaking for Joyce when he claimed in a footnote about the heads that "this historico-literary technique, here inaugurated, is a preparation for the employment of the same method, but on the grand scale, a stylistic *tour de force*, in a later episode, the *Oxen of the Sun*."[8] Joyce never said where he got the idea from, either. The placards he was receiving from Darantiere, however, were not like American galley proofs (which are long sheets of text, longer than single pages of a book) but instead consisted of large pieces of paper, about twenty-eight inches wide by eighteen inches high, eight book pages printed only on one side of each sheet. A placard was arranged in columns, with the first page printed above the second, the third above the fourth, and so forth. Joyce looked at these placards, column after column, while he was thinking about his newspaper episode. If he read them visually as well as verbally, they might have reminded him of a newspaper. Whatever inspired him, he transformed the appearance of his pages into something suggesting a newspaper on these proofs.

Typically, having made the decision to redesign the episode, Joyce carried the process as far as he could. He revised the heads—only about half of them appear on the first proofs in their published form—and honed their initial pattern of moving from stately dignified ones at the beginning to slangy colloquial ones at the end.[9] This results in a kind of double linearity to the printed text: the narrative proceeds in its own way, telling the ongoing story of Leopold Bloom and Stephen Dedalus on June 16, 1904, whereas the heads offer a separate sequence of linguistic change. The reader can take the heads and the text as separate narratives, follow one and ignore the other, or negotiate the shifting relationships between each head and the text that follows it, and, given all these possible relationships between the heads and the text, the so-called linearity of the printed text breaks down completely.

Furthermore, the heads sever any sense of a seamless connection between the written words and spoken narrative. Until this point in *Ulysses*, as anyone who has listened to an audio version of it knows, the book can be read aloud like almost any nineteenth-century novel. But what about the heads? Do you say them in a declamatory voice, as you might for a newspaper head or subhead? Most readers probably would, but Joyce himself offered another option. When he recorded a page of "Aeolus" in 1924, the only recording he ever made from *Ulysses*, he rather surprisingly read the one head in the section he chose, "FROM THE FATHERS" (*U* 7:841), as part of Stephen Dedalus's interior monologue. And an extreme case, a head from the middle of the episode—"? ? ?" (*U* 7:512)—can be seen but not heard or read aloud at all. It makes sense only as a sequence of printed signs on a page.

Like Martha Clifford's letter, the heads have looked different in various printings of *Ulysses*. In the first editions from Shakespeare and Company, they appeared in large bold type. The 1961 Modern Library edition makes them even larger and bolder relative to the text. Conversely, in the 1932 Odyssey Press edition they are capitalized but not in bold type and no larger than the text for the body of the episode, and the designer of the Gabler edition made them smaller than even the uppercase letters in the text below them and lighter than in the Odyssey Press printing. The most unusual presentation occurs in the rare Limited Editions Club version from 1935 (best known for its illustrations by Henri Matisse), where the text is printed on large pages with two columns per page and the heads appear in varying fonts that reflect their development from what Gilbert describes as "dignified" to "vulgar."

In discussing the heads, Gilbert provides an intriguing example of how a reading of *Ulysses* can depend on the particular pages that happen to be in front of the critic. In *James Joyce's "Ulysses*," which is based on the Shakespeare and Company editions and is informed by Gilbert's work on the translation of Joyce's novel into French, he called the "Aeolus" heads "captions"—"the text is split up into brief sections, each headed with a caption composed in the journalistic manner"—and a footnote to this sentence says that "the style of the captions is gradually modified in the course of the episode; the first are comparatively dignified, or classically allusive, in the Victorian tradition; later captions reproduce, in all its vulgarity, the slickness of the modern press."[10] Five years later, in the introduction to the double-columned, multi-font Limited Editions Club version, Gilbert says of "Aeolus" that "the structure resembles that of the front page of a daily newspaper, and it is interesting to note how the style of the headlines employed gradually declines from mid-Victorian dignity to the vulgar slickness of the modern press."[11] Here is Gilbert reading McGann's bibliographical code. The differing terms—captions, headlines—and his comparison of the text with the front page of a newspaper in one piece but not in the other are based on the non-linguistic features of the text: the sizes of the pages, their layouts, the fonts used for their texts. Either passage from Gilbert in isolation would give the impression that he is talking about *Ulysses* itself, but, more precisely, in each case he describes the text as printed in specific ways in the pages of particular editions. *Ulysses* in print is very much a text of pages as well as words.

■

I want to spend a few pages considering the idea of a "page" on a computer screen. I originally wrote these words on a handheld device I owned in the late 1990s and early 2000s. Its tiny display bore little resemblance to pages except that, unlike either a desktop or laptop computer screen (but like more recent e-book readers or an iPhone in one of its display options), it was taller than it was wide. Eventually, I uploaded the words into a full computer and copied them into a word-processing document, where they joined words I had already written. Once there, I knew how many pages these thoughts about pages would occupy when I printed them out, and from that number I could estimate how many pages they would occupy when they were published.

I like to think I was using cutting-edge technology for its time, of course, but working this way is actually rather retrograde. You would think that the page would be one of the first concepts to disappear with computer text, and there have been many attempts to use terminology not associated with print for writing on the screen as a way of differentiating it from writing that will eventually appear in print. For example, in HyperCard, an early hypertext software writing and reading program for Macintosh computers, each unit was called a "card," and Storyspace, another hypertext authoring and reading program, uses the phrase "writing space," as does one of Storyspace's authors, Jay David Bolter. Hypertext theorists employ words like "node," "screen," or, in George Landow's term adapted from Roland Barthes, "lexia." But even though, as Bolter has argued in *Writing Space*, using computers for word processing employs only a small part of the machine's capabilities, many of us work this way much of the time.[12] Instead of embracing the new ways of writing that computers make possible (Bolter uses outline processors as his example), we have resorted to a halfway measure. The computer lets us easily perform such tasks as moving text around and italicizing words, and it allows us to display different fonts in a single document and to insert images and other graphics, but for the most part word-processing programs allow us to generate documents that could have been produced on a typewriter.

A similar halfway situation seems to have developed regarding pages. A definition of "page" crept into the fourth edition of the *American Heritage Dictionary* (2000) that wasn't there in the third (1992): "A webpage." The use of "page" in such terms as Web page or home page has become so ubiquitous that "page" now refers almost as easily to the Web as to print, but the use of "page" for Web units is actually quite odd. A Web page consists of the text and graphics that load when you give your browser an "http://" command along with a URL, but what your browser displays can turn out to be a single word or an entire novel. Thus, the visible boundaries of a written or printed page—boundaries implied in such definitions as "a leaf or one side of a leaf, as of a book, letter, newspaper, or manuscript," "the writing or printing on one side of a leaf," "the type set for printing on one side of a leaf" (all from the *American Heritage Dictionary*)—are not part of the concept of a Web page, since that kind of page can be much larger than any monitor is capable of displaying at one time.

I am curious about how these units on the Web came to be called pages. No one seems to know. For instance, Robert Cailliau, who along with Tim Berners-Lee invented the World Wide Web, in response to my question about when and how the word "page" become the main term used for the part of a Web site that is on the screen, answered simply, "No idea."[13] Unlike other aspects of the Internet, Berners-Lee and Cailliau conceived of the Web from the start as a hypertext-based system. Hypertext, which Landow defines as "text composed of blocks of words (or images) linked electronically by multiple paths, chains, or trails," had already acquired various terms for its units: "nodes," "screens," "spaces," or "cards" for the individual screens and "links" for the connections between them.[14] In some systems, such as Ted Nelson's Project Xanadu, the units linked together were thought of as documents—that is, broadly conceived elements that, more than nodes or screens, can be imagined in terms of print and books—and Mark Bernstein, Christopher Keep, and Mark Feltham have each speculated that early developers of the Web first thought of sites as documents, this emphasis leading to the designation of the smaller units as "pages."[15] However it happened, the adoption of the term seems to have been rather casual: Berners-Lee writes in *Weaving the Web* that, as he planned the World Wide Web, "every node, document—whatever it was called—would be fundamentally equivalent in some way." The choice of terminology was part of the process by which, as

John Seely Brown and Paul Duguid have argued, "the Web made the informationally dense and inscrutable Internet intelligible . . . by relinquishing the mystique of information for the language of the document. Pages structure the Web. Bookmarks help us find our way back to where we have been. Indexes and tables of contents organize it." As Bolter puts it, though, this development is hardly surprising or unique: "We always understand a particular medium in relation to other past and present media forms."[16] Calling these Web units "pages" gives them a kind of familiarity, especially since the term for the larger unit, "site," lacks any analogy to print. Web pages might look and act very different from printed ones, and they constantly remind us in both positive and negative ways that they are not print, but the term "page" puts a limit on the disorientation. If the Web can (or once could) make us feel lost in a strange new world, the presence of "pages" can make us feel a little bit at home.

Possibly, maybe even probably, "page" became part of Web terminology at the same time "home" did. Mark Bernstein from hypertext publisher Eastgate Systems speculates that "home page" came into use as an analogy to HyperCard's "home card": an option in HyperCard was always to "go Home." Home pages can be analyzed in fascinatingly varied ways. For Wade Rowland, in *Spirit of the Web*, "the 'personal home page' developed early and spontaneously. . . . These personal pages are a unique feature of the Web that is endlessly moving as an expression of human diversity and the universal desire to share information." Welcome to my (virtual) home, the door is always open. For Bolter, the purpose of a home page is "nothing other than identity construction." For Jonathan Rosen, in *The Talmud and the Internet*, the stakes are even higher. For Rosen, a Web home page is an assertion of rootedness that we make in a state of metaphysical and spiritual homelessness:

> When the Jewish people lost their home (the land of Israel) and God lost His (the Temple), then a new way of being was devised and Jews became the people of the book and not the people of the Temple or the land. They became the people of the book because they had no place else to live. That bodily loss is frequently overlooked, but for me it lies at the heart of the Talmud, for all its plenitude. The Internet, which we are continually told binds us all together, nevertheless engenders in me a similar sense of Diaspora, a feeling of being everywhere and nowhere. Where else but in the middle of Diaspora do you *need a* home page?[17]

We return to our home pages to connect with others, to define ourselves, to root ourselves. On the printed pages of *Ulysses*, though, Leopold Bloom—typed page from Martha Clifford hidden safely in his pocket, newspaper page with its Plumtree's Potted Meat ad reminding him of his incomplete home long since discarded—just wants to go home.

A sidenote: Late in his work on *Ulysses* Joyce prepared a schema of the book, listing the eighteen episodes and including eight categories of information for each one. This chart has proved to be a mixed blessing; many of its entries have baffled critics who have tried to connect them with the text itself. One of these problematic items is for episode 4, "Calypso," where the entry for "Correspondences" says "Calypso—The Nymph, Dlugacz: The Recall: Zion: Ithaca." It presumably inspired Stuart Gilbert's comment in *James Joyce's "Ulysses,"* the book in which the schema was first published, that "Darkness is of the prison-house, the shackles of the flesh, all that withholds Mr Bloom from Zion, Odysseus from Ithaca."[18] The equation of Zion and Ithaca might seem excessive in relation to Bloom's respectful but dismissive reaction to a newspaper notice that he reads inviting people to purchase tracts of land in Palestine and plant trees on them (*U* 4:191–200), but this correspondence is provocative in relation to the triangulation of *Ulysses*, home, and Talmud/Diaspora/home page.

■

You might want to "go home" on a Web site, but with books the important thing is not to "lose your place." A book's title page—or its companion, the spine—identifies the book among the confusion of all the others that surround it. A Web home page serves that function, too, but it also provides a secure place of rest and stability within a site. (With books, you'd probably use a paper, cloth, or plastic bookmark to create your own secure place.) A sure sign of a badly designed Web site is that you cannot get back to where you came from or get home easily. Even worse is when you cannot get anywhere in the site at all, when you are, as the clichéd expression goes, "lost in cyberspace." In that case, you probably invoke a hierarchy of home pages, leaving the site's lost page behind as you eagerly click the button that will take you to the home page you have designated for your browser.

A digital presentation of an annotated *Ulysses* would have to be well designed, including easy navigability. If you want beginning-level definitions and identifications, you need to be able to find them without being encumbered by unwanted scholarly treatises, but if you want more advanced information you need to be able to get it without being burdened by simple identifications of names and details you already know. What would it mean to go home? What page would that be? I suspect that "home page" as a digital location of identification or return applies mostly to the kinds of personal, informational, or commercial sites that now dominate the Web. But hypertext author Michael Joyce has discussed other structures in his distinction between "exploratory" and "constructive" hypertexts.[19] A constructive hypertext is one in which the author builds a new structure; the reader makes choices among links provided by the author. This is the principle of most electronic hypertext fictions, including Michael Joyce's own *Afternoon: A Story* and Shelley Jackson's *Patchwork Girl*. Readers of these fictions and others like them, I would guess, rarely return "home." Rather, they wander around, maybe interested, maybe frustrated, probably both. They go back to where they were. They consult the map view if one is available. Going "home," however, in these hypertext fictions doesn't mean returning to a place of security. It is more like closing a book.

A hypertext centered on a text like *Ulysses* is what Michael Joyce calls an exploratory one. There is, in a sense, a center: a preexisting work, now put into the network. Reading this kind of hypertext, you move out from and back to the central text. You might stay away from that text for quite a while. You might read all of the *Odyssey*, follow several newspapers for June 16, 1904, or watch a slide show of photographs from the Dublin of that day. But going back to *Ulysses*, to wherever you were in it, to wherever Leopold Bloom is in his wanderings, and not to the front page would be going home.

Ulysses on the screen, and *Ulysses* as part of an electronic network, can never be the same as *Ulysses* in the pages of a book. It is 732 pages long in the first Shakespeare and Company edition, 792 in the Odyssey Press printing, 783 in the 1961 Modern Library edition, and 644 in the 1986 paperback Gabler edition. Digitally, on the "Finnegans Web" site it comprises 18 (very long) pages, each episode of the book presented as a single scrolling page with lines indicating the page divisions in the paperback Gabler editions, and on my iPhone it takes up anywhere from around 700 to over 20,000 screen pages, depending on the font and font size that I select. Even at 20,000 screens, the digital text loses all sense of the bulk that makes the printed versions so distinctive and also so imposing, but, more important, it cannot exist in isolation, separated by its covers from other books on the shelf. If it is part of a linked network, its words will be connected to all kinds of other material, including to other parts of itself. As Landow has stated, "If one put a work conventionally considered complete, such as *Ulysses*, into a hypertext format, it would immediately become 'incomplete'"—a digital *Ulysses* is like a home without Plumtree's Potted Meat.[20]

On a textual level, however, *Ulysses* has always been both complete and incomplete. It is complete within the pages of a printed edition. But McGann once took a sentence from "Lestrygonians" describing men eating lunch at the Burton pub—"A man spitting back on his plate: halfmasticated gristle: gums: no teeth to chewchewchew it" (*U* 8:659–60)—and claimed that, depending on your interpretation of the relationship between the manuscripts and the printed text, *Ulysses* is complete without the word "gums," which was not present in the book from 1922 until 1984, or with the word, which Gabler included in his edition.[21] In McGann's analysis, you can eat just as well or as badly whether or not the text spells out "gums." Maybe the home that is *Ulysses* is complete, or incomplete, in print or on a screen, with or without Plumtree's Potted Meat. (A quibble: McGann's argument is correct in principle but unfortunately inaccurate in its specific example. In isolation, the passage he cites makes equal sense whether or not it contains "gums" after "gristle." But, at two later points in *Ulysses*, Bloom recalls the scene from the Burton and specifically remembers the gums: "That chap in the Burton, gummy with gristle" [*U* 11:569–70] and "Chap in the Burton today spitting back gumchewed gristle" [*U* 13:876].)

For Landow, questions about a work's completeness or incompleteness relate not to what words might or might not be in it but to its place in an intertextual network. On one level, of course, *Ulysses* is as complete as any literary work; Richard Ellmann calls it "one of the most concluded books ever written."[22] But it is problematic whether a book called *Ulysses*, which uses Homer's *Odyssey* as a structural grid, can ever be considered "complete" in itself. Readers often accompany their reading with secondary books on *Ulysses*. They also bring their previous experiences with them, and they accumulate information about *Ulysses* in their heads or in notes on separate sheets or in the margins of *Ulysses* itself. If Joyce's novel can be called "complete" in print form, that largely means that its pages can exist without any other printed markings within covers that contain no other works. A digital *Ulysses* has to dispense with the covers and the boundaries they provide— "home" shifts from a house in the neighborhood of print to an apartment in a large high-rise complex—and with the physicality of the pages. What can it provide as compensation?

Returning to the concept of the page can indicate what a digital presentation of *Ulysses* can contribute. It retains McGann's linguistic code and some features of his bibliographical code: fonts, paragraph layouts, line units, even page divisions. But it can also give readers options regarding whether or not to retain these bibliographic features. One reader might want to work with the pages of a particular print edition, whereas another might find it more important to fit all of Martha Clifford's letter on the screen at one time. Readers can create much of the bibliographical code in ways that are not possible in books by making the fonts larger or smaller or by changing the font entirely. With more than one version of *Ulysses* possibly available, readers are able to alter the page to whichever form of the text they prefer. No single visual display is "the page," which is always the content and form that a particular reader chooses at a given time.

It is more, of course. An electronic page includes links, the potential connections between one digital unit and another. Links are often considered to be neutral connectives, but as Nicholas Burbules argues, they are far more dynamic, provisional, and even rhetorical: they open up the page to some external screens but not to others; they are "rhetorical moves that can be evaluated and questioned for their relevance." The page is framed by a window, which, as Bolter says in *Writing Space*, "marks out a space for a particular unit of verbal text, graphics, or both."[23] The page can also include sound, with or without any visual indication.

Thus, the digital page both is complete in itself and also links outward. It is silent, and it speaks. It is two things at once. In Bolter's words, it oscillates between its two states or sets its two states in dialogue with each other, consistent with Rosen's sense of both the Talmud and the Internet as places where conflicting realities can "live side by side" in an "ambidextrous" culture.[24] And it reflects the dominant pattern in *Ulysses*, in which oppositions that are set up always remain present, neither side canceling out the other.

Rosen suggests in *The Talmud and the Internet* that "we are passing, books and people both, through the doors of the computer age and entering a new sort of global Diaspora in which we are everywhere—except home."[25] The fictional Leopold Bloom knows how problematic "home" is: even when you are there, you are not fully home. But he also knows how to resist simple solutions: while he was out wandering on June 16, 1904, reading and placing ads, his home acquired two kinds of potted meat—Plumtree's and Blazes Boylan's—and, for Molly Bloom at least, home did become an abode of bliss. Yet, as Molly affirms in her monologue at the end of the novel, it still remained incomplete without Leopold. Uprooting the pages of *Ulysses* from their print materiality and moving them into a new, uncertain digital one will change *Ulysses*, along with our sense of the page. Surrounded by and linked into a vast network of other verbal, visual, and aural texts, the pages of *Ulysses* will experience a new kind of fullness and an equally new, and fuller, incompleteness—home is incomplete and an abode of bliss at the same time.

9

Mobile Notes

Annotating *Ulysses* in Print and on a Screen

The footnote, once considered the treasure of a special artistic talent—the inscription on the pedestal of a monument—has sunk in reputation to a bauble dropped to the bottom of a scholar's page or tossed onto a heap at the back of a book. And yet a note, whether an expository addendum to a text, an annotation, or a reference, exhibits an intriguingly complex set of possible relationships with the text to which it refers. When the work in question is *Ulysses* and the medium is digital, a rethinking of the entire question of notes and annotations becomes possible, even necessary.

Undergraduate English students probably first encounter annotations and footnotes in *The Norton Anthology of English Literature* or another college textbook. They squint to decipher the tiny bits of information at the bottom of a page and then return to the text at the top either appreciative or frustrated. They seem to quickly form a judgment that footnoted annotations are useful places to find what they need to know, repositories of strangely arcane and irrelevant displays of knowledge, or simply verbiage.*

Graduate students learn that creating notes as references to, and also as extensions of, the main text's argument is an essential part of scholarly work, and the first stage in my professional relationship with notes con-

---

*Or bits of information not directly relevant to the main text: I first wrote this essay in digital hypertext format for the Web (as "'James Joyce's *Ulysses* in Hypermedia': Problems of Annotation") and then reconceived it for print. I thought I had originally written a thoroughly hypertextual, multi-pathed document, but when I reworked it into a print-based essay I discovered to my shock that each screen flowed seamlessly into the next as if they had all been conceived as paragraphs in print in the first place.

sisted of becoming proficient at writing them. The second stage involved reading other people's notes with interest and also skepticism, occasionally reading the notes before and maybe even in place of the main text. In the third stage, I tended to stop reading most notes, often skipping them whenever a text included them. In the fourth (current) stage, I welcome the chance to write without using them when that is possible.

This is a chapter about annotation, however, so I will include some notes. Doing this in a print text is a routine activity, but it is a different matter in a digital one. On a screen, for one thing, I can't easily provide footnotes. The bottom of the screen doesn't mean the same thing spatially as the foot of a page (text on top, note at bottom). I could provide notes at the end of long electronic "page," but that would be only a screen imitation of a printed text. Since notes can appear as new screens, no longer at the bottom or end and no longer necessarily subordinate to a primary text, they don't have to be short in order to meet printing requirements or to avoid overwhelming the main text.

■

In *The Footnote: A Curious History*, Anthony Grafton documents how, for a long time, the writing of footnotes involved particular, uncommon skills and was even considered a special talent. (A second book on footnotes, a spirited defense of them, is Chuck Zerby's *The Devil's Details*.) For the most part, this isn't the case now, as several examples illustrate. Gérard Genette, appropriately in a footnote, quotes a clever disparaging remark from the French writer Alain: "A note is the mediocre attached to the beautiful." In his poem "The Scholars," William Butler Yeats contrasts "young men, tossing on their beds" and writing poems inspired by passionate emotions with the "old, learned, respectable bald heads" of their editors and annotators. And, sustaining the unlikely combination of footnotes and beds, Grafton relates a wonderfully witty quip from Noel Coward[1]—to the effect that having to read a footnote resembles needing to go downstairs to answer the door while making love.*

---

*In a footnote—where else?—Grafton notes that Coward attributed a stronger version of the remark to John Barrymore, who, according to Barrymore's biographer Cole Lesley, "expressed the opinion that having to look at a footnote was like having to go down to answer the front door just as you were coming."

Scholars have talked about footnotes in various ways. Patricia White employs Gaston Bachelard's phenomenological account of space, in which the attic represents pattern and framework and the cellar stands for irrationality, to account for our tendency to value the text on the top of a page to the detriment of the note at the bottom. John Lavagnino neatly captures the sense of frustration that notes can elicit when he talks about commentary's "social ineptitude": it is never there when you want it, invariably there when you do not. (Perhaps the most notorious recent annotation is Richard J. Finneran's note to "He" in "That He might be nobly breeched," line 13 of Yeats's poem "Wisdom": "Jesus Christ, son of God in the Christian religion.") Demonstrating how hot and controversial a topic annotation can be, in an article in the *Chronicle of Higher Education* Rodger Beehler gives several examples of intrusive notes as part of his claim that modern annotation "gives new meaning to the idea of wrestling with a text."[2]

In the eighteenth and nineteenth centuries, writers sometimes included their own footnotes and marginal commentaries in their novels and poems for serious, comical, or satirical purposes, as in Pope's *Dunciad*, Fielding's *Tom Jones*, Sterne's *Tristram Shandy*, and Coleridge's "Rime of the Ancient Mariner." In the late twentieth century and into the twenty-first, they appear in novels usually to be ridiculed or caricatured, often to stunning or hilarious effect. In Vladimir Nabokov's *Pale Fire* (1961), for example, a novel in the form of an annotated edition of a poem, the annotator desperately tries to commandeer the poem to give it a meaning that the poet refused to provide. In one chapter of Jonathan Coe's novel *The House of Sleep* (1997), a sleepy film-journal editor inadvertently omits one footnote number from a filmmaker's annotated memoir, causing all the subsequent notes to refer, sometimes scandalously, to the wrong cue in the text (note 4 is supposed to annotate what is erroneously numbered 3 in the text, etc.). As a result, a sentence from the memoir in which the director talks about his wife—"Marsha is delightfully candid about her earlier career, and has never made any secret of the fact that she started out in the business by starring, under my own direction, in a series of sex movies"—which is supposed to be annotated with the a note identifying the films ("Their titles, for the record, were *Wet Knickers*, *Pussy Talk* and *Cream on My Face*"), is instead annotated in this way: "Much praised, recently, by Denis Thatcher, who said that they had given him 'six of the most enjoyable hours of my life.' His wife Margaret later joked that he was 'stiff for hours afterwards.'" The note with the porn-film titles ends up annotating the sentence "Among the most prized possessions in our library are several books recommended to her during an audience with Pope Paul VI, who said that they were among the most inspiring and influential works he had ever read." The Thatcher note is supposed to annotate "This [country] club, the flagship of my chain I might add, has already played host to some distinguished visitors, and boasts among its attractions no fewer than two rather challenging eighteen-hole golf courses."[3]

Other contemporary examples abound. A mock mathematical-theory article that occupies twelve pages of Gilbert Sorrentino's novel *Mulligan Stew* (1979) contains 114 footnotes, all of which are essentially non sequiturs. Mark Z. Danielewski in *House of Leaves* (2000) and David Foster Wallace in both the novel *Infinite Jest* (1996) and the essays in *Consider the Lobster* (2006) prove themselves to be obsessive and master footnoters, all three books even containing notes to their notes. And Jenny Boully's *The Body* (2002) and Mark Dunn's *Ibid* (2004) are two works consisting entirely of footnotes without a main text.

(A historical distraction, best relegated to a footnote except for its length: In the nineteenth century, a self-annotating text could sometimes be unintentionally comic. In *Very Bad Poetry*, Kathryn Petras and Ross Petras present an excerpt from "The Homeward-Bound Passenger Ship" by the mid-nineteenth-century, and appropriately named, English poet Edward Edwin Foot. In it, a footnote at the end of the line "The captain scans the ruffled zone" helpfully describes the last phrase as "A figurative expression, intended by the Author to signify the horizon," and a note to the word "See" in the line "See, if you can, their lifeless forms!—" annotates the word as "Imagine." The editors also provide a complete untitled short poem by Foot, which they say "deserves special notice for the ratio of poem text to footnote text" and also for the footnotes' startling inability to clarify the poem in any way:

> Altho' we[‡] mourn for one now gone,
> And he—that grey-hair'd Palmerston,[§]
>   We will give God the praise,—
> For he, beyond the age of man,[**]
> Eleven years had over-ran
>   Within two equal days.

[‡]The nation.
[§]The Right Honourable Henry John Temple, Viscount Palmerston,

K.G., G.C.B., etc. (the then Premier of the British Government), died at "Brockett Hall," Herts., at a quarter to eleven o'clock in the forenoon of Wednesday, 18th October, 1865, aged eighty-one years (all but two days), having been born on the 20th October, 1784, The above lines were written on the occasion of his death.
"Scriptural limitation.)[4]

In a text destined for print publication such as this one, I can refer to footnotes without reproducing most of them because we are all so familiar with notes and annotations that we know what is meant. But mistakes such as those in *The House of Sleep* make no sense in a digital environment, where the need to number notes disappears. (A parallel error in a digital text might concern misconnected links.) In the early 2000s I sold my two-story house and bought a one-floor apartment, so I had to begin relating even to the part of the Noel Coward quip about going downstairs to answer the door from memory and no longer from direct experience. Talking about annotating *Ulysses* in a digital presentation involves changes of these kinds.

■

Annotations can seem to exist at a level of fact, but Martin Battestin lists three variables that always affect annotation: the assumed audience, the nature of the text being annotated, and the nature of the annotator. Traugott Lawler emphasizes the second variable, the text being annotated and its presumed attitude toward annotation, when he suggests that "perhaps the central question to ask, before we start annotating a text, is whether the text itself embodies an attitude to annotation." Several critics have attempted to describe this complex relationship. For example, Peter Cosgrove remarks that a footnote leads a "double existence," both outside the text giving information and inside it hindering its progression. Lavagnino considers ways in which this double existence can be seen in terms of conflict: the text versus the commentary or the commentary (as supposedly objective "fact") versus the more valued act of criticism. Less neutrally, Ralph Hanna characterizes annotation in terms of power and aggression both toward the author and toward the presumed audience.[5]

Jacques Derrida captures these paradoxes neatly when he describes the "double bind" of annotation: the text says to read it in silence but at the same time cries out for response from the reader: "we see how [the] law text, which makes the law, produces at the same time a double bind: it says to the reader or auditor, 'Be quiet, all has been said, you have nothing to say, obey in silence,' while at the same time it implores, it cries out, it says, 'Read me and respond: if you want to read me and hear me, you must understand me, know me, interpret me, translate me, and hence, in responding to me and speaking to me, you must begin to speak in my place, to enter into a rivalry with me.'"[6] This response, of course, often appears in the form of commentary and annotation in footnotes.

■

Ulysses serves as an excellent test case of Lawler's suggestion that an annotator should always ask about the text's attitude to annotation. Texts are exhibited throughout *Ulysses*, and its characters respond to, comment on, even actually annotate texts. The entire "Scylla and Charybdis" episode features Stephen Dedalus's theory of *Hamlet*, in which detail after detail in *Hamlet* and Shakespeare's other works is interpreted in the light of biographical information. Less loftily and less aggressively, Leopold Bloom annotates an advertisement for Alexander Keyes, Tea, Wine, and Spirit Merchant, as he talks to the editor of the *Freeman's Journal* about placing the ad in the newspaper (*U* 7:120–63). And the newspaper editor recounts how a Dublin newsman cabled classified information about a local murder to a New York newspaper by providing an elaborate annotation of an ad that his New York colleagues had in front of them (*U* 7:626–77).

In many different ways, then, texts exist in *Ulysses* to be commented on and to be annotated. Because so much information in the book is obscure—Dublin details from 1904, specific information from Irish history, allusions to popular culture from the late nineteenth and early twentieth centuries, references to Homer's *Odyssey*, and phrases in Latin and Greek (which someone turning to *Ulysses* might have been expected to know when the book was published in 1922 but which are increasingly beyond the experience of those people now)—readers have often looked for help in annotations, and such information has been provided for them. Four collections of annotations in English exist. Two are book-length: Weldon Thornton's *Allusions in "Ulysses"* (1968) and Don Gifford and Robert J. Seidman's *"Ulysses" Annotated* (1988). The other two are editions of *Ulysses*: the Penguin 20th-Century Classics *Ulysses: Annotated Student's Edition* (1992), with notes by Declan Kiberd; and the Oxford World's Classics *Ulysses: The 1922 Text*

(1993), with notes by Jeri Johnson. Both these editions offer endnotes to accompany the text.

All these notes have proven both useful and frustrating. In different ways, they provide much valuable information and leave a great deal out that a reader might want; they make mistakes along with providing reliable information; and they mix interpretation with more factual details. To use them, a reader must either keep a separate book open next to *Ulysses* or flip to the back of a large paperback. The annotations in the *Ulysses* editions are, understandably, aimed at students and provide the kinds of information that beginning readers probably need and want. The Thornton and Gifford-Seidman books provide information that more advanced readers as well as beginners might look for.

These annotators necessarily take a pragmatic approach: they have a job to do, and they set out to do it. They don't worry much about the relationship of the notes to the text—although Gifford and Seidman offer the bizarre suggestion that a reader might want to look at their notes first and then turn to *Ulysses*.[7] But, as soon as the medium changes, and especially when, as in a digital presentation, the notes can begin to occupy the same visual space as the text, such questions need to be addressed.

■

Presenting any print-based text in digital format inevitably changes it, and those changes affect annotation in important ways. A passage from *Ulysses* can help to illustrate issues regarding both annotations in general and *Ulysses* in a digital presentation. The three variables for annotation that Battestin mentions—the nature of the text, the assumed audience, and the annotator—all figure into the example. So does the question of an annotation's social ineptitude or grace that Lavagnino raises: Is the annotation needed or unnecessary? Does it say too much or too little? Does it try to answer the right questions or the wrong ones? Does it provide the information that its presumed audience wants and needs? Is it appropriate to *Ulysses*, the text it annotates?

The passage I want to focus on occurs at the end of "Lotus Eaters." Leopold Bloom walks along a street in Dublin after spending some time in a church and then in a chemist's shop, and Bantam Lyons, a man he knows slightly and likes even less, approaches him. Bloom mainly wants to get rid of Lyons as quickly as he can, and after a brief conversation Lyons walks away.

Bloom is pleased with himself for extricating himself from Lyons so easily and effortlessly:

> Bantam Lyons's yellow blacknailed fingers unrolled the baton. Wants a wash too. Take off the rough dirt. Good morning, have you used Pears' soap? Dandruff on his shoulders. Scalp wants oiling.
> —I want to see about that French horse that's running today, Bantam Lyons said. Where the bugger is it?
> He rustled the pleated pages, jerking his chin on his high collar. Barber's itch. Tight collar he'll lose his hair. Better leave him the paper and get shut of him.
> —You can keep it, Mr Bloom said.
> —Ascot. Gold cup. Wait, Bantam Lyons muttered. Half a mo. Maximum the second.
> —I was just going to throw it away, Mr Bloom said.
> Bantam Lyons raised his eyes suddenly and leered weakly.
> —What's that? his sharp voice said.
> —I say you can keep it, Mr Bloom answered. I was going to throw it away that moment. Bantam Lyons doubted an instant, leering: then thrust the outspread sheets back on Mr Bloom's arms.
> —I'll risk it, he said. Here, thanks.
> He sped off towards Conway's corner. God speed scut. (U 5:523–42)

First-time readers are unlikely to pay much attention to Bloom's repeated words, "I was just going to throw it away" and "I was going to throw it away that moment." Bloom himself doesn't consider them to be anything special, just part of his attempt to shoo Lyons away. But Lyons seems to treat them as very meaningful, although the text declines to say why or even which of the words he responds to.

Three of the four sets of notes I've mentioned annotate these lines. Gifford and Seidman, in a first, long note to the race itself, mention the event that Lyons thinks Bloom alludes to:

> **Ascot. Gold cup**—The Gold Cup, one of the two main annual events of the British racing calendar, was to be run that day at Ascot Heath, twenty-six miles from London, at 3:00 p.m. "The Gold Cup, value 1,000 sovereigns with 3,000 sovereigns in specie in addition, out of which the second shall receive 700 sovereigns added to a sweepstakes

of 20 sovereigns each . . . for entire colts and fillies. Two miles and a half. The field: M. J. de Bremond's Maximum II; age 5. Mr. W. Bass's Sceptre; age 5; A. Taylor. Lord Ellesmere's Kronstad; age 4; J. Dawson. Lord Howard de Walden's Zinfandel; age 4; Beatty. Sir J. Miller's Rock Sand; age 4; Blackwell. Mr. W. Hall Walker's Jean's Folly; age 3; Robinson. Mr. F. Alexander's Throwaway; age 5; Braime. M. E. de Blashovits's Beregvolgy; age 4. Count H. de Pourtale's Ex Voto; age 4. Count H. de Pourtale's Hebron II; age 4. M. J. de Soukozanotte's Torquato Tasso; age 4. Mr. Richard Croker's Clonmell; age 3." "Selections for Ascot Meeting. Gold Cup—Zinfandel." "Tips from 'Celt': Gold Cup—Sceptre." (as reported in the *Freeman's Journal*, 16 June 1904, p. 7.) The race was won by the dark horse Throwaway, a twenty-to-one shot; see 14.1128–33n [a reference to a note to a later "Oxen of the Sun" passage].

In a second note annotating Bloom's spoken words, Gifford and Seidman emphasize again why Lyons thinks the words are significant:

> **throw it away**: See preceding note. The point is that Bloom has just unwittingly given a tip on the Gold Cup race.[8]

Kiberd in his note combines some factual information with an interpretation of Joyce's passage:

> *throw it away*: later, when a horse called *Throwaway* wins the Ascot Gold Cup, Lyons will circulate a rumour that Bloom has won money on the bet: another example of the treachery of misunderstood language. The newspaper-phallus is now "thrown away" by Bloom before he opts for his narcissistic bath.[9]

In contrast, Johnson limits her brief note to factual information:

> *Ascot Gold Cup*: an important event for Dubliners in *Ulysses*; the actual Gold Cup, an annual event, was run in 1904 at Ascot (in England) at 3:00 p.m., 16 June.[10]

Some clear and certain statements—factual and with an unproblematic relationship to the passages, and all of which will become clear later in *Ulysses*—can be said about Bloom's two remarks, "I was just going to throw it away" and "I was going to throw it away that moment." There really was a horse race, the Gold Cup, at Ascot in England on June 16, 1904. Lyons mentions this when he asks to see Bloom's newspaper, and Bloom recognizes it, even though he seems to have no idea which horses are entered in the race. There really was a horse named Throwaway in the race, a horse that ran as a twenty-to-one outsider. Throwaway went on to win the race. A group of Dubliners—all of whom bet on Sceptre (even Lyons, who temporarily followed up on the tip that he thought Bloom gave him but who was later dissuaded from the bet)—talk in a pub, and one of the men reports Bloom's conversation with Lyons. As a result, the men believe that Bloom, in what they see as typical of Jews, had an inside tip on Throwaway, won a pile of money on the race, and stingily failed to share his winnings with the other men by buying them a round of drinks. Bloom is almost injured in an attack as a result (*U* 12:1548–58). He eventually reads a newspaper account of the race, but whether or not he connects the results of the race even then with his remark earlier in the day to Lyons isn't clear (*U* 16:1274–85).

An annotation can point out a range of details, including, as in the Throwaway passage, information that the book will reveal only later on. But how much should it say? Should beginning readers, in a note to a passage at this early point in the novel, be given information they will learn only later on?

I see no clear answer to this question. People will respond according to their sense of the experience of reading a book like *Ulysses*, or what they think it should be, and this will affect their answers to questions about whether readers should or should not be given information ahead of when they will encounter it in the novel, or whether the task of guiding readers through the book occasionally or even often involves violating some of Joyce's patterns of revealing information. My students tend to be divided, or, perhaps more accurately, conflicted: in the abstract they tell me that they don't think they should be told anything ahead of its appearance in the book, but in practical terms they welcome any information that gives them a sense of how this bewildering and mystifying novel (which is how *Ulysses* appears to most of them as they read the early episode "Lotus Eaters") actually works.

Thus, even if annotators agree on an assumed reader who is experiencing *Ulysses* for the first time, they won't necessarily agree about how much information should be included in a note. The audience might be constant, but the annotators' sense of how *Ulysses* works will crucially affect how they construct the note. And what if the presumed audience changes? For second-time or more experienced readers, there is no need to maintain the secret of Throwaway. For these readers, the questions annotators have to ask themselves involve such issues as how much to say, in what order, and whether anything should be left out.

■

So we are talking about a rhetoric and even an ethics of annotation: how to present information effectively, what order to present it in, how much to say and to omit, how to distinguish indisputable fact from interpretation. This is a matter both of accuracy and also of tact. A change in the medium can affect how annotators might think about both. The general situation regarding annotation and some questions about the activity (such as how much information to include and how to order the information) remain relatively constant no matter what the medium. They are equally relevant and problematic for print annotations and for digital ones. But, for several reasons, digital presentation opens up new possibilities and therefore new angles to the questions.

For one thing, there is much less restriction regarding the amount of space that annotations can take up in digital presentations. Print annotations typically need to be kept short, or to take up less space than the primary text, or to fill up fewer than, say, five hundred pages, but these kinds of limitations disappear in digital formats. Also, there is no need to posit only one kind of audience, whether first-time readers, or students plus some more experienced readers, or scholars. Because information can be doled out as users request it, a digital presentation can plan for several different levels of readers. In the Throwaway example, it is possible to posit a readership that includes both people who should not be told anything about Bloom's throwaway phrase, "I was just going to throw it away," and also people who won't be bothered or compromised by being told everything that can be said about the phrase.

For digital presentation, the question then becomes how to present the information, how to be tactful. While I was pondering questions like the ones I have been asking here, I helped run and participated in a monthlong online discussion regarding annotation on the J-Joyce e-mail listserv.[11] We discussed several possible presentations. One is to construct the information in layers, so that a series of screens starts with basic factual and identifying information and then expands into more elaborate details and ultimately into various interpretations. Beginning readers can start with the basic information and, only if they want it, move on to fuller annotations. Advanced readers can choose to start with the more advanced details and interpretation and skip the basic identifications that they probably already know.

A related question involves how much information beginners should be told. It is counterproductive (and one of the reasons that students often don't read printed annotations) to give beginners more information than they want. If they are looking for a simple definition of a word or identification of a detail, a long paragraph full of scholarly exegesis is overkill. It might turn them off to the annotations, and maybe even to the book itself. It seems most useful to make the first-level annotation as simple and short as is realistically possible (five words? ten? twenty-five? whatever will suffice in each case) and then give readers easy access to more information. If a reader wants only a quick fix on a word or phrase in order to keep reading, the least intrusive annotation is probably the most successful one.

■

From the Throwaway example, or from almost any other passage from *Ulysses* that might be given (or, for that matter, from any other work)—and with the differences between print and screen presentation in mind—several questions about annotation can be formulated. None of them have clear answers, and, in some cases, the possible answers for a digital presentation will be different from those for a print one. (The original online version of this chapter displays eight different ways of presenting the annotations to the "Lotus Eaters" passage.) I will close with seven questions and some thoughts in response to them.

(1) What should be annotated?

Clearly, something needs to be said about the conversation between Bloom and Lyons, which at first glance seems either inconsequential or bewildering. But, since the digital format permits a layered series of screens, it is possible, even desirable, to resist mentioning in the first instance the reason why Bloom's remark about throwing away the newspaper becomes so significant. An initial note to those words might be a simple "watch-this-space" symbol, or the note might be limited to the mention in the text of the horse race and say something similar to Johnson's note, which merely indicates that a horse race took place in England on that day. A link from that initial note can take readers to more information.

(2) What, if anything, should be not annotated?

Probably nothing that is known should be kept out of the annotations, but most of the details should be reserved for second- and higher-level notes.

(3) Should information be presented differently for first-time readers than for later ones? If so, how can this be done?

In a digital presentation, the note aimed at beginning readers should present only the barest factual information. More elaborate options, such as highlighting the relationship of Bloom's remark to the horses in the race (as Gifford and Seidman's first note does) or indicating what Bloom has inadvertently conveyed with his remark (as does their second note), or presenting the annotator's interpretive spin on the passage (as in Kiberd's note), can be reserved for the notes aimed at more advanced readers.

(4) How should the information be presented, given the many possibilities opened up by computer links?

Many options exist, each with advantages and disadvantages. The one option that should not be followed is the print one, in which all the included information comes out as one short or long note. Since it takes little time or effort to get from one screen to another, the information can be parceled out in increasingly complex layers, with different kinds of materials, such as words and images, presented on separate screens. A designer can choose among various possible formats for the presentation, such as putting the annotations in pop-up windows or in frames, indicating that certain words are triggers for links or hiding that fact, and requiring the reader to click the mouse or merely to hold the cursor on a word for a few seconds to call up an annotation.

(5) Can there be too much information? Too little? Is there a desirable mean?

Obviously, an annotator can present too little information. In print, space considerations sometimes force the annotator into this position. Too much? This is probably a matter of context. Beginning readers who want a quick definition of a word or identification of a person or place or historical event in order to understand a passage will probably find an annotation less than helpful, to the point of uselessness, if it goes on and on with all kinds of scholarly knowledge, especially if the information the readers want isn't easy to find within the exposition. And yet other readers will probably desire the extra information, and even some beginners will become interested enough in the topic to be inspired to stop their reading to learn more.

The best solution to this situation, and one that digital presentation can do well, is the method I've already outlined: give in the first instance only a short introductory note, but provide clearly marked links in that note that lead to more information. Readers who do not want anything more can quickly move back to the text, and those who do can follow the links that are provided.

(6) Is there a line between information and interpretation? If so, how do we proceed in order not to cross it? If not, how do we construct annotations?

In one sense, any annotation is interpretation. Even if the information is completely factual, such as the historical detail about the Gold Cup race on June 16, 1904, the decision to provide the annotation involves an interpretation regarding what matters in the text of *Ulysses*. Of the existing annotations to the Throwaway passage, Johnson's stays most strictly at what might be called a factual level. Gifford and Seidman's first (to some extent) and second (to a much greater degree) annotations move into the realm of interpretation by deciding, or assuming, that telling readers information that they will not encounter in the book for hundreds of pages is an acceptable practice. Kiberd's note rests at the other extreme on the fact-interpretation scale from Johnson's: it seems to exist mainly to provide the annotator's interpretation of the passage.

In a digital presentation, the annotations at the first level for beginning readers work best if they come close to Johnson's practice. Notes aimed at advanced readers can adopt procedures like Gifford and Seidman's, and eventually the annotations can become fully interpretive. However, digital presentation need not remain single-voiced in the way a print book usually is, so whenever an interpretation appears, a conflicting or complementary one, or one simply in a different voice, can also be presented, even giving readers the opportunity to close off all interpretations except one if they wish to. The default position, that *Ulysses* can be interpreted in many ways and in many voices and not by a single "authority," would remain in place.

(7) Do these questions change for different categories of information (historical, other languages, intertextuality)?

A short note with links to more detailed information might be a desirable norm for annotations, but not all details from *Ulysses* will lend themselves to such well-ordered annotations. Some passages cannot be discussed at all except at the level of interpretation. In the J-Joyce listserv discussion of annotation, Andrew Blom suggested one such detail: it involves an Italian exclamation, "Già," near the end of "Proteus" (*U* 3:392–96). Gifford and Seidman annotate the word as an adverb, meaning "already" or "Let's go. Let's go."[12] Blom suggests, however, that the word is an exclamation and derives from the German *ja*. He translates it as something like "yes," "sure," "of course," or "right," as in "That's me, all right. Yeah, sure." If neither translation is erroneous, then no single note can provide a quick first annotation. The initial note will itself be an interpretation.

A similar and even more direct situation exists regarding the incomplete phrase that Leopold Bloom writes in sand on a beach at the end of "Nausicaa." He writes "I." and then "AM. A." before he covers over the letters with sand (*U* 13:1256–69). The text never specifies what else Bloom intended to write, if anything. Annotators who choose to comment on "I. AM. A." can do so only at the level of interpretation, since any consideration of what Bloom might be writing can be only speculation.

The complications that this question opens up do not affect the appearance of the annotations or how readers call them up, but they do suggest that the separation between factual information and interpretation is a thin, perhaps nonexistent, one and also that some first-level notes will have to be content to say something like "critics disagree on the meaning of this detail."

■

Early on in *Ulysses*, Leopold Bloom thinks about a time when Molly asked him to make love with her. He recalls her saying, "Give us a touch, Poldy. God, I'm dying for it" (*U* 6:79–80). A reader can interrupt an experience of this memory by turning to one of the published sets of annotations to find "a touch" defined as "slang for sexual intercourse"[13] and might find the note helpful in increasing the erotic implications of "touch" or even in extending the response into the emotional—"touched," since Bloom is remembering the lovemaking that produced his and Molly's son Rudy, who died eleven days after he was born. Or the reader might find the note intrusive, socially inept, even "touched" in the sense of unbalanced or demented. Footnoted annotations, whether in print or in an electronic format, can be all of these. Whether a note is an inscription on a monument's pedestal or a Calder-like mobile floating on a screen, the possibility of working in digital formats can provoke us into thinking anew, or again, about the value, utility, and challenges of annotations.

10

The Case of the Snuffed Footnote

A Report from the Stacks

It was only a minor puzzle—I knew that, I knew that. But it got to me, and it was as tenacious as a bookworm inching closer and closer to the paste in the binding. I couldn't stop thinking about those simple but treacherous words: R. M. Weber, *Dichtung und Dichter*, Berlin, 1890. A footnote is shorthand for an entire world contained in a book. Why was this world remaining so hidden?

A researcher thrives on asking questions and trying to answer them. Often you feel like a gumshoe. Maybe you don't walk down mean streets, but cramped and dark library stacks can be nasty, too, and you risk your eyesight, back, and nasal passages as you seek the answer to a puzzle that you know is buried somewhere in an old book or journal. Footnotes, even ones fancily dressed up in meticulous Modern Language Association style—those dandies, those femmes fatales—can lead you into cul-de-sacs and blind alleys.

Two fellow Joyceans, Daniel Ferrer in Paris and Jed Deppman in San Antonio and then Oberlin, and I were putting together a book of eleven French essays by genetic critics, including one on Joyce and paragraphs. Besides translating the essays, we also needed to edit them, and that involved modifying some of the notes the authors provided and adding new ones. One of the essays (not the one on Joyce) referred to what sounded like a bizarre late-nineteenth-century book of literary criticism that discusses poetry in terms of human sexual organs. It named an author and a title but provided no other bibliographical information. I like things to be neat and consistent and full, and as I began to flesh out the partial references for notes like this one I found myself braving the library stacks again and again in search of answers.

Ferrer declared himself an agnostic in matters of bibliographical completeness. He seemed to wonder why I was bothering with some of the questions I posed to him. But when you hear Research's call, you need to marshal your courage and follow your gut instincts, and when online searches prove insufficient, you have to be brave and go wherever is necessary, even into the bowels of the library. It's dark in there, and dusty and lonely, and we all know of some people who went in and never came out, but you can't keep thinking about the danger, you can't let it get to you. Despite what anyone says, you know that too much depends on finding the answer to the question.

■

A statement in one of the essays we were translating intrigued me from the moment I first saw it. The author was providing a quick history of manuscript study and indicated that the establishment of European manuscript libraries in the nineteenth century, particularly the Goethe- und Schiller-Archiv in Weimar, Germany, inspired this kind of work at the end of the century. But, he went on, a tendency of critics to rely slavishly on models from the natural sciences marred much of this work, and as an especially egregious example he cited a book from 1890, which the French text named *Poésie et poètes* (Poetry and Poets) by R. M. Weber. Weber considered poetry to have a physiology, and believed its mechanisms could be given reproductive and anatomical terms: semen, potency, uterus. The French text gave no source for Weber, and when we wrote to the author, he couldn't help us. He had written the essay in the 1970s, he told us. He no longer had his notes and working papers and remembered nothing about Weber. He could find only a brief reference: R. M. Weber, *Dichtung und Dichter*, Berlin, 1890. It wasn't much to work with, but we had already identified quotations when we started with no reference information at all. R. M. Weber, *Dichtung und Dichter*, Berlin, 1890—I'd do what I could with it. (In chapter 3 I quoted an entry from one of Paul Valéry's notebooks describing a fertilized embryo as the beginning of the process of creating a poem, but Valéry surely wasn't the elusive author we were seeking.)

We had the option of simply printing this reference as a note. It is a complete bibliographic entry, after all, since Modern Language Association format doesn't require publishers' names for pre-1900 books, and a less obsessive type than I am probably would have put it in without further ado. But Weber's book aroused my curiosity, and I tried to find it. Following my usual procedure, I looked up the author and the book in various online library catalogs: the University of Toronto (always my first search, because I live in Toronto and can easily get to the university's Robarts Library), the New York Public Library (I also spend a lot of time in New York and am familiar with this library's catalog system and with the library itself), the Library of Congress, the British Library, and the Bibliothèque Nationale. I had been able to identify almost every book I searched for, and even almost every quote within each book, by sitting at home at my computer and finding the entry in one of these catalogs, then going to a library and looking at the book itself. But none of the libraries listed Weber's *Dichtung und Dichter*. None showed anything by R. M. Weber or a book with that title by any other author. Nor did any catalogs I searched from German libraries.

I wrote to friends and colleagues who work in German literature, and I looked in specialized histories of German literary criticism and in such other histories of criticism as William K. Wimsatt and Cleanth Brooks's *Literary Criticism: A Short History*, volume 4 (The Later Nineteenth Century) of René Wellek's eight-volume *History of Modern Criticism, 1750–1950*, and (even though I knew I wouldn't find anything in this) the entries on German criticism in a book I had coedited, *The Johns Hopkins Guide to Literary Theory and Criticism*. No one I asked had heard of Weber or his book, and none of the books mentioned him. Some of my correspondents advised me to let it go: it was the essay's author, after all, who had identified Weber, they tried to reassure me, and if the name was wrong, the mistake was his. Maybe I should have taken this advice, but by now I was caught in the grip of that note. I was really puzzled and intrigued. Minor critics get forgotten, certainly, but how could someone who claimed that poetry had sex organs be unknown to absolutely everyone?

■

Weber couldn't simply have disappeared like some body in a Philip Marlowe mystery. Something had to be wrong with the reference. Maybe the author's name was wrong, or maybe the title. Perhaps Weber and the book weren't German but rather French or English. Maybe *Dichtung und Dichter* wasn't a book at all but an article published in a Berlin journal or encyclopedia in 1890. I wrote again to people asking about journals or encyclopedias that might have published an article or entry with claims like the ones made here and about names that might be similar to Weber. I asked my questions to everyone I ran into at the annual MLA convention. But no one could suggest anything.

I kept searching for "R. M. Weber" on Google: hits directed me to sites such as one on cricket mating songs, which was poetry of a kind and also sexual but, I suspected, not what I sought. One day I thought I might be facing a purloined-letter situation: maybe I kept missing the answer because it was right in front of me. The essay we were translating originally appeared as the afterword to a collection of French genetic-criticism essays. Maybe Weber was mentioned in one of those essays. I looked through them, but he wasn't there.

All the approaches I had tried led nowhere, so I began to assume that the name R. M. Weber was the problem. I went back to Wellek's chapter on German criticism in volume 4 of his history, pages I had only skimmed before in search of the name Weber. I read them more closely, this time looking for other people who might be our Weber. If I were to find anyone, he would be an obscure, largely forgotten critic; as Wellek's account made clear, *all* German literary critics from the late nineteenth century are now obscure and forgotten. On page 302 I found a paragraph-long account of a critic who, according to Wellek, "has a gift of witty and often malicious characterization and frequently shows real critical acumen" but who "likes to characterize writers by their physique, the style of their beards, the manner of their walk." Well, here was something. Wellek concludes that this writer was "clever, affected, and often absurd." His name was Richard Moritz Meyer. He lived from 1860 to 1914 and worked and published in Berlin. This seemed to be it. The first two initials matched, and someone reading Meyer or reading about Meyer (since by now I thought that our author's account came not from direct contact with "Weber"'s work but from a secondary discussion of it) could easily mistake the five letters in Meyer for those in Weber. And the two differing letters would explain why my searches in the various libraries' "W" sections had led me nowhere.

I went back to the online catalogs and found the titles of more books by Meyer than I could possibly want. All were published in Berlin, many in the 1890s. Several titles were promising: *Poetics* (Berlin, 1888; this and the titles that follow are my own literal English versions of the titles of these untranslated German books); *Old German Poetry Described According to*

Its Formal Principles (Berlin, 1889); *Nineteenth-Century German Literature* (Berlin, 1900); *Outline of Modern German Literary History* (Berlin, 1902); *Forms and Problems* (Berlin, 1905). James Henry Spohrer, Germanic Collections librarian at the University of California at Berkeley, whom Deppman had contacted and who was e-mailing us with advice and suggestions regarding the Weber problem, mentioned Meyer's *Literary-Historical and Biographical Essays* (Berlin, 1911), which he thought might include an essay with a title like "Dichtung und Dichter." None of these books dated from 1890, but Spohrer also suggested looking at an index to German periodical writings called the *Bibliography of German Periodical Literature, Including Collective Works*. Armed with all the book titles and call numbers, I trudged off to the Robarts Library once again, now in search of the critic I had begun to think of as Weber/Meyer.

I got on the elevator, pushed the button for the eleventh floor, and avoided making eye contact with my fellow passengers, all of whom might have distracted me from my quest or pilfered my results had they ascertained what I was looking for. The library played to the hilt the first stage in the Janus-faced game that makes these institutions so notorious: its shelves possessed most of the books on my list. Each one was longer than the one before, and I wondered what I would do with them given my rusty (to say the least) German. I flipped the pages of one book after another, looking for the German words for "semen," "potency," and "uterus"—*Same* or *Samen, Potenz, Gebärmutter*. As soon as I found them I would have identified the book our author had cited, and I began mentally composing the e-mail message I would write to my skeptical colleagues announcing the solution to the problem. However, after a few hours and hundreds and hundreds of dusty pages (where did he find the time and energy to write so much and yet remain so little known?), I found nothing. The library had shown its other face once again: after promising so much, it yielded little.

The periodical-literature bibliography remained. All the volumes of this reference work were on the shelves of one stack in the Robarts Library Reference Room, but the aisle leading to that stack was roped off! The ceiling was unstable, the reference librarian told me. Apparently the administrators of the Robarts Library felt compelled to protect me from Meyer or to protect him from me by using a ruse of architectural instability. But was I going to let the small matter of the ceiling falling on my head stop me in my quest? As the other researchers, secure at their desks and carrels, tsk-tsked me in that manner unique to denizens of reference rooms, I climbed under the plastic yellow "Danger" tapes, planning to dash over to the appropriate stack (all my years as a runner would help me here), quickly pull out the volumes for the years 1885 to 1900, and escape to safety. But I discovered that the bibliography volumes were not produced chronologically (volume 4 covered 1891–92, 5 was for 1889–90, others were far more erratic—who knew that a German reference series could be so disorganized?), and it took a while to locate the years I needed, even longer than it normally would have because I kept glancing apprehensively at the ceiling. At last I found the volumes I needed and hightailed it out of there. Something by Meyer was listed in almost every one I looked at, and a few entries from 1890 and the years around it in the Berlin-based *Journal of German Antiquity and German Literature* seemed promising. I located the issues of this journal and Meyer's reviews in them. But, again, I found nothing. Nothing at all! Reluctantly, I had to admit that Richard Moritz Meyer was not our R. M. Weber.

■

I was back at square one, and part of me realized it was time to stop the quest. But possible new steps to take kept popping into my head, especially in the middle of the night. I returned over and over again to the online library catalogs, searching for Weber and for *Dichtung und Dichter*, and then, not expecting much, I did a new Google search on the phrases "R. M. Weber," "R. M. Meyer," and "Richard Moritz Meyer." Weber turned up nothing useful, of course—just the fornicating crickets. But the Meyer searches led to the titles of two recent essays on the critic. The links didn't lead to the texts of the essays, but they named the authors and gave the authors' university affiliations. I went to the Web sites of the two universities and searched for the authors. I couldn't find any information on one of them, but the University of Hamburg's site gave me an e-mail address for the other, Hans-Harald Müller. I wrote to him immediately, laying out the problem and all my attempts so far to link Weber to Meyer.

All successful mystery cases need a break, and Harry Müller provided this one's. Meyer isn't the person you're seeking, his e-mail message told me. He was a legitimate genetic critic. A better candidate—same initials, similar last name—would be Richard Maria Werner, who used ideas from the natural sciences and Darwin to talk about literature. Müller even gave me a reference for a review from 1900 of a book by Werner whose title contained the words that had eluded me for so long: *Vollendete und Ringende: Dichter und Dichtungen der Neuzeit* (Cases Resolved and Unresolved: Poets and Poetries of the Modern Period).

So I returned to the reference works and online library catalogs, this time searching for Werner. I'm not sure I wanted to find anything, since I was a little disappointed by the prospect of Werner. In my various formulations of the note I would eventually write for our Weber, I took for granted that his actual name contained five letters in the form "_e_er," and this new name didn't fit that pattern. Werner was not mentioned anywhere, not even in Wellek's *History of Modern Criticism*—here was someone so obscure that he didn't even make it into an account of forgotten obscurities. But he wrote a phenomenal amount. His dates were right (1854–1913), and he wrote about literature, but he wasn't published in Berlin. I noted a few of the titles: the book Müller had mentioned from 1900; another with a similar title, *Modern German Poets and Thinkers* (1914); and one especially intriguing title because of both the structure of its title and its date: *Lyrik und Lyriker: Eine Untersuchung* (Lyric Poetry and Poets: An Analysis; Hamburg and Leipzig, 1890).

I schlepped to the Robarts Library again—down St. George Street in a pouring rain. My researcher's innate optimism helped to carry me along to some extent, but my bookbag was as heavy as the rain after all the disappointments and dashed hopes I had experienced so far. As I started to work, though, I saw that the various strands of my little puzzle were starting to connect in ways I never would have guessed. It turned out that the 1900 review of Werner's book that Müller had mentioned was by, of all people, Richard Moritz Meyer, and Meyer had also reviewed *Lyrik und Lyriker* in the October 4, 1891, issue of the *Journal of German Antiquity and German Literature*, the periodical I had perused a few weeks back when Meyer was my target. (The review, interestingly enough, was misdated to match the date in our author's fragmentary reference for Weber: Berlin, December 1890.) The library didn't possess most of the Werner titles on my list, but it did own *Lyrik und Lyriker*. I found it easily, an impressive old, thick volume with tie-strings around it. No one had untied it for years—perhaps, I guessed, not since 1890. I had come to expect these German volumes to be long, and this one was no exception: 650 pages! I took a deep breath (not too deep, since the book was ferociously dusty) and began my search for the words *Same* or *Samen*, *Potenz*, and *Gebärmutter*.

The last page of the preface caught my eye. A phrase in quotation marks was "Physiologie der Lyrik" (physiology of the lyric), something very close to our essay's claim that R. M. Weber's goal was to give "une physiologie de la poésie." Werner said that he would have used that phrase for his book's title if another recent book had not been called *Physiologie der Liebe* (Physiology of Love). I looked around for the other three words, assuming that they must be somewhere nearby, probably in the preface as well. (Maybe I wouldn't have to look at the book's other six hundred pages.) But—and why should this have surprised me by now?—I couldn't find them.

So it was on to the entire book. From the contents page I saw that some chapters were named "Die Befruchtung" (Fertilization), "Inneres Wachstum" (Inner Growth), and "Geburt" (Birth)—the words I sought had to be in at least one of those chapters. But, as I leafed through the pages, they weren't jumping out at me, as I half expected them to do. On page 24, though, in a section of the first chapter ("Einleitung," Introduction) called "Zur Begründung" (Preliminaries), I saw the phrase "ein Ei befruchtet wird" (an egg will be fertilized) and then, a few lines later, one of my words: *Same* (semen, sperm, seed—Werner was saying that scientists know how eggs get fertilized but don't know why in one case a seed fertilizes an egg as a male embryo and in another as a female). My spirits lifted; the dust began to smell like a meadow; I knew I was in the right territory. But I didn't find anything else to help me in the remaining six hundred pages.

I decided to try one last course of action before giving up and admitting that, even though I suspected that Werner was our Weber, I couldn't prove it. As a last resort, I looked at the preface and the section around page 24 once again, and, since the preface was only five pages long and the other section just three, I decided to translate the passages carefully rather than loosely. I found a German-English dictionary and set to work. As I struggled through pages 24 and 25, I began to get a sense of what I think had gone on to cause all this trouble when our author wrote the original French essay. Werner makes comparisons between scientists studying processes of conception and birth and researchers studying the psychology of poetic creation. We can know how semen fertilizes an egg, for example, but we do not know why one particular act of conception produces a male embryo and another a female. Likewise, we can investigate how a poem came into being, even to some extent what went on inside the poet as the poem was developing, but what caused a particular poetic embryo to develop into a specific poem cannot be known. Such questions go beyond artists' possible self-awareness, Werner says. Nevertheless, just as natural scientists continue to investigate aspects of life that they do not and maybe cannot know, so literary critics can't be stopped when they reach an unknowable topic. Where there is a possibility of further knowledge, there is a right to investigate. Fortified by an analogy between biological conception and birth and the gestation and growth of poems, Werner goes on to ask where we might look for evidence of the latter, and he suggests poets' letters and diaries. By that point, he is talking like what we (especially my two coeditors, our author, and I) now would call a genetic critic.

I read no farther into *Lyrik und Lyriker*. I didn't expect the rest of the book to add anything to my quest. So I don't know if, as Werner's book went on, what seemed to me like a relatively restrained attempt to construct an analogy between scientific and literary investigation became wilder, more reductive, and more jargon-ridden. That is certainly possible—but in an 1890 review in the *Journal of German Antiquity and German Literature*, Werner seems to chide G. Beyer (these names! here was another near-Weber/Meyer/ Werner) for his fondness for uncontrolled metaphorical adjectives in a book on German poetics.

I no longer had any doubt that our essay's attribution of R. M. Weber's *Dichtung und Dichter* was actually a reference to R. M. Werner's *Lyrik und Lyriker*. What I think happened was this: our author did not read Werner's book itself but rather someone's account of it (perhaps even Meyer's 1891 review, dated Berlin 1890, which includes the phrase "Physiologie der Lyrik"). That account paraphrased Werner's argument using more direct biological terminology than Werner himself had used. When our author incorporated that account into his essay (the one we translated), the account's descriptive paraphrases evolved into what seemed to be quotations from the book itself. At the same time, R. M. Werner's *Lyrik und Lyriker* morphed into R. M. Weber's *Dichtung und Dichter*, perhaps because, once the German title became the French *Poésie et poètes*, the French could be translated back into German either way. I have no idea whether this is what actually happened, but it was the best solution I could come up with, and it let me sleep. I especially like the possibility that Meyer's review might have figured into the sequence of events. I don't think this is particularly likely, but if it did, then R. M. Weber was somehow constructed out of both R. M. Meyer and R. M. Werner.

All researchers know that you can no more expose your unprotected back to your associates than you should let your finger slip out from the endnotes section at the back of a book. You can never rest easy and consider a problem solved. In my euphoria over identifying Weber as Werner, however, I forgot all this. I wrote to Jed Deppman and Daniel Ferrer and also to James Spohrer and Harry Müller to tell them about Werner and to lay out my evidence. Harry thought that another Werner book might be a better source, but everyone agreed that, for the purpose of providing an accurate reference in our translation of the essay, the mystery was solved. I felt like I was on top of the stacks. I even convinced my wife that we should let our hair down (so to speak—I don't have enough left to let down) and indulge in a Friday evening in the neighborhood branch of the public library or even in a bookstore and try to get reacquainted.

Jed, Daniel, and I considered possible ways of incorporating our solution into the essay. We could present the correct Werner information in the translated text and not mention the author's original reference to Weber at all, give the correct information in the translated text but indicate the original reference in a note, or translate the author's original formulation but correct the reference to Werner in a note. We even considered the earlier suggestion: simply translate the original reference to Weber and not mention Werner. Now that we knew the answer, we could wallow in magnanimity.

We showed our findings to the author and asked him how he would like us to proceed. Did he want us to silently replace Weber with Werner?

No.

Name Werner but indicate the original reference to Weber?

No, no.

Give only the original Weber?

Non, non, non.

Instead, he blindsided us. He *reworded* the paragraph (!). He REMOVED all the names (!!). He insisted on speaking only in general terms about "some nineteenth-century critics" who turned to the natural sciences for concepts and tools!!!

My heart sank as if it were the 650 pages of *Lyrik und Lyriker* falling to the library floor.

And that is how the paragraph appears in our book. No R. M. Weber, no R. M. Meyer, no R. M. Werner, none of that gritty specificity that provides so much sustenance to a researcher. We followed the operations manual: posed a question; advanced, investigated, and rejected various hypotheses; and eventually found a solution—all exactly the way a research project is supposed to proceed. But no one who picks up our book will know that this little project was ever even initiated, much less solved. In our acknowledgments we thank James Henry Spohrer and Hans-Harald Müller for their help in solving a puzzle whose results are nowhere in the volume.

I can't let it go, I can't let it go. Those dusty journal volumes and tied-up books in the Robarts Library stacks: they are the world the footnote promises! I won't allow it to remain hidden. Yes, the footnote must circulate. I owe that to you, R. M. and R. M. and R. M., and to researchers everywhere. Here it is at last, in all its MLA-complying, eyesquint-inducing, scholar-enthralling glory:*

---

*Richard Maria Werner, *Lyrik und Lyriker: Eine Untersuchung* (Hamburg and Leipzig: Verlag von Leopold Voss, 1890), xi, 24–26.

Epilogue
Privacy in Bloom

Ever since I first read *Ulysses*, Leopold Bloom has provided the clearest and most dependable image I've found of the kind of person I'd like to be, someone who lives an ordinary life and survives it with optimism, good humor, integrity, and dignity. A thirty-eight-year-old canvasser for ads, a graduate of what he terms the "university of life" (*U* 15:840, 17:555–56), a Jewish outsider in lower-middle-class Catholic Dublin, Bloom lives through one day in all its twists and turns and ups and downs. In many ways, June 16, 1904, is an ordinary day—"the dailiest day possible," Joyce's fellow novelist Arnold Bennett called it—but Bloom does attend the funeral of an acquaintance who died suddenly earlier in the week from an alcohol-induced heart attack and, most important, lives through the hours knowing that at 4:00 his wife will be unfaithful to him (and, in the second half of the book, has cuckolded him) with her concert manager.[1] From the outside, and to his fellow Dubliners, Bloom is practically invisible and silent. They acknowledge him only to scorn him. Joyce gives us access to Bloom's inner life, however, and it is his thoughts, responses, reactions, daydreams, and fantasies that make him, for me, a figure of great sympathy, even of heroism.

We have access to a full range of Bloom's thoughts during his day—serious thoughts, trivial ones, happy, sad, generous, selfish, licit, illicit. Joyce lets us eavesdrop on his plans for his own life and his ideas for improving Dublin civic life (bury people vertically to save space in cemeteries), and on his attempts to recall poems and plays he has read and seen, often with mistakes. We also accompany him into his outhouse where we watch him and eavesdrop on his thoughts as he defecates: "Hope it's not too big bring on piles again. No, just right" (*U* 4:509–10). Later, we read the hilarious account of him masturbating and then follow his post-orgasmic thoughts, and we share his recollections of connubial lovemaking with Molly and his only half-serious plans, if even that, for his own adulterous affair with Martha Clifford. In one of the most extraordinary sections of *Ulysses*, we witness, as if paraded on a stage, Bloom's unconscious mind, the desires and drives, fears and wishes to which he has no conscious access. He would surely be mortified to learn that anyone else knew about this part of his being, or even to know about it himself. (Declan Kiberd remarks about even Bloom's conscious thoughts that if they "were to be made public, there would be outrage.")[2] If Leopold Bloom is a sympathetic, dignified, and heroic character, he is also one who has had much of what we would consider his privacy ripped from him by his creator.

I've thought about Leopold Bloom in many ways over the years, but never before in terms of privacy. He is a literary character, after all, a creation of words. But my sense of his dignity and heroism is connected to my voyeuristic interest in his inner life, to my access to what, if he were a living human being, he surely would want to keep private. And, of course, the playing field is uneven: I don't have to give anything away, or expose any part of myself, as I read *Ulysses*—except privately. No one knows how much or how little I'm affected by the book, how deeply or shallowly I respond, with how much interest or boredom, sympathy or hostility, unless I choose to make those reactions public.

Because I'm a professional literary critic and scholar, and a university professor, I do reveal at least some of those responses. Like most academics, I have made a tacit deal regarding my privacy. When I write literary criticism or scholarship, I write about an author or a work, not directly about myself. This ensures me a kind of protection, since I communicate through my ideas, my ability to discover and marshal evidence, and my skill at writing clear, relatively neutral, academic prose. I speak to a small audience, in most of my writings to those people interested in *Ulysses*. Within this tiny group I become a semi-public or sometimes public figure. Likewise, at my university, along with my colleagues I become a figure of interest and gossip among the students who pass through my department. In these roles I have found that I like being recognized and acknowledged, and I feel a little stung when I'm not. To the extent that I am a public person at all, it is only within these few narrow worlds. Outside of them, I remain private, and I think I know how my temperament has led me to this position of severely circumscribed celebrity within a much larger anonymity.

I love listening to the National Public Radio show *Car Talk*, even though I've never had the slightest interest in cars and no longer even own one. Tom and Ray Magliozzi once mentioned the Car-O-Scope, a questionnaire they offered on their Web site that was designed to tell you whether your car was the best match for your personality. What they were trying to find out from their questions was clear: if the only two jobs in the world were an accountant or a social worker, I'd choose to be an accountant; I like the inside of my car to be tidy; white-water rafting and skydiving hold no appeal whatsoever for me. I felt confident that the Car-O-Scope would conclude that the Subaru Forester I owned then and I were indeed made for each other. But one question threw the profile out of whack: "It would drive me nuts being married to an artist-type."[3] For not only can I imagine being married to an artist, I am married to one, and without being driven noticeably off the road. (The Forester, after all, had all-wheel drive.) Furthermore, unlike me, Molly Peacock is a writer who has often written about very personal aspects of her outer, inner, and sexual life in her poems and prose works.

When Molly and I married in 1992, both of us by then in our mid-forties, she was well established as a poet, and I knew that, by entering her world, I was granting her freedom to write about anything that happened with me and also to write indirectly or even directly about me. I found myself surprisingly unthreatened by this, feeling a kind of protection in knowing that she would never expose in her poems anything about me that I really wanted to keep to myself. I even felt flattered, I realized, when she wrote about me, whether about ordinary events like eating meals together or feeding our cats or intimate ones like making love or lying in her mother's bed the night after her mother died. I also got accustomed to the odder experience of hearing her perform these poems at public readings, feeling a mixture of pride and embarrassment in knowing that the strangers seated around me were learning things about me that I wouldn't have talked about. (I fell into the habit of sitting in the front row so that I couldn't see the rest of the audience and they couldn't see my face.) And I even adjusted to the more bizarre experience of hearing Molly intersperse these poems with others that are about someone else, even though some people in the audience thought they were learning something about me.

Poems are condensations and crystallizations, but prose is usually much more direct. Shortly after we got married, Molly began writing a memoir, a book she published in 1998 as *Paradise, Piece by Piece*. Her focus in the book was her own growth and development and the crucial life decisions she has made, including her choices to become a poet and not to have children. But, in addition to being married to her as she was writing the book, I figure into both themes of her book in other ways, because Molly and I were high school sweethearts in suburban Buffalo in the mid-1960s. We dated, "went steady" through a year and a half of high school and one year of college at different universities, and were each other's first lover. (And so I knew the living Molly before I met the fictional one.) We broke up at the end of our first college year and lost touch for eighteen years.

Then, reading the *New York Times Book Review* one Sunday morning in December 1984 in London, Ontario, where I had lived for nine years after being hired by the University of Western Ontario's English Department, I saw a review of what turned out to be Molly's second book of poems, *Raw Heaven*. I found the book, and just after that, in a fluky coincidence, a friend sent me her address. I knew I had to write her. I did, and she quickly wrote back. She lived in New York City, where I often visited, and we arranged to meet for a drink. We began getting together for lunch or dinner whenever I visited New York, and for seven years we enjoyed a platonic friendship. Since we were both deep into psychotherapy and working through various family problems, I was grateful for her firsthand recollections of me and my family from so many years ago. She provided me with the only accounts of those years, other than my own memories, that I was able to obtain.

In June 1991, when the publisher W. W. Norton canceled my contract for a Norton Critical Edition of *A Portrait of the Artist as a Young Man*, Molly was the only person I knew who had a writer's experience with publishers, and I phoned her for advice about this professional crisis. After the first few calls, we began talking at least once every day. She couldn't help me much with my canceled contract, but as we spoke on the phone evening after evening for a couple of weeks, our conversation became less professional and more personal and then romantic. I invited her to visit me, and, even though over the past seven years we had never done more than hug each other as we met or departed, she said she'd come. Within hours of her arrival we were lovers again, and within six months, even though we had jobs in different cities, we decided to get married. We did that the next summer in an announced elopement to a small town in Washington State for a combined wedding-honeymoon.

A few months after our wedding, Molly's mother died, and Molly began to talk more and more about her own life as a story she had to tell. I supported her as she began to write her memoir, but as she worked on it I found myself in an unexpected position in relation to my privacy. I was surprised and, I realized, pleased to see that she was including parts of my life in her story, not poetically but narratively, not veiled but undisguised. However, I was being written about solely as I appeared to someone else and as I figured in someone else's life. I was a subsidiary figure, a secondary character, in another person's story.

Trust was essential. I knew Molly to be a decent, honest person who wrote to explore her own inner and outer life, not to depict others badly or cruelly, to seek revenge, or to boost herself at someone else's expense. But she is, after all, a writer, and can you ever really trust a writer? She gets the last word. I had to learn to treat some details from my life as interesting anecdotes that I would enjoy making public, and so I got prepared for the world to learn about the time in 1964 when I went to Molly's house and found a note on an unlocked door instructing me to go into the living room, take off all my clothes, and go into the bathroom. I found her there in a bubble bath, where she invited my seventeen-year-old eyes to feast on the sight of her naked body. I nearly forgot my anxiety about her parents suddenly coming home as I tripped on the edge of the tub in my eagerness to join her. (They did return, but we were out of the tub, drying off, and managed to escape.) Or about our first weeks as college freshmen, three hundred miles apart from each other, when she visited me and we made love for the first time, not as in the glow of a romantic Hollywood movie but in a freezing room in an empty motel twenty hitchhiked miles out of town. She wanted to recount these events, and details about me entered and left her book as she reworked her story for her own purposes over six years.

As I read the drafts that Molly showed me, I sometimes seemed to be mainly a pawn in her story. Incidents from my life got shortened or dropped because they didn't fit the book's evolving narrative arc. I wondered whether readers would see me as a figure who in any way resembles the person I think I am. For the first time I thought sympathetically about Richard Best, that minor character in *Ulysses* who listens, unconvinced, to Stephen Dedalus's theory that Shakespeare based his plays on barely transformed events in his life. Best was a historically real person—Joyce uses his actual name—who became a distinguished translator, scholar, and director of the National Library of Ireland. He did not share the unflattering mannerisms and verbal tics that Joyce, partly to revenge himself on the literary figures who he felt had snubbed him years earlier, gave him in print. Fiction and reality blended uncomfortably in Best's life, as he made clear when he responded with annoyance to a BBC interviewer that he was *not* a fictional character but a living being.[4] Best's protests were hopeless, of course: readers of *Ulysses* who know his story may feel a moment's sympathy for him, but any interest they have is in the character and not the flesh-and-blood person. Was I about to become a Richard Best? Were readers going to respond to and maybe even analyze someone else's written portrait of me?

I came to see that a distinction has to be made between exposure, which is against a person's will, and disclosure, which isn't. It made me uncomfortable to realize that the world would know things about my illnesses, professional setbacks, and smaller moments of vulnerability, especially since I don't have the kind of personality that easily reveals such information. That's not the same thing, however, as having your towel suddenly swiped away—an involuntary full monty. I felt more like an actor justifying a nude scene in a film. I used to think that beautiful stars were just showing off their perfect bodies. But as I had to think about my life in its imperfect nakedness, with all the anxieties that provoked, I came to understand the insecurity that these actors must feel but also came to know that, sometimes, the story simply won't work unless the players are fully disrobed.

Letting someone write about that first delicious sight of nakedness or the near comic (Molly and I can now admit) loss of virginity is one thing, but illness and family complications seemed like another matter. In the early 1980s I suffered through two bouts of melanoma, and, in fact, when I first wrote to Molly after I saw the review of *Raw Heaven*, she had just learned about my cancer from a friend of mine and thought I was dying and writing to say good-bye to everyone I knew. When the cancer was new and I was terrified, I talked about it to anyone who would listen, but most people didn't want to hear, and I gradually stopped saying much. Many people who have come to know me since then don't know about it at all. But it seemed essential to Molly's story about our reunion: when we re-met, she had to meet me and my illness, and when we decided to marry, she had to take the cancer along with the rest of me. Janna Malamud Smith claims in her book *Private Matters* that knowing another person "depends on a safe place, a wish to tell honestly, and a listener who can bear to hear."[5] Molly became that listener for me, and since she felt that her story wasn't complete without the melanoma, it became part of her memoir.

My family was a different matter. I gave Molly a release, first informally and eventually legally, to write about my life undisguised and uncensored, but I didn't give her the same right to use my family's private lives. To tell the complex family stories, even though my story is incomplete without them, would involve crucial violations of their privacy. This is the one aspect of my life that I asked Molly to omit from her book, and she agreed to do that.

In the years after Molly wrote *Paradise, Piece by Piece*, though, I often thought about this omission and eventually realized that if I want to understand and talk about my past and how it has affected the person I've become and the choices I've made, I can't speak about myself but not also about my family. Molly has written about her mother's odd combination of neglect and encouragement toward her: in order to push her away and keep her at a safe distance, her mother encouraged her to write or paint or do anything creative, as long as she did it independently. As a result, Molly learned quickly that artistic expression was a positive thing and also that she had an audience, and she has said that she thinks she first began to write in order to reach her mother. Whenever she talks about this, or I read one of her written accounts of it, I almost envy her: if you have to grow up in a neurotic household, you're not often lucky enough to come out of it with your creative instincts encouraged.

As I recount in chapter 2, I remember weekly visits to my grandmother, my father's mother, when I was seven or eight. My father, who was quiet, serious, extremely intelligent, and also remote and very hard to know, packed my brother, my sister, and me into the car and took us to visit her apartment about a mile away from our house. Once we were there, we all sat uncomfortably while my grandmother asked perfunctorily about my mother and then went on to various bits of small talk. My mother—affectionate, loud, and funny—was the kind of person who hardly ever expressed anger, but, in the earliest memories I have, she wasn't speaking to her mother-in-law or to her own brother, who lived in Florida. Over the years, she extended the cut-off list to her sister (off and on), my grandmother's entire family, almost every good friend she ever had, and her second son, my brother. The cut-offs have continued to this day, with my generation repeating the pattern. I've continued to speak to everyone, however, even if at a distance of at least a hundred miles, ever since I left Buffalo for college when I was eighteen.

If Molly learned to create in the hopes of breaking through her mother's wall, I learned to play it very safe in, I eventually saw, a desperate attempt to avoid doing anything that would cause my mother to close the window in her wall and shut me out. I was in my mid-thirties, several years into psychotherapy for what I thought was help in adjusting to my cancer, before I even began to see that there was any problem with my family (never mind that I was already divorced and severed from several formerly close friends), and older still before I began to gain even the small degree of control that I think I now have over my responses to these ruptures.

I went to college to be a math major. I was very good at math in high school, but surely equally important at the time was the psychological neutrality of math. But I got deflected by literature, and specifically by *Ulysses*, which I read at the start of my sophomore year and fell in love with almost instantly. (Three months after Molly Peacock and I broke up, still on the rebound, I met Molly Bloom.) Leopold Bloom hooked me, and from my fascination with Bloom I came to love everything else in *Ulysses*: many of its other characters, its exuberance, its wordplay, its games and puzzles, and especially its view of humanity and of how to live in a modern world. Novels, I was discovering, were saying things that no living person ever said to me, even things I would have been frightened to hear said aloud. No other book spoke to me, or has ever spoken to me, as *Ulysses* does, and in its wonderful and beautiful way, about life's setbacks and tragedies but also about its basic comedy, about how to live and to react to setbacks and betrayals, about the inner strength, dignity, and heroism of an outwardly unassuming and unnoticeable person, and about the sheer exuberance and joy of communicating through language.

"It really makes sense you left math for literature," Molly wrote about me in her poem "The Wheel," and of course it does, even though, when I changed my major, I had shown no aptitude for literature or desire to work with it on any of the psychological or vocational tests I was given in high school and college.[6] Literature gave me access to a world I needed to enter, and talking and writing about it provides me with both the outlet and the safety of relative anonymity that I have to accept as the legacy of my upbringing. Although I've taught a wide range of courses in twentieth-century literature, textual criticism and scholarly editing, electronic hypertext, and film, it is always *Ulysses*, and with it Leopold Bloom, that I come back to, my own Ithaca. I was nineteen years younger than Leopold Bloom when I first read his story, and I'm many more than nineteen years older than him now. The novel has changed very much for me over the years, but my love for it remains as strong as ever. I practically stopped teaching it for several years in the 1980s and early 1990s: students found the book too lengthy, too difficult, too male, and I found the struggle to convince them of its worth too discouraging. But in the mid-1990s I changed my attitude and teaching strategies and found myself reenergized. I threw away all my lecture notes and started teaching without the security I thought they provided me—a major act for someone both as anal-retentive and as shy as I am. Many of my students (although certainly not all) still resist the book more than I would wish, but when one or two people in a class of fifteen or twenty begin to respond strongly, I feel that I have succeeded in my job as a teacher, and I also see new versions of myself as I was when I discovered the book in 1966.

So can a choice to live a life writing about and teaching the creative works of other people be related to issues of privacy? For me, literary scholarship and teaching seem like a calling, not so much because of the poetry and fiction itself (although I am happy to play my small part in promoting an awareness of and love for literature in an age when it needs all the advocates it can find) as because of the balances they provide me between privacy and disclosure, safety and risk, criticism and creativity. I'm lucky to have found *Ulysses*—a novel that for me is about living with opposites—when I did, just as I am lucky to have encountered wonderful teachers and to have twice found the living Molly. Near the end of *Ulysses*, we read a report of Leopold Bloom's assessment of his day: "He had not risked, he did not expect, he had not been disappointed, he was satisfied." What satisfies him are "To have sustained no positive loss. To have brought a positive gain to others. Light to the gentiles" (*U* 17:349–50, 352–53). I'm not a gentile, but Bloom and *Ulysses* have repeatedly given me "a positive gain," something much more important than this relatively modest formulation of the source of Bloom's satisfaction.

Receiving that gift meant being able to say yes to Leopold Bloom, to Molly Bloom, and to *Ulysses*, just as Molly Peacock and I eventually reaffirmed our teenage yeses to each other as middle-aged vows. Joyce knew how profound and complex this simple word could be and how different it is each time it is uttered, whether by Molly Bloom throughout her monologue or by a reader throughout a lifetime of encounters with his novel. Following Joyce and violating Leopold and Molly Bloom's privacy provoked my original attachment to *Ulysses*; studying Joyce's manuscripts allowed that affirmation to become an imaginative connection with another mind at work; and opening the doors on my own privacy helps me better understand and explain, to myself and to others, why many years ago I said to *Ulysses* that I would, yes, and over and over again have continued to say that I will, yes.

Appendix 1. Remarks on the National Library of Ireland's Newly Acquired Joyce Manuscripts

On May 30, 2002, The National Library of Ireland held a press conference in its Front Hall to announce its acquisition of a previously unknown collection of Joyce manuscripts. At the library's request I read a short statement about the documents on that occasion, and I reprised it on June 18, 2002, as part of a plenary talk at the Eighteenth International James Joyce Symposium in Trieste. The text of those remarks follows.

This is an incredible day for the National Library, for Ireland, and for lovers of James Joyce's works and of literature everywhere. All at once, six of Joyce's notebooks, sixteen drafts of *Ulysses* (any one of which would be a cause of excitement on its own), and some typescripts and proofs for *Finnegans Wake*—all completely unknown until now—become part of the National Library of Ireland's collection. The National Library joins the ranks of the major collections of manuscripts of the works of Ireland's greatest novelist.

Writers themselves often cannot or will not speak directly about their creative processes, and Joyce was certainly no exception to this. But the notes, drafts, manuscripts, typescripts, and proofs for their works can speak, and, because they are less guarded than the writers might be, they can even take us closer to the creative process than might the writers' own accounts. The documents can lead us into an area of literary research that sheds a unique and profound light on literature and on human creativity. Often preserved by the authors themselves, the pages can show us the words the authors wrote, those they eliminated or replaced, their false starts and new beginnings, their responses to mistakes the typists or printers made—all the ways the works moved from conception to completion. The documents can't give us direct access to the mental activities that accompanied the writing, but, if the record is complete enough, they can provide incredibly valuable and fascinating evidence of creativity in action. James Joyce provides the best example we have in the English-speaking world of the excitement and value of an author's manuscripts, and the manuscripts take us as close as we can get to Joyce at work.

For over fifty years, we have had a huge amount of manuscript material for Joyce's works, and collections have been established at the University at Buffalo; Cornell, Yale, Harvard, and Princeton universities; the British Library; the Rosenbach Museum and Library in Philadelphia; the Universities of Texas and Tulsa; and the National Library of Ireland. Some important documents, such as fair copies and proofs, survive for *Dubliners* and *A Portrait of the Artist as a Young Man*, but from the start it was the materials for *Ulysses* and *Finnegans Wake* that were thrillingly voluminous. These papers allowed a detailed picture of Joyce at work to emerge. The notebooks revealed the sources he read and used in *Ulysses* and *Finnegans Wake*; the drafts showed the various episodes in gestation and development; and the later typescripts and proofs documented the unbelievable way Joyce built up the books by adding words and phrases to the typed and printed pages as they passed under his eyes—up to a third of the words in parts of *Ulysses* first entered the book in this way. Full as it was, the manuscript record was incomplete, but it allowed scholars to put together as detailed a picture of an artist in the process of creating a major work of Western culture as any record could be imagined to permit.

For the most part, the existing Joyce collections were in place by 1960. No other major documents surfaced in almost forty years, and the record seemed fixed. Then, in 2000, a draft of the "Circe" episode of *Ulysses* came to light, and the National Library of Ireland purchased it. The next year, even more surprisingly, came a draft of the "Eumaeus" episode—hardly anyone knew this draft existed, and almost no one knows who bought it at auction. (I certainly don't.) These two documents opened up the tantalizing possibility that yet more materials survived. Now, all at once, we are presented with two notebooks from Joyce's early adult years, a few documents for *Finnegans Wake*, and, especially, four notebooks full of notes for *Ulysses* and sixteen drafts of *Ulysses* covering almost half (eight) of the book's eighteen episodes. Once again, *Ulysses* demonstrates without a doubt that it is the novel of the twentieth century.

Some of these documents are like long-separated siblings who, after years, even generations, of not knowing about each other's survival are brought together and allowed to reunite. A draft of the "Sirens" episode of *Ulysses* in the National Library collection is the first half of an incomplete early draft of that episode in a copybook held at Buffalo, and a draft of the "Cyclops" episode is the second half of a Buffalo copybook. Together, the four copybooks represent the complete draft stage of those two episodes. Buffalo also possesses six copybooks that contain parts of a single early draft stage of the "Oxen of the Sun" episode—Joyce numbered them 1, 2, 4, 6, 7, and 8 in large red-orange Roman numerals—and these manuscripts are now joined and completed by the National Library's copybooks numbered 3, 5, and 9. Four seemingly stray pages of notes for *Finnegans Wake* fit securely into the middle of a Buffalo *Wake* notebook from which they somehow got separated seventy or so years ago.[1] And Joyce's early notes on aesthetics—quotations and questions he wrote down in 1903, which were first quoted in Herbert Gorman's biography in 1939 and often reproduced from that printed source—are now available for us to read in the handwritten document that Joyce let Gorman transcribe and publish.[2]

Other manuscripts are like relatives whom a family never even knew to exist. The Buffalo collection possesses an early draft of "Proteus," the third episode in *Ulysses*, and this document has long been considered the earliest surviving draft of *Ulysses*. The National Library's collection contains an even earlier version of "Proteus." The "Sirens" episode, eleventh in *Ulysses*, is often seen as a turning point in the book because Joyce decided, for the first time, to make his fictional form match his subject matter in a radical way—here, he wrote an episode about music in the form of a fugue. The National Library's collection contains a very early draft of "Sirens," in the same copybook as the "Proteus" draft, and it shows the episode in a state before Joyce decided to impose the musical form on it. The National Library collection also contains a second draft of "Circe" to join the library's previously acquired one, so now the once-empty record between the early draft at Buffalo and the fair copy at the Rosenbach Museum and Library is filled with not one but two intermediate states of development of the longest and most complex episode in *Ulysses*.

And we have never had any drafts at all of "Scylla and Charybdis," the episode in which Stephen Dedalus expounds his theory of *Hamlet* in the National Library of Ireland, or of the last two episodes, "Ithaca" and "Penelope"— "Ithaca" with its questions and answers about Leopold Bloom's return home to No. 7 Eccles Street with Stephen, Stephen's departure, and Bloom's reunion with Molly after his day out in Dublin and her day at home with Blazes Boylan; and "Penelope" featuring Molly's monologue. The earliest document we have had for these three episodes is the fair copy, the Rosenbach Manuscript. The National Library's collection contains drafts of all three episodes. As an indication of how an author's use of even the simplest words in the language can make a difference, I can think of no better example than the end of "Penelope," where the National Library's draft shows that, as Joyce first composed Molly's last words, she thought, "and I said I would," before he crossed out "would," substituted "will," and then wrote the final word, "yes." That final verb "will" ("and yes I said yes I will Yes" [U 18.1608–9]), so forward looking a memory as a future-tense verb, so decisive in its assertion of human will—how amazing to think that it was once locked in a subjunctive tense, a memory restrained both grammatically and emotionally.

As I have been indicating, the greatest excitement in the National Library's new collection lies in the materials for *Ulysses*. Joyce took eight years to write his book, and his readers have now spent eighty years responding to it, analyzing it, or, as Richard Ellmann put it, "learning to be James Joyce's contemporaries, to understand our interpreter."[3] The drafts are all working documents that precede the fair copy—they show the episodes in states of gestation and in flux, and we can observe Joyce trying out ideas, strengthening some and discarding others, in ways that we cannot in the later typescripts and proofs, where his revisions mostly serve to augment an existing, fixed pattern. The other *Ulysses* materials are notebooks, page after page of notes. Each time Joyce used a note, he crossed it out in a red, blue, or green crayon, and some of the pages are marvels of Technicolor cross-outs. Most of the notebooks are from late stages of Joyce's work, but one, tantalizingly, dates from his early work, a stage of his writing of *Ulysses* that has been almost completely undocumented until now. Once these notes are deciphered and analyzed, they might turn out to provide the most drastic alterations of all to our sense of how Joyce conceived and wrote *Ulysses*.

The French genetic critic Louis Hay has written that "Manuscripts have something new to tell us: it is high time we learned to make them speak."[4] For decades now, we have been learning how to listen to manuscripts. On this great day, thanks to Mr. and Mrs. Alexis Léon's private offer of these materials to the National Library of Ireland, the library's and Ireland's gift to the literary, cultural, and scholarly world presents us all with an extraordinary, unprecedented opportunity to discover the "something new" that these manuscripts can tell us specifically about James Joyce and more generally about the mysteries and marvels of human creativity.

Appendix 2. Extant Manuscripts for *Ulysses* as of Summer 2002

A Chart

In trying to assess the changes in the archive of *Ulysses* manuscripts as a result of the National Library of Ireland's acquisition of new materials in 2002 and the "Circe" and "Eumaeus" documents that surfaced in the two previous years, I prepared a chart that compares the state of the archive up to 2000 with that from after the National Library's announcement of its new collection. To make this chart as complete as possible, for each extant document I've indicated its present location, its catalog number if one exists, and any published photoreproductions or transcriptions. A manuscript in the National Library is labeled with the abbreviation "NLI" and the library's manuscript number. This chart fills in and supplements the episode-by-episode list of extant manuscripts that I provided in *James Joyce's Manuscripts: An Index*.

Documents that existed before 2000 are designated by regular type, and those that have come to light since that date are in boldface type. An arrow indicates that a document leads directly to the next extant stage. A document's position in a column indicates its approximate place in the composition sequence for an episode: the columns are subject to small and large corrections and do not indicate relationships between manuscripts for different episodes.

The chart covers the documents for Joyce's work on each episode up to the Rosenbach Manuscript. At some point during his work on each episode he produced a final working draft or fair copy, and from that point on his revisions function almost exclusively to refine and especially to augment the episode's existing shape. The Rosenbach Manuscript is the extant docu-

Table 1. Extant Manuscripts for *Ulysses* as of Summer 2002

NOTES	Alphabetical Notebook (Cornell item 25; *Archive* 7:109–56; *Workshop* 92–105—partially used for *Ulysses*) / **NLI 36,639/3**	Buffalo VIII.A.5 (*Archive* 12:129–66; *Notes and Early Drafts* 11–33)	British Library 49975 (*Archive* 12:2–95; *Notesheets*)	Buffalo V.A.2 (*Archive* 12:97–125; *Notes and Early Drafts* 55–118) / **NLI 36,639/4, NLI 36,639/5/A, NLI 36,639/5/B**
TELEMACHUS				Rosenbach MS
NESTOR				Rosenbach MS
PROTEUS	**NLI 36,639/7/A**	Buffalo V.A.3 (*Archive* 12:238–58) →		Rosenbach MS
CALYPSO				Rosenbach MS
LOTUS EATERS				[lost final draft] / Rosenbach MS
HADES				[lost final draft] / Rosenbach MS
AEOLUS				[lost final draft] / Rosenbach MS
LESTRYGONIANS				[lost final draft] / Rosenbach MS
SCYLLA AND CHARYBDIS	[LaHune item 254; Slocum item 5.b.iii—now lost]	**NLI 36,639/8/A–C**		[lost final draft] / Rosenbach MS
WANDERING ROCKS				Rosenbach MS
SIRENS	**NLI 36,639/7/A**	**NLI 36,639/9/**; Buffalo V.A.5 (*Archive* 13:32–56)		[lost final draft] / Rosenbach MS
CYCLOPS	Buffalo V.A.8 (*Archive* 13:83–132; *Notes and Early Drafts* 152–77) / **NLI 36,639/10** →	Buffalo V.A.6 (*Archive* 13:134a–h; *Notes and Early Drafts* 178–87)		Rosenbach MS
NAUSICAA		Buffalo V.A.10 (*Archive* 13:175–214) /Cornell 56A–B (*Archive* 13:215–44)		[lost final draft] / Rosenbach MS

OXEN OF THE SUN	Buffalo V.A.11–12 (*Archive* 14:5–56) / **NLI 36,639/11/ A–B** →	Buffalo V.A.13–18 (*Archive* 14:59–132) / **NLI 36,639/11/C-F**	Cornell (uncatalogued; draft of pp. 61–65; *Archive* 14:135–39) → pp. 61–66 of Rosenbach MS	[lost final draft] / Rosenbach MS
CIRCE	Buffalo V.A.19 (*Archive* 14:201–59; Notes and Early Drafts 191–249) →	**NLI 36,639/12** →	**NLI 35,958 (Quinn MS)**	Rosenbach MS
EUMAEUS		**"Eumeo" (current location unknown)** →	Buffalo V.A.21 (*Archive* 15:321–68)	Rosenbach MS
ITHACA		**NLI 36,639/13**		Rosenbach MS
PENELOPE		**NLI 36,639/14**		Rosenbach MS /Buffalo V.A.22 (*Archive* 16:293–97)

ment representing the final-working-draft/fair-copy stage, but it is problematic, since only part of it is the working draft used by the typist for the next stage, whereas the other part is a fair copy which perhaps Joyce made from the working draft in order to sell John Quinn a better looking manuscript.[1] When the Rosenbach Manuscript is the document that was used to prepare an episode's typescript, I have listed only it in the last column. When a lost working draft was presumably used for the typescript, the last column says "[lost final draft]/Rosenbach MS."

A few observations: the pre-2000 chart (the documents in regular type) looks as I imagined it would, with some clusters of extant manuscripts accompanied by many gaps. Flush with excitement from seeing all the new manuscripts, I eagerly anticipated the dramatically different results that I would see when I added the new manuscripts that surfaced in late 2000 and early 2001, and especially those from May 2002. What I saw when I finished it was more manuscripts (with some drafts now completed), somewhat fewer gaps, but basically still several clusters of extant manuscripts accompanied by many missing ones. While an extraordinary number of notes, drafts, and other documents for *Ulysses* are extant, a large amount is not. For eight of the eighteen episodes of *Ulysses*, even now no pre–Rosenbach Manuscript materials exist at all.

I can think of at least two possible explanations for the patterns of extant and non-extant documents:

1. Joyce's working habits changed. As he moved into what in *"Ulysses" in Progress* I called the middle stage ("Wandering Rocks," "Sirens," "Cyclops," "Nausicaa," "Oxen of the Sun"), he started taking more notes and saving more of his papers.[2] Before 2000 only one pre-middle-stage, pre–Rosenbach Manuscript document—the Buffalo "Proteus" draft—was extant. Since late 2000 a few more drafts from early episodes have become extant, but the number remains very small: two drafts for "Proteus" and one for "Scylla and Charybdis."

2. The pattern of extant manuscripts is related to where the documents ended up. Buffalo in the 1940s and 1950s and the National Library in 2002 acquired manuscripts that were in Paris. Cornell has materials that remained in Trieste. The National Library materials, in particular the manuscripts for "Sirens," "Cyclops," and "Oxen of the Sun" that are parts of the same draft stages as documents at Buffalo, highlight how easily documents that Joyce produced as a single draft stage of an episode became separated from each other. This isn't particularly surprising, since he probably didn't pay close attention to a manuscript's location once he had finished using it. The separation of two linked documents, one perhaps tossed into one pile in Paris and another into a different pile, or one left in Trieste and the other sent to Paris, was likely more accidental than planned. Scholars first encountered this situation when the earlier collections were established and Buffalo acquired one "Nausicaa" copybook, which ended up in Paris, while Cornell obtained two other copybooks from the same draft stage of the episode that remained behind in Trieste.

When Rodney Wilson Owen studied the sparsely documented early years of Joyce's work on *Ulysses*, he investigated Joyce's use of notes from the so-called "Alphabetical Notebook" at Cornell (transcribed as "The Trieste Notebook" in Robert Scholes and Richard Kain's *Workshop of Daedalus*) and concluded that "the presence of the notebook echoes in 'Proteus,' 'Scylla,' and to a lesser extent in 'Sirens' and 'Wandering Rocks' suggests these episodes were among the earliest planned."[3] Probably not coincidentally, the only two pre-middle-stage episodes for which any drafts have survived are "Proteus" and "Scylla and Charybdis" (two draft stages would be extant for both episodes if the "Scylla" manuscript that Buffalo thought it had acquired when it bought the La Hune collection had reached Buffalo), and, with the two new drafts of "Sirens" at the National Library—perhaps the most tantalizing and unexpected materials in the new collection—a third episode is accounted for. Given this pattern, the complete absence of pre–Rosenbach Manuscript drafts for "Wandering Rocks" remains puzzling. If they ever do surface, they will probably be fascinating.

The new *Ulysses* materials will likely have only a minimal impact on the text of *Ulysses*. Almost all of them (the only exceptions are the three late *Ulysses* notebooks and the typescript of the schema) precede the Rosenbach Manuscript, or fair copy, stage. Once an episode reached that stage, whether in the extant Rosenbach Manuscript or in a missing final working draft, Joyce considered it finished, even if only provisionally and temporarily, and from then on his revisions mostly involved improving and augmenting an existing pattern. Those documents—the Rosenbach Manuscript and the typescripts and proofs that came after it—provide the most important materials for a textual editor to work with.

Although the new National Library materials will likely have only a small impact on editions, they will be of great interest to genetic critics. As in all his drafts, we can watch Joyce trying out ideas, sketching passages, rejecting some words and phrases, and expanding and revising others. These new documents will help genetic critics, as well as other critics interested in literary creation, catch a glimpse of the writing process that produced such a work as *Ulysses* and better understand some of the particularities and pleasures of both the writing process and *Ulysses* itself.

Notes

Introduction

1. Gilbert, *Joyce's "Ulysses,"* 1st ed., vi; Kevin Dettmar mentions the best-of-the-century lists in "James Joyce and the Great Books"; Goldberg, *James Joyce*, 94; French, *Book as World*, 268; Sherry, *James Joyce: "Ulysses,"* 105; Attridge, *Joyce Effects*, 120; Lewis, *Time and Western Man*, 90.

2. Schwartz, "'In greater support of his word,'" 88; Jones, "Memorial Dublin" and "Ghosts through Absence" (both forthcoming); Schwartz, "'In greater support of his word,'" 86.

3. See Bénéjam, "Stephen and the Venus of Praxiteles."

4. De Biasi, "Horizons for Genetic Studies," 125 (his italics).

5. Alexander Calder in 1933, quoted in Simon, "Alexander Calder," 53; Pierre, "Painting and Working in the Abstract," 234; Mancusi-Ungaro, "Movement as Lifeblood and Death-Knell," 195.

6. W. P. Williams and Abbott, *Introduction to Bibliographical and Textual Studies*, 152.

7. For a brief introduction to genetic criticism, see Deppman, Ferrer, and Groden, "Introduction," and the same authors' "Genetic Criticism." For elaboration on the changes in genetic criticism, see my "Before and After," esp. 163–69.

8. Gifford and Seidman, *"Ulysses" Annotated*, 32.

9. Valéry, "Ego Scriptor," in *Cahiers/Notebooks*, 2:475.

10. Ellmann, *James Joyce*, 430.

11. Poe, "The Philosophy of Composition," 743.

12. Hay, "History or Genesis?" 207.

13. McKenzie, *Bibliography and the Sociology of Texts*; McGann, *A Critique of Modern Textual Criticism*; McGann, *The Textual Condition*, esp. 13–14. A concise introduction to traditional bibliography and textual criticism is in W. P. Williams and Abbott's *Introduction to Bibliographical and Textual Studies*.

14. W. W. Greg, "Bibliography—an Apologia" (1932), cited in McKenzie, *Bibliography and the Sociology of Texts*, 9; Loizeaux and Fraistat, introduction to *Reimagining Textuality*, 5.

15. Bishop, *Riding with Rilke*, 33–36; the "portal" quotation is on 36.

16. Atlas, "Confessing for Voyeurs," 25; S. Smith and Watson, *Reading Autobiography*, xii.

17. Veeser, "Introduction," x–xii, quote on x; Grimes, "We All Have a Life."

18. Tompkins, "Me and My Shadow," 25; Freedman, "Autobiographical Literary Criticism," 12; Behar, "Dare We Say 'I'?" B2.

19. Attridge, *Joyce Effects*, 118 (his italics).

20. Phillip Lopate quoted in Atlas, "Confessing for Voyeurs," 25.

21. Bechdel, *Fun Home*, esp. 201–32.

22. Carlton, "Rereading *Middlemarch*, Rereading Myself," 244; E. Brown, "Between the Medusa and the Abyss," 225; Carlton, "Rereading *Middlemarch*, Rereading Myself," 239; Atlas, "Confessing for Voyeurs," 25.

23. Lejeune, "Auto-Genesis."

24. Dickens, *David Copperfield*, 1. In a message posted on the Joyce-Ulysses Yahoo listserv in June 2007, Richard Stack identified a statement similar to Stephen's "that striking of that match" passage in Collins's 1873 novel: "That trifling action decided the whole future course of her life" (Collins, *The New Magdalen*, 19). *The New Magdalen* also contains several other phrases that are the same as or close to ones in *Ulysses*: "messenger" (39, 72, 74, 91, 104, 132, 155; cf. *U* 7:762, the line before Stephen's "striking of that match" thought: "Messenger took out his matchbox thoughtfully and lit his cigar"), "I see it in your face" (42; *U* 15:3663–64 and *P* 50), "the dead alive" (63, a chapter title; cf. *U* 6:974–75: "the grey alive"), and the proverbial "Coming events cast their shadows before" (82, a chapter title; *U* 8:526).

25. Atlas, "Confessing for Voyeurs," 25.

26. Carlton, "Rereading *Middlemarch*, Rereading Myself," 242; Behar, "Dare We Say 'I'?" B1.

27. S. Smith and Watson, *Reading Autobiography*, 3.

Chapter 1. The Archive in Transition

1. Slote, "Preliminary Comments," 21. See also Selley, "The Lost 'Eumaeus' Notebook."

2. Buffalo's collection is cataloged in Spielberg, *Joyce's Manuscripts and Letters*, and the Cornell collection in Scholes, *Cornell Joyce Collection*. For a checklist of the Joyce manuscripts known to exist in 1980, listed both by Joyce work and by library collection, see my *James Joyce's Manuscripts*. Photoreprints of the documents mentioned here are in *Archive*, vols. 12–27.

3. Gheerbrant, *James Joyce*, item 254; and Slocum and Cahoon, *Bibliography of James Joyce*, item 5.b.iii, p. 140. See also Spielberg, *Joyce's Manuscripts and Letters*, vii.

4. Gorman, *James Joyce*, 96–99, 133–38; *CW* 141–48; Scholes and Kain, *Workshop of Daedalus*, 52–55, 81–91; Joyce, *Occasional, Critical, and Political Writing*, 102–7.

5. Wim Van Mierlo discusses this notebook in "The Subject Notebook."

6. Killeen, "Seller of Joyce Trove," 9 (my ellipsis); "Behind the Scenes," 22.

7. Killeen, "Vast Joyce Manuscript Archive Arrives," 9.

8. D. T. Max quotes the remark, based on my transcription, in his *New Yorker* profile of Stephen James Joyce, "The Injustice Collector," 37.

9. For a brief description of the individual manuscripts, see my "National Library of Ireland's New Joyce Manuscripts," 25–28. Luca Crispi's forthcoming online catalog of the James Joyce Collection at the National Library of Ireland will offer much fuller descriptions.

10. Hay, "Does 'Text' Exist?" 73.

11. Buffalo MS V.A.22; *Archive* 16:297. The Rosenbach Manuscript does not contain the last "sentence" of "Penelope," which is in this Buffalo document.

12. Buffalo TS V.B.16.c, three sets of Harvard placards, Texas page proofs; *Archive* 16:349, 21:368, 21:370, 21:375–76, 27:277.

13. The words are on page 19r (39) of the National Library's "Penelope" draft (NLI MS 36,639/14). I thank Daniel Ferrer for pointing out to me that the change was a *currente calamo* revision, and Luca Crispi for confirming the sequence of Joyce's writing.

14. Ellmann, *James Joyce*, 516.

15. McGann, "The Monks and the Giants," 87.

16. Buffalo MS V.A.5; *Archive* 13:32–56.

17. Groden, *"Ulysses" in Progress*, 124–25.

18. Ellmann, *"Ulysses" on the Liffey*, between 187 and 188; Gilbert, *Joyce's "Ulysses,"* rev. ed., [30]; *L* 1:129.

19. For their help in interpreting Joyce's list, I thank Stephen Adams, Ruth Bauerle, Zack Bowen, Timothy Martin, and Adrienne O'Henly.

20. Owen, *Joyce and the Beginnings of "Ulysses,"* 67–68. For the Cornell notebook, see Scholes, *Cornell Joyce Collection*, 12, item 25 (where it is called "The Alphabetical Notebook"); Scholes and Kain, *Workshop of Daedalus*, 92–105 (where it is called "The Trieste Notebook" and transcribed); and *Archive* 7:109–56. Further and fuller discussion of the new "Sirens" manuscripts is in Ferrer, "What Song the Sirens Sang."

21. Joyce, *Ulysses: A Critical and Synoptic Edition*, 1:418, 3:1738.

22. Joyce, *Ulysses: A Facsimile of the Manuscript*, "Scylla and Charybdis," fol. 13; Joyce, *Ulysses: A Critical and Synoptic Edition* 1:418, 3:1738; *Archive* 12:357.

23. Gifford and Seidman, *"Ulysses" Annotated*, 221.

24. St. Thomas Aquinas, *Summa Contra Gentiles*, book 1, chapter 91, section 3.

25. Noon, *Joyce and Aquinas*, 57.

26. Herr, "Theosophy, Guilt, and 'That Word Known to All Men,'" 51–52. Herr wrote this article before the publication of Gabler's edition of *Ulysses*.

27. Gifford and Seidman, *"Ulysses" Annotated*, 221 (their italics). For a different analysis of the passage, including textual arguments for including or not including it in the text of *Ulysses*, see Finneran, "'That Word Known to All Men' in *Ulysses*."

Chapter 2. When First I Saw, Part 1

1. Kevin Dettmar mentions these various best-of-the-century lists in "James Joyce and the Great Books."

2. Fordham, "'Circe' and the Genesis of Multiple Personality," 509.

3. Hay, "Does 'Text' Exist?" 73.

4. Kiberd, *"Ulysses" and Us*, 66.

5. Joyce, "A Portrait of the Artist," 60.

6. Woolf, "Modern Fiction," 151, 155. Woolf made the same argument in the same words in the earlier "Modern Novels."

7. Joyce, "A Portrait of the Artist," 60.

Chapter 3. From Monument to Mobile

1. Peake, *James Joyce*, 196–97.
2. Blamires, *The New Bloomsday Book*, 58–59; Schwarz, *Reading Joyce's "Ulysses,"* 122; Schwaber, *The Cast of Characters*, 154; Peake, *James Joyce*, 197.
3. Sultan, *The Argument of "Ulysses,"* 115–16; Duffy, *The Subaltern "Ulysses,"* 170; McGee, "Machines, Empire, and the Wise Virgins," 87.
4. First set of placards: *Archive* 18:67–68, 18:87; second set of placards: *Archive* 18:95; first set of page proofs: *Archive* 23:69–71; three subsequent sets of page proofs: *Archive* 23:69–71, 23:85–87, 23:101–3.
5. *Archive* 18:95; *Ulysses*, Odyssey Press ed., 152; *Archive* 18:21.
6. Rosenbach Manuscript, "Aeolus," 32; "Aeolus" typescript: Buffalo TS V.B.5, p. 17; *Archive* 12:302.
7. Bowers, *Textual and Literary Criticism*, 4, 5.
8. Wellek and Warren, *Theory of Literature*, 137, 57, 91.
9. Stauffer, "Genesis," 43–44 (my ellipsis).
10. McGann, "*Ulysses* as a Postmodern Work," 185.
11. Rabaté, *Joyce and the Politics of Egoism*, 203.
12. Larbaud, "The *Ulysses* of James Joyce," 102; also Benco, "James Joyce in Trieste," 57.
13. Budgen, *Joyce and the Making of "Ulysses,"* 172.
14. Groden, *"Ulysses" in Progress*, 4, 23.
15. Ibid., 4.
16. Ibid., 200–201 (ellipsis added).
17. Litz, *The Art of James Joyce*, v; Litz, "Uses of the *Finnegans Wake* Manuscripts," 103.
18. Crispi and Slote, *How Joyce Wrote "Finnegans Wake,"* 5.
19. Wellek and Warren, *Theory of Criticism*, 73, 91.
20. James, *The Art of the Novel*, 27, 119, 119, 121, 140.
21. See, for instance, ITEM's journal *Genesis: Manuscrits/Recherche/Invention*, and Deppman, Ferrer, and Groden, *Genetic Criticism*.
22. Stauffer, "Genesis," 41.
23. Grésillon, "Slow: Work in Progress," 110, 108 (her italics, my ellipses).
24. De Biasi, "Horizons for Genetic Studies," 125 (his italics); Contat, Hollier, and Neefs, "Editors' Preface," 2 (my ellipses); Hay, "Does 'Text' Exist?" 75 (his italics).
25. Groden, *"Ulysses" in Progress*, 23; Contat, Hollier, and Neefs, "Editors' Preface," 1.
26. Valéry, "Poetry," in *Cahiers/Notebooks*, 2:219; Valéry, "Ego Scriptor," in *Cahiers/Notebooks*, 2:475 (his italics; my ellipsis).
27. Bellemin-Noël, "Psychoanalysis and the Avant-texte," 31 (his italics).
28. Ferrer, "Clementis's Cap," 230, 230; Ferrer, "Production, Invention, and Reproduction," 51; Ferrer, "Clementis's Cap," 234 (in all cases, his italics, my ellipses).
29. MacLeish, "Ars Poetica," 1284; Bowman, "Genetic Criticism," 644.
30. Grésillon, "**Still** *Lost Time*," 155 (her bold text); Debray Genette, "Flaubert's 'A Simple Heart,'" 93.
31. Ferrer and Rabaté, "Paragraphs in Expansion," 133; McGann, *The Textual Condition*, 13–14.

32. Ferrer and Rabaté, "Paragraphs in Expansion," 149 (my ellipsis).
33. Rabaté, *Joyce and the Politics of Egoism*, 196, 202, 207, 207.
34. Gilbert, *Joyce's "Ulysses,"* rev. ed., 179.
35. Frank, "Spatial Form in Modern Literature," 10, 12, 63 (my ellipsis).

Chapter 4. When First I Saw, Part 2

1. Bellemin-Noël, "Psychoanalysis and the Avant-texte," 31 (his italics).
2. Ferrer, "Production, Invention, and Reproduction," 51.
3. Ferrer, "Clementis's Cap," 234 (his italics).
4. British Library "Cyclops" notesheet 8:68; *Archive* 12:11; *Notesheets*, 115; *U* 12:68.
5. British Library "Cyclops" notesheet 5:76; *Archive* 12:7; *Notesheets*, 102; *U* 12:1628-30.
6. British Library "Cyclops" notesheet 5:1; *Archive* 12:7; *Notesheets*, 100; cf. *U* 18:846-47.
7. For example, see Buffalo MS V.A.8, pp. [20v] and [21r] (Joyce's 21v and 22r); *Archive* 13:124-25. Joyce skipped 16 when he numbered the copybook's pages.
8. Buffalo MS V.A.6, p. 2r; *Archive* 13:134c; *Notes and Early Drafts*, 181.
9. Buffalo MS V.A.6, p. 2v; *Archive* 13:134d; *Notes and Early Drafts*, 182. Here and in other quotations from the manuscripts, to indicate Joyce's revisions I have retained some of the symbols that Hans Walter Gabler used for the synoptic text in *Ulysses: A Critical and Synoptic Edition*. A pair of carets (^ / ^) indicates the first revision to a passage. Text that Joyce deleted and replaced with other text is indicated by angle brackets (< / >); text that Joyce deleted without a replacement is indicated by square brackets ([/]). See Joyce, *Ulysses: A Critical and Synoptic Edition*, esp. x.
10. Buffalo MS V.A.6, p. 1v; *Archive* 13:134b; *Notes and Early Drafts*, 179.
11. Buffalo MS V.A.6, p. 6; *Archive* 13:134f; *Notes and Early Drafts*, 185.
12. British Library "Cyclops" notesheet 3:36-39; *Archive* 12:4; *Notesheets*, 92. A third version of the poem, falling between the British Library version and the one in Buffalo MS V.A.6, is in the National Library of Ireland's "Cyclops" MS 36,639/10, p. 1v.
13. Buffalo MS V.A.8, p. 1r; *Archive* 13:85; *Notes and Early Drafts*, 152.
14. Buffalo MS V.A.8, p. [21r] (Joyce's 22r); *Archive* 13:125; *Notes and Early Drafts*, 170.
15. Luca Crispi's forthcoming online catalog of the Buffalo Joyce collection will offer a correct description of the "Cyclops" drafts and will also include documents that Buffalo acquired after Spielberg prepared his catalog in 1962.
16. Litz, *The Art of James Joyce*, 6, 9.
17. Grésillon, "Slow: Work in Progress," 110 (her italics; my ellipsis).
18. Ellmann, *James Joyce*, 467-69.

Chapter 5. *The James Joyce Archive* and Hans Walter Gabler's Edition of *Ulysses*

1. Riddell, "People's Joyce," 57, 72b. I learned about Riddell's parody in Dettmar's "James Joyce and the Great Books."
2. Hayashi, *James Joyce*, 10.
3. Shillingsburg, *Scholarly Editing in the Computer Age*, 3.

4. Dettmar, "James Joyce and the Great Books." Ernst and Lindey's statements are reproduced in Moscato and LeBlanc, *The United States of America v. One Book Entitled "Ulysses" by James Joyce*, 243, 255–56. See also Kelly, *Our Joyce*, 92–140, and Vanderham, *James Joyce and Censorship*, 91–99.

5. Budgen, *Joyce and the Making of "Ulysses,"* 172 (my ellipsis).

6. The history of Buffalo's Joyce collection is documented in three essays in Maynard, *Discovering James Joyce*, which is the catalog of an exhibition mounted at the University at Buffalo's Anderson Gallery in summer 2009: Basinski, "Foreword and Acknowledgments," esp. 11–15; Silverman, "Why Buffalo?" (a reprint of a 1964 article); and Crispi, "Sylvia Beach's Joyce Collection at Buffalo." See also Spielberg, *Joyce's Manuscripts and Letters*, vii.

7. Scholes, *Cornell Joyce Collection*, esp. v–vii. See also Mizener, *The Cornell Joyce Collection*.

8. Garland Publishing Inc. Records, Princeton University. Consulted April 26, 2005.

9. In a special "25th Anniversary of the *James Joyce Archive*" issue of *Genetic Joyce Studies* from summer 2002, Hayman and Gabler present their own accounts of working on the *Archive*. The issue also includes articles on working with the *Archive* by Bill Cadbury, Luca Crispi, R. J. Schork, and Fritz Senn.

10. Herring, review of *James Joyce Archive*, 97, 87.

11. Ibid., 97.

12. J. P. P[ostgate], "Textual Criticism," 715 (my ellipses).

13. See Slote, *"Ulysses" in the Plural*, 3; Buffalo MSS V.D.1.a, p. 11, and V.D.1.b, p. 2; and Spielberg, *Joyce's Manuscripts and Letters*, 89–90.

14. A succinct account of copytext editing is in W. P. Williams and Abbott, *Introduction to Bibliographical and Textual Studies*, 82–83, 87–102. The most complete discussion and justification of the issue of "final authorial intention" is Tanselle's "Editorial Problem of Final Authorial Intention." For German editing see Gabler, Bornstein, and Pierce, *Contemporary German Editorial Theory*, especially Gabler's introduction, 1–16.

15. Parts of this account of Gabler's edition are a condensed version of sections of my afterword to the 1993 *Ulysses: The Gabler Edition*.

16. The phrase "the work as he wrote it" is in Gabler's afterword to *Ulysses: A Critical and Synoptic Edition*, 3:1891, and "*Ulysses* as Joyce wrote it" is in his afterword to the 1986 *Ulysses: The Corrected Text*, 649, and in his foreword to the 1993 *Ulysses: The Gabler Edition*, xvii.

17. Gabler, afterword to *Ulysses: The Corrected Text*, 649.

18. McDowell, "New Edition Fixes 5,000 Errors," 1, C9; Gabler, afterword to *Ulysses: The Corrected Text*, [650].

19. Gabler, foreword to *Ulysses: A Critical and Synoptic Edition*, 1:viii; McGann, "*Ulysses* as a Postmodern Work," 174.

20. Remnick, "War over 'Ulysses'"; Kidd, "Errors of Execution in the 1984 *Ulysses*"; Gabler, "A Response to: John Kidd, 'Errors of Execution in the 1984 *Ulysses*.'"

21. The conference talks and discussions were transcribed and published in a special issue of the *James Joyce Literary Supplement*: "*Ulysses*: The Text—The Debates of the Miami J'yce Conference."

22. Groden, "A Response to John Kidd's 'An Inquiry into *Ulysses*,'" 81, 108.

23. "Inside Publishing," 11.
24. Mahaffey, "Intentional Error," 183, 172 (her italics); Knowles, *The Dublin Helix*, 1–4, esp. 3.
25. McGann, "*Ulysses* as a Postmodern Work," 182.
26. Spoo, "*Ulysses* and the Ten Years War," 108, 110–11 (my ellipsis).
27. Mays, "Gabler's *Ulysses* as a Field of Force," 10, 12.
28. Bornstein, *Material Modernism*, 138, 138–39.

Chapter 6. Revisiting the "Cyclops" Manuscripts, Part 1

1. Groden, *"Ulysses" in Progress*, 4–5, 200–203 (ellipsis added).
2. Ibid., 51, 21, 4; palimpsest: 4, 23, 32.
3. Barthes, "From Work to Text," 57–58 (his italics, my ellipses).
4. The concept of intertextuality, developed by Julia Kristeva in her reading of Bakhtin, is summarized concisely by Barthes in "Theory of the Text," 39.
5. Gabler, "Textual Criticism," 713. The quoted passage is not in Gabler's revised "Textual Criticism" entry in the second edition of *The Johns Hopkins Guide to Literary Criticism and Theory*.
6. Cerquiglini, "Variantes d'auteur et variance de copiste," 118. Scholars working on and editing manuscripts of other authors have also argued that the relationship between early drafts and published work need not be one of preliminary to final state of a work. See, for example, Silver, "Textual Criticism as Feminist Practice," esp. 204ff.
7. Buffalo and Cornell have numbered their holdings; see Spielberg's and Scholes's catalogs of the two collections. The notes are Buffalo MS V.A.2; the lists are Buffalo V.A.7 and Cornell item 55; the "Cyclops" drafts are Buffalo V.A.8, completed by National Library of Ireland MS 36,639/10, and Buffalo V.A.6, with short passages in Buffalo V.A.2, V.A.7, and V.A.9; the typescripts are Buffalo V.B.10.a and 10.b; and Buffalo's proofs are V.C.1. Groden, *"Ulysses" in Progress*, 120–21, provides a tabular account of the "Cyclops" documents (not including, of course, the National Library draft, which the library acquired in 2002). Except for the National Library draft and the Rosenbach Manuscript, the "Cyclops" documents are reproduced in *Archive*, vols. 12, 13, 19, and 25.
8. Hay, "Does 'Text' Exist?" 70.
9. Groden, *"Ulysses" in Progress*, 115–65, esp. 139, 151–52; *Notes and Early Drafts*, 124–49, esp. 128, 149; Gabler, "Joyce's Text in Progress," 230.
10. Buffalo MS V.A.8, pp. 1r, 20r; *Archive* 13:85, 121; *Notes and Early Drafts*, 152, 166. See chapter 4, note 9, for an explanation of the symbols in the transcriptions from the manuscripts.
11. Budgen, "Further Recollections of James Joyce," 320 (Budgen's ellipsis). See also Groden, *"Ulysses" in Progress*, 124.
12. Barthes, "Theory of the Text," 33.
13. Gilbert, *Joyce's "Ulysses,"* rev. ed., [30].
14. Groden, *"Ulysses" in Progress*, 126–28.
15. Buffalo MS V.A.8, pp. 11r, 12r; *Archive* 13:105–7; *Notes and Early Drafts*, 161–62.

16. Groden, *"Ulysses" in Progress*, 139.
17. Gabler, "Joyce's Text in Progress," 229.
18. Groden, *"Ulysses" in Progress*, 129.
19. Bakhtin, "From the Prehistory," 47 (his italics).
20. Ibid., 65, 61.
21. Groden, *"Ulysses" in Progress*, 124.
22. Bakhtin, "From the Prehistory," 48–49.
23. Booth, *Rhetoric of Fiction*, 71 and throughout; Hayman, *"Ulysses": The Mechanics of Meaning*, 84 and throughout.
24. Buffalo MS V.A.8, pp. 11v, 12r; *Archive* 13:106–7; *Notes and Early Drafts*, 162.
25. Groden, *"Ulysses" in Progress*, 124, 130–31; Buffalo MS V.A.8, p. 1r; *Archive* 13:85; *Notes and Early Drafts*, 152.
26. Groden, *"Ulysses" in Progress*, 130–31.
27. Buffalo MS V.A.8, p. 1v; *Archive* 13:86; *Notes and Early Drafts*, 154; Groden, *"Ulysses" in Progress*, 125.
28. Buffalo MS V.A.8, p. 1v; *Archive* 13:86; *Notes and Early Drafts*, 154, 153; Groden, *"Ulysses" in Progress*, 125. A question mark at the start of a word indicates that the transcription of Joyce's handwriting is uncertain.
29. Groden, *"Ulysses" in Progress*, 126.
30. Buffalo MS V.A.8, p. 2r; *Archive* 13:87; *Notes and Early Drafts*, 154.
31. Buffalo MS V.A.8, p. 1r; *Archive* 13:85; *Notes and Early Drafts*, 152–53; Groden, *"Ulysses" in Progress*, 125. The second layer of revision is indicated by rotated carets (> / <).
32. Buffalo MS V.A.8, p. 1v; *Archive* 13:86; *Notes and Early Drafts*, 154.
33. Bakhtin, "From the Prehistory," 76.
34. Ferrer, "What Song the Sirens Sang," 60, 66 n. 19.
35. Gabler, "Joyce's Text in Progress," 219.
36. Groden, *"Ulysses" in Progress*, 55.
37. Gabler, "Joyce's Text in Progress," 228.
38. See also *Ulysses: A Critical and Synoptic Edition*, 1:616.
39. Hay, "Does 'Text' Exist?" 68–69.
40. *L* 1:128; Joyce to Pound quoted in Ellmann, *James Joyce*, 416; Gabler, "Joyce's Text in Progress," 224.
41. Ellmann, *James Joyce*, 521.
42. Gabler, "Joyce's Text in Progress," 229.
43. Hay, "Does 'Text' Exist?" 75 (his italics); McGann, "The Monks and the Giants," 87.
44. Buffalo MS V.A.8, p. 22r, MS V.A.6, fol. 2r; *Archive* 13:125, 134c; *Notes and Early Drafts*, 170, 181; Groden, *"Ulysses" in Progress*, 133–34, 135–37; cf. *U* 12:1628–30.
45. Groden, *"Ulysses" in Progress*, 135, 137.

Chapter 7. Revisiting the "Cyclops" Manuscripts, Part 2

1. The British Library notesheets are reproduced in *Archive* 12:2–95 (the "Cyclops" notes are on 12:2–13) and transcribed by Phillip Herring in *Joyce's "Ulysses" Notesheets in the Brit-*

ish Museum (81–124 for "Cyclops"). The Buffalo notebooks are VIII.A.5 (*Archive* 12:129–66; transcribed by Herring in *Notes and Early Drafts*, 1–33) and V.A.2 (*Archive* 12:97–125; *Notes and Early Drafts*, 35–118; "Cyclops" pages are *Archive* 12:114–16 and *Notes and Early Drafts*, 95–100). In addition, the "Alphabetical Notebook" held in the Cornell University Library (item 25; *Archive* 7:109–56) and transcribed as "The Trieste Notebook" in Scholes and Kain, *Workshop of Daedalus*, 92–105, though not primarily a *Ulysses* notebook, contains some notes that Joyce used in *Ulysses*. On the basis of Madame France Raphael's transcriptions in the 1930s of Joyce's unused notes in his many notebooks, Danis Rose and John O'Hanlon attempt to re-create a lost *Ulysses* notebook (MS VI.D.7 in Spielberg's Buffalo catalog, *Joyce's Manuscripts and Letters*); see Joyce, *James Joyce: The Lost Notebook*. Rose isolates another lost *Ulysses* notebook, but it turns out to consist of transcriptions of the unused notes not from a single notebook but from the four National Library gatherings of notes; see Buffalo MS VI.D.4; *James Joyce: The Lost Notebook*, ix, xxi; and Rose, *Textual Diaries of James Joyce*, 37. The National Library of Ireland's policy is to refer to the documents by collection number followed by document number; its four notebooks are MSS 36,639/3, 36,639/4, 36,639/5/A, and 36,639/5/B. Wim Van Mierlo discusses notebook 36,639/3 in "The Subject Notebook."

2. "Cyclops" notesheets 5:18–19, 5:20, 5:29, 5:41–42; *Notesheets*, 100–101.

3. National Library of Ireland MS 36,639/3, p. 15r, and Weininger, *Collected Aphorisms*, 20. See also Killeen, *"Ulysses" Unbound*, 258. I thank Luca Crispi, Vincent Deane, and Wim van Mierlo for sharing their ideas about the National Library notes with me.

4. Owen, *Joyce and the Beginnings of "Ulysses,"* 4.

5. See, for example, Groden, *"Ulysses" in Progress*, 142.

6. See Joyce, *"Ulysses:* Episode Twelve [first part]," 50–52; Groden, *"Ulysses" in Progress*, 161–62; National Library of Ireland MS 36,639/4, p. 6r, MS 36,639/5/A, p. 8v, and MS 36,639/5/B, p. 9v.

7. Groden, *"Ulysses" in Progress*, 119 n. 6.

8. Buffalo MS V.A.8, p. [24r] (Joyce's 25r); *Archive* 13:131; *Notes and Early Drafts*, 174; National Library of Ireland MS 36,639/10, pp. 1r, 2r; cf. *U* 12:1122. See chapter 4, note 9, for an explanation of the symbols in the transcriptions from the manuscripts.

9. Buffalo MS V.A.8, p. [22r] (Joyce's 23r); *Archive* 13:127; *Notes and Early Drafts*, 146, 177 n. 58.

10. See Daniel Ferrer's account of the "Sirens" part of National Library of Ireland MS 36,639/7/A in "What Song the Sirens Sang," esp. 57–60.

11. Budgen, *Joyce and the Making of "Ulysses,"* 154.

12. The list includes scenes for the episode's first half and is the missing companion to Buffalo MS V.A.7, a single page that lists events from the episode's second half. See *Archive* 13:136; *Notes and Early Drafts*, 129–30; and Groden, *"Ulysses" in Progress*, 122.

13. The next draft is Buffalo MS V.A.6; *Archive* 13:134a–h; *Notes and Early Drafts*, 178–87. The fair copy is in Joyce, *Ulysses: A Facsimile of the Manuscript*.

14. See Groden, *"Ulysses" in Progress*, 119 n. 6.

15. See Litz, *The Art of James Joyce*, 12. Litz quotes a comment by Valery Larbaud from 1922. See also Budgen, *Joyce and the Making of "Ulysses,"* 174, and Gorman, *James Joyce*, 238.

16. Joyce prepared the better-known schema in fall 1921 to help Valery Larbaud as he put together a lecture on *Ulysses*, and he permitted Stuart Gilbert to publish this schema in *James Joyce's "Ulysses"* (rev. ed., [30]). Earlier, in September 1920, he sent an Italian schema to Carlo Linati (*SL* 270–71), which is transcribed and translated in Ellmann, *"Ulysses" on the Liffey*, between 187 and 188.

17. *Notes and Early Drafts*, 4.

18. On this point see Ferrer, "What Song the Sirens Sang," 53–62. The National Library "Proteus"-"Sirens" draft is MS 36,639/7/A.

19. Groden, *"Ulysses" in Progress*, 133.

20. The "Ithaca" draft is National Library MS 36,639/13.

21. Owen, *Joyce and the Beginnings of "Ulysses,"* 65–68, 113.

22. *Notesheets*, 16.

23. Deppman, Ferrer, and Groden, "Introduction," 11.

24. Max Saunders quoted in Fordham, "'Circe' and the Genesis of Multiple Personality," 507.

25. Greenblatt, "The Death of Hamnet," 42, for both quotations.

26. Budgen, *Joyce and the Making of "Ulysses,"* 15, 17; Ellmann, *James Joyce*, 436; *L* 1:135.

27. Ellmann, *James Joyce*, 467–68, 279.

28. Gorman, *James Joyce*, 239, 241; Maddox, *Nora*, 149.

29. Budgen, *Joyce and the Making of "Ulysses,"* 327; Ellmann, *James Joyce*, 438–39; McCourt, *Years of Bloom*, 89–91, 217–38.

30. See also Crispi, "Manuscript Timeline 1905–1922."

31. On responses to Joyce's work, see Fordham, "'Circe' and the Genesis of Multiple Personality," esp. 507, 511, and 515, and Nash, *Joyce and the Act of Reception*.

32. Gillespie, *Inverted Volumes Improperly Arranged*, 93–96; see also the more extended bibliographical descriptions in Gillespie with Stocker, *James Joyce's Trieste Library*.

33. Darnton, "What Is the History of Books?" 111–12, 124.

34. Bush, "James Joyce," 524, for both quotations (my ellipsis). Bush quotes Arnold Goldman's review of Richard Ellmann's revised *James Joyce*, "'Now' in the 'Post-Now' Era," 1.

35. Brief accounts of Zurich at this time are in Budgen, *Joyce and the Making of "Ulysses,"* 30–35; Gorman, *James Joyce*, 260; and, echoing Gorman, Ellmann, *James Joyce*, 446–47.

36. Svevo, *James Joyce*, [14]; Benco, "James Joyce in Trieste," 53. Regarding Joyce's lectures and articles, see McCourt, *Years of Bloom*, esp. 98–121, and Spoo, "Tropics of Joycean Discourse," 819.

37. Budgen, *Joyce and the Making of "Ulysses,"* 187 (my ellipsis); Budgen, *Myselves When Young*, 199. Budgen quotes "Dooleysprudence" (*CW* 246, 247), although the extant versions of the poem say "coolest chap" rather than Budgen's "coolest card" (see *Archive* 1:310, 1:314).

38. Ellmann, *James Joyce*, 472; Budgen, *Joyce and the Making of "Ulysses,"* 166; Gorman, *James Joyce*, 241–42 (my ellipsis); Ellmann, *James Joyce*, 383.

39. Stoppard, *Travesties*, 65.

40. Gorman, *James Joyce*, 229–30; Benco, "James Joyce in Trieste," 55; Ellmann, *James Joyce*, 389.

41. Eugene Jolas, "My Friend James Joyce," 4 (also quoted in Hartshorn, *James Joyce and Trieste*, 66); Ellmann, *James Joyce*, 441; Sherry, *Joyce: "Ulysses,"* 11 (my ellipsis).

42. Kiberd, introduction to *Ulysses: Annotated Students' Edition*, ix; Spoo, "'Nestor' and the Nightmare," 139; Barham, *Forgotten Lunatics of the Great War*, 389 n. 12. I was led to Barham's book by Alistair Stead's note, "Great War *Ulysses*."

43. Manganiello, *Joyce's Politics*, 153; Kiberd, introduction to *Ulysses: Annotated Students' Edition*, ix.

44. Spoo, *Joyce and the Language of History*, 177 n. 24. Spoo elaborates on this topic in "'Nestor' and the Nightmare," where he cites E. L. Epstein's claim that Stephen's thoughts about the students' hockey game feature "disguised World War I imagery" (138, citing Epstein, "Nestor," 23).

45. Fairhall, *Joyce and the Question of History*, 167, 194. Fairhall quotes Budgen, *Joyce and the Making of "Ulysses,"* 67–68.

46. Buffalo MS V.A.8, p. 19v; *Archive* 13:120; *Notes and Early Drafts*, 169 (my ellipses). The next draft is in MS V.A.6, p. 3; *Archive* 13:134c; *Notes and Early Drafts*, 180–81.

47. Ellmann, *James Joyce*, 464–65.

48. Spoo, "'Nestor' and the Nightmare," 148.

49. Budgen, "Joyce's Chapters of Going Forth by Day," 363.

50. Ellmann, *James Joyce*, 704; Manganiello, *Joyce's Politics*, 43.

51. Gorman, *James Joyce*, 234.

52. See Ellmann, *James Joyce*, 399; Manganiello, *Joyce's Politics*, 164–65; and Joyce, *Lost Notebook*, xxii–xxv, and Rose and O'Hanlon's supplemental "Afterword (Note and erratum received *trop tard*)."

53. Nolan, *James Joyce and Nationalism*, 129, 130.

54. Radford, "King, Pope, and Hero-Martyr," esp. 311 and 322 n. 24; Jones, "Memorial Dublin" and "Ghosts through Absence" (both forthcoming), with references to Duffy's *Subaltern "Ulysses."*

55. Watson, "The Politics of *Ulysses*," 41.

56. Gibson, *Joyce's Revenge*, 107, 103–4.

57. Watson, "The Politics of *Ulysses*," 48 (my ellipsis), 44, 54.

58. Sherry, *Joyce: "Ulysses,"* 11. In "*Százharminczbrojúgulyás-Dugulás*: Bloom, Hungary, and the Spectre of the Citizen Haunting Post-Communist Europe," a lecture delivered at the Twentieth International James Joyce Symposium in Szombathely, Hungary, on June 16, 2006, Ferenc Takács discussed ways in which Joyce's Citizen in "Cyclops" prefigured nationalist leaders who arose in new or newly reformed nations following the end of World War I and again after the collapse of the Soviet Union in the late 1980s. See Radford, "King, Pope, and Hero-Martyr," 320, for a similar discussion.

59. Gibson, *Joyce's Revenge*, 117, 113; Fairhall, *Joyce and the Question of History*, 183 (the phrase "knowable community" is from R. Williams, *The Country and the City*, 165, and "imagined community" is from Anderson, *Imagined Communities*); Gibson, *Joyce's Revenge*, 107–8.

60. Gibson, *Joyce's Revenge*, 123.

61. Radford, "King, Pope, and Hero-Martyr," 320.
62. Hartshorn, *James Joyce and Trieste*, 112; Ellmann, *James Joyce*, 417.
63. See *L* 1:114–15, 1:123; 2:418 n. 3, 2:436–37; and Norburn, *A James Joyce Chronology*, 82–83, 86, 95. I have used Norburn's concise compendium of events in Joyce's life here and elsewhere in this chapter.
64. Information in this paragraph comes from the Mayo Clinic's online articles about iritis, uveitis, and glaucoma.
65. Gottfried, *Joyce's Iritis*, 10, 9, 12, 12. See also the essays by Ruth Frehner, Christa-Maria Lerm Hayes, Fritz Senn, and Ursula Zeller, in Zeller, Frehner, and Vogel, *James Joyce: "gedacht durch meine Augen"/"thought through my eyes."*
66. Budgen, *Joyce and the Making of "Ulysses,"* 173.
67. Slocum and Cahoon, *Bibliography of James Joyce*, 140; and Spielberg, *Joyce's Manuscripts and Letters*, vii n. 1. For a discussion of the "Proteus" draft see Ferrer, "What Song the Sirens Sang," 53–57.
68. Christie's New York, "James Joyce's *Ulysses*," 14, 21.
69. Selley, "The Lost 'Eumaeus' Notebook," 6–9, 11–14, 16–17, 19–27. See also Slote, "Preliminary Comments."
70. Gorman, *James Joyce*, 254; cf. Ellmann, *James Joyce*, 427.
71. Rushing, "The English Players Incident," 384.
72. Ellmann, *James Joyce*, 447.
73. See, for example, ibid., 426–28, 439–47.
74. *Every Man's Own Lawyer*, 54th ed., listed in Gillespie, *Inverted Volumes Improperly Arranged*, 94, and Gillespie with Stocker, *James Joyce's Trieste Library*, 93.
75. Rushing, "The English Players Incident," 373; cf. Gorman, *James Joyce*, 254. The four poems are in Joyce, *Poems and Shorter Writings*, 122–25 (poems 26, 27, 30, and 31), and three of them are in *Archive* 1:316–17, 1:320–21, and 1:321.
76. Rushing, "The English Players Incident," 387.
77. Ellmann, *James Joyce*, 462; Gorman, *James Joyce*, 263.
78. Ellmann, *James Joyce*, 459n; Shakespeare, *Troilus and Cressida*, 1009; Ellmann, *James Joyce*, 412.
79. Ellmann, *James Joyce*, 448; *P* 171.
80. Ellmann, *James Joyce*, 448–52; Budgen, *Myselves When Young*, 187–94, especially 194.
81. Ellmann, *James Joyce*, 451.
82. Rushing, "The English Players Incident," 377.
83. Ellmann, *James Joyce*, 449–50; *U* 11:860, 11:889.
84. Ellmann, *James Joyce*, 457, 480–81; Weaver to Joyce, July 6, 1919, in Weaver, "Harriet Weaver's Letters to James Joyce," 181–82; *SL* 240–41; and Lidderdale and Nicholson, *Dear Miss Weaver*, 157–60.
85. Ellmann, *James Joyce*, 457, 481, 467–68.
86. Maddox, *Nora*, 149; Shloss, *Lucia Joyce*, 67.
87. Ellmann, *James Joyce*, 433; Budgen, *Myselves When Young*, 188; Ellmann, *James Joyce*, 445.

88. Here and in the rest of this paragraph, I thank Luca Crispi for helping to set me straight regarding the different handwritings on these pages.

89. Buffalo MS V.A.8, p. 10r; *Archive* 13:103; *Notes and Early Drafts*, 160; *U* 12:1198–99.

90. Eliot, *The Waste Land*, [14]–15, 139 (*The Waste Land*, 1.164). I thank Sebastian Knowles for directing me to Vivien Eliot's remark on *The Waste Land*'s manuscript pages.

91. Gorman, *James Joyce*, 254; Ellmann, *James Joyce*, 459.

92. Joyce to Pound quoted in Ellmann, *James Joyce*, 416; Joyce to Weaver in *L* 1:128.

93. *L* 1:205, quoted in Fordham, "'Circe' and the Genesis of Multiple Personality," 518.

94. Ferrer, "Clementis's Cap," 234 (his italics).

Chapter 8. Mobile Pages

1. Buffalo MS V.A.3, p. 15; *Archive* 12:253. Ferrer and Rabaté discuss this sequence of word options in "Paragraphs in Expansion," 144–45.

2. Gifford and Seidman, *"Ulysses" Annotated*, 62.

3. McCarthy, "*Ulysses* and the Printed Page," 62.

4. McGann, *The Textual Condition*, 13–14.

5. Gifford and Seidman, *"Ulysses" Annotated*, 131.

6. Photoreproductions of three of the four pages I describe in this and the next paragraph are in *Archive* 18:3, 18:12, and 18:13.

7. Knowles, *The Dublin Helix*, 37.

8. Gilbert, *Joyce's "Ulysses,"* rev. ed., 179 n. 1 (his italics).

9. Groden, *"Ulysses" in Progress*, 105–10.

10. Gilbert, *Joyce's "Ulysses,"* rev. ed., 179 and 179 n. 1.

11. Gilbert, introduction to *Ulysses*, xii. I thank Paul Meahan for calling Gilbert's introduction to my attention.

12. Gillies and Cailliau, *How the Web Was Born*, 128; Cohen, *Getting Started with Storyspace*, 11–29, esp. 13; Landow, *Hypertext 3.0*, 3; Bolter, *Writing Space*, 29–32.

13. Robert Cailliau, e-mail to me, March 16, 2001.

14. Landow, *Hypertext 3.0*, 2.

15. Nelson, "Opening Hypertext," 53. Mark Feltham, e-mail to me, March 11, 2001; Christopher Keep, e-mail to me, March 12, 2001; and Mark Bernstein, e-mail to me, March 16, 2001, in different ways all speculate about an initial connection of Web "pages" to a concept of documents.

16. Berners-Lee with Fischetti, *Weaving the Web*, 16; J. S. Brown and Duguid, *Social Life of Information*, 182 (my ellipsis); Bolter, "Identity," 18.

17. Mark Bernstein, e-mail to me, March 16, 2001; Rowland, *Spirit of the Web*, 309 (my ellipsis); Bolter, "Identity," 20; Rosen, *Talmud and the Internet*, 14 (his italics).

18. Three typings of the schema are reproduced in *Archive* 12:174a–b; Gilbert, *Joyce's "Ulysses,"* rev. ed., 144–45.

19. M. Joyce, "Siren Shapes," 41–42.

20. Landow, *Hypertext 3.0*, 113.

21. McGann, "*Ulysses* as a Postmodern Work," 191.

22. Ellmann, preface to *Ulysses*, xiv.

23. Burbules, "Rhetorics of the Web," 117; Bolter, *Writing Space*, 67. In an earlier version of this chapter I presented two screenshots showing different presentations of a passage from "Lotus Eaters," one with the text alone and the other cluttered with verbal and visual secondary information. See "James Joyce's *Ulysses* on the Page and on the Screen," 161 and 171, including the text surrounding the screenshots.

24. Bolter, *Writing Space*, 63, 117; Rosen, *Talmud and the Internet*, 85.

25. Rosen, *Talmud and the Internet*, 15–16.

Chapter 9. Mobile Notes

1. Alain quoted in the *Robert Dictionary*, cited in Genette, *Paratexts*, 319 n. 1; Yeats, "The Scholars," in *Poems*, 141; Grafton, *The Footnote*, 69–70, 70 n. 16. In the footnote Grafton cites Lesley, *Remembered Laughter*, xx.

2. White, "Black and White and Read All Over," 84–85; Lavagnino, "*Pale Fire*," 82; Yeats, *Poems*, 223, 665; Beehler, "In Editing a Good Novel," B14. To be fair, in his edition of Yeats's *Poems*, Finneran says in his headnote to the Explanatory Notes that "some of these notes will doubtless strike some readers as superfluous. However, it should be remembered that this edition will be distributed throughout the world. It thus did not seem possible to assume a 'common body of knowledge' which all readers of this volume would share" (624).

3. Coe, *House of Sleep*, 270–71. I thank John Lavagnino for recommending Coe's novel to me.

4. Both poems are in Petras and Petras, *Very Bad Poetry*, 39. To avoid confusion with my own endnote numbers, I have replaced the original footnote numbers in *Very Bad Poetry* with symbols.

5. Battestin, "Rationale of Literary Annotation," 4; Lawler, "Medieval Annotation," 97; Cosgrove, "Undermining the Text," 148; Lavagnino, "*Pale Fire*," 82; Hanna, "Annotation as Social Practice," 181–82.

6. Derrida, "This Is Not an Oral Footnote," 202.

7. Gifford and Seidman, *"Ulysses" Annotated*, xvi.

8. Ibid., 98, 99 (their italics and ellipses).

9. Kiberd, notes to Joyce, *Ulysses: Annotated Students' Edition*, 979 (Kiberd's italics).

10. Johnson, notes to Joyce, *Ulysses: The 1922 Text*, 801.

11. The discussion took place in November and December 1998. A condensed version of the messages is available at http://publish.uwo.ca/~mgroden/annocond.html.

12. Gifford and Seidman, *"Ulysses" Annotated*, 66.

13. Ibid., 107.

Epilogue

1. Bennett, review of *Ulysses*, 220.

2. Kiberd, *"Ulysses" and Us*, 108.

3. Car Talk (Tom and Ray Magliozzi), "Car Talk Car-O-Scope."

4. Ellmann, *James Joyce*, 363–64.
5. J. M. Smith, *Private Matters*, 225.
6. Peacock, "The Wheel," in *Original Love*, 20–21, and *Cornucopia*, 177.

Appendix 1. Remarks on the National Library of Ireland's Newly Acquired Joyce Manuscripts

1. Buffalo MS VI.B.17; *Archive* 33:2–56. The National Library's pages would fit between notebook pages 54 and 55; see *Archive* 33:29.

2. Gorman, *James Joyce*, 95–99, 107, 133–38. The notebook page that is transcribed on page 107 is also reproduced photographically among the illustrations between pages 184 and 185.

3. Ellmann, *James Joyce*, 3.

4. Hay, "History or Genesis?" 207.

Appendix 2. Extant Manuscripts for *Ulysses* as of Summer 2002

1. Groden, *"Ulysses" in Progress*, 205–17.

2. Ibid., 37–52, 115–65.

3. Owen, *Joyce and the Beginnings of "Ulysses,"* 68. For details about the "Alphabetical Notebook"/"Trieste Notebook," see chapter 1, note 20.

Works Cited

Adams, Robert Martin. *Afterjoyce: Studies in Fiction after "Ulysses."* New York: Oxford University Press, 1977.
Albee, Edward. *The American Dream.* 1961. In Albee, *"The American Dream" and "The Zoo Story."* New York: Signet, 1963.
———. *The Sandbox.* 1960. In Albee, *"The Sandbox" and "The Death of Bessie Smith."* New York: Signet, 1963.
———. *Who's Afraid of Virginia Woolf?* 1962. New York: Pocket Books, 1963.
American Heritage Dictionary of the English Language. 3rd ed. Boston: Houghton Mifflin, 1992. 4th ed. Boston: Houghton Mifflin, 2000.
Anderson, Benedict. *Imagined Communities: Reflections on the Origin and Spread of Nationalism.* London: Verso, 1983.
Aquinas, St. Thomas. *Summa Contra Gentiles.* Trans. Joseph Rickaby. 1905. http://maritain.nd.edu/jmc/etext/gc1_91.htm.
Arnheim, Rudolf, W. H. Auden, Karl Shapiro, and Donald A. Stauffer; introduction by Charles D. Abbott. *Poets at Work: Essays Based on the Modern Poetry Collection at the Lockwood Memorial Library, University of Buffalo.* New York: Harcourt, Brace, 1948.
Atlas, James. "Confessing for Voyeurs: The Age of the Literary Memoir is Now." *New York Times Magazine*, May 12, 1996, sect. 6, p. 25.
Attridge, Derek. *Joyce Effects: On Language, Theory, and History.* Cambridge, UK: Cambridge University Press, 2000.
Bachelard, Gaston. *The Poetics of Space.* 1958. Trans. Maria Jolas. New York: Orion Press, 1964.
Bakhtin, M. M. "From the Prehistory of Novelistic Discourse." Ca. 1940. In *The Dialogic Imagination: Four Essays.* Ed. Michael Holquist. Trans. Caryl Emerson and Holquist. Austin: University of Texas Press, 1981. 41–83.
Barham, Peter. *Forgotten Lunatics of the Great War.* New Haven: Yale University Press, 2004.
Barney, Stephen A., ed. *Annotation and Its Texts.* New York: Oxford University Press, 1991.
Barthes, Roland. "From Work to Text." 1971. In *The Rustle of Language.* Trans. Richard Howard. New York: Hill and Wang, 1986. 56–64.

———. "Theory of the Text." 1973. Trans. Ian McLeod. In *Untying the Text: A Post-Structuralist Reader*. Ed. Robert Young. Boston: Routledge and Kegan Paul, 1981. 31–47.
Basinski, Michael. "Foreword and Acknowledgments: James Joyce in Buffalo, New York." In Maynard, *Discovering James Joyce*, 11–17.
Battestin, Martin C. "A Rationale of Literary Annotation: The Example of Fielding's Novels." *Studies in Bibliography* 34 (1981): 1–22. Also http://etext.lib.virginia.edu/bsuva/sb/.
Bechdel, Alison. *Fun Home: A Family Tragicomic*. Boston: Houghton Mifflin, 2006.
Beehler, Rodger. "In Editing a Good Novel, the Best Footnote Is ^{0}." *Chronicle of Higher Education*, March 9, 2001, B14–B15.
Behar, Ruth. "Dare We Say 'I'?" *Chronicle of Higher Education*, June 29, 1994, B1–B2.
"Behind the Scenes: Counting the Cost of James Joyce." *The Phoenix*, August 16, 2002, 22–23.
Bellemin-Noël, Jean. "Psychoanalysis and the Avant-texte." 1982. Trans. Jed Deppman. In Deppman, Ferrer, and Groden, *Genetic Criticism*, 28–35.
Benco, Silvio. "James Joyce in Trieste." 1930. Trans. anon. In *Portraits of the Artist in Exile: Recollections of James Joyce by Europeans*. Ed. Willard Potts. Seattle: University of Washington Press, 1979. 49–58.
Bénéjam, Valérie. "Stephen and the Venus of Praxiteles: The Backside of Aesthetics." In *Cultural Studies of James Joyce*. Ed. R. Brandon Kershner. *European Joyce Studies* 15 (2003): 59–76.
Bennett, Arnold. Review of *Ulysses*. 1922. In *James Joyce: The Critical Heritage*. Ed. Robert Deming. 2 vols. London: Routledge and Kegan Paul, 1970, 1:219–22.
Berners-Lee, Tim, with Mark Fischetti. *Weaving the Web: The Original Design and Ultimate Destiny of the World Wide Web by Its Inventor*. San Francisco: HarperSanFrancisco, 1999.
Bishop, Ted. *Riding with Rilke: Reflections on Motorcycles and Books*. Toronto: Viking Canada, 2005; New York: Norton, 2006.
Blamires, Harry. *The New Bloomsday Book: A Guide through "Ulysses."* 1966. 3rd ed. London: Routledge, 1996.
Blom, Andrew H. Message sent to J-Joyce Internet discussion list, November 29, 1998. Online. http://publish.uwo.ca/~mgroden/annocond.html. Posted April 2001.
Bloom, Harold, Paul de Man, Jacques Derrida, Geoffrey Hartman, and J. Hillis Miller. *Deconstruction and Criticism*. New York: Continuum, 1979.
Bolter, Jay David. "Identity." In *Unspun: Key Concepts for Understanding the World Wide Web*. Ed. Thomas Swiss. New York: New York University Press, 2000. 17–29.
———. *Writing Space: Computers, Hypertext, and the Remediation of Print*. 1991. 2nd ed. Mahwah, N.J.: Lawrence Erlbaum, 2001.
Booth, Wayne C. *The Rhetoric of Fiction*. 1961. 2nd ed. Chicago: University of Chicago Press, 1983.
Bornstein, George. *Material Modernism: The Politics of the Page*. Cambridge, UK: Cambridge University Press, 2001.
———, ed. *Representing Modernist Texts: Editing as Interpretation*. Ann Arbor: University of Michigan Press, 1991.

Boully, Jenny. *The Body: An Essay.* 2002. Athens, Ohio: Essay Press, 2007.
Bowers, Fredson. *Textual and Literary Criticism.* Cambridge, UK: Cambridge University Press, 1959.
Bowman, Frank Paul. "Genetic Criticism." *Poetics Today* 11 (1990): 627–46.
Brown, Ellen. "Between the Medusa and the Abyss: Reading *Jane Eyre*, Reading Myself." In Freedman, Frey, and Zauhar, *The Intimate Critique*, 225–35.
Brown, John Seely, and Paul Duguid. *The Social Life of Information.* Boston: Harvard Business School Press, 2000.
Brown, Susan. "The Mystery of the Fuga per Canonem Solved." *Genetic Joyce Studies* 7 (Spring 2007).
Budgen, Frank. "Further Recollections of James Joyce." 1956. In Budgen, *Joyce and the Making of "Ulysses,"* 314–28.
———. *James Joyce and the Making of "Ulysses."* 1934. Bloomington: Indiana University Press, 1960. Also http://libtext-dev.library.wisc.edu/cgi-bin/JoyceColl/JoyceColl-idx?type=browse.
———. "Joyce's Chapters of Going Forth by Day." 1941. In *James Joyce: Two Decades of Criticism.* Ed. Seon Givens. 1948. Augmented ed. New York: Vanguard Press, 1963. 343–67.
———. *Myselves When Young.* London: Oxford University Press, 1970.
Burbules, Nicholas C. "Rhetorics of the Web: Hyperreading and Critical Literacy." In *Page to Screen: Taking Literacy Into the Electronic Era.* Ed. Ilana Snyder. London: Routledge, 1998. 102–22.
Bush, Ronald. "James Joyce: The Way He Lives Now." *James Joyce Quarterly* 33 (1996): 523–29.
Cadbury, Bill. "Thoughts on the Necessity of Redoing the *Archive.*" *Genetic Joyce Studies* (Summer 2002 Special Issue).
Carlton, Peter. "Rereading *Middlemarch*, Rereading Myself." In Freedman, Frey, and Zauhar, *The Intimate Critique*, 237–44.
Car Talk (Tom and Ray Magliozzi). "Car Talk Car-O-Scope." http://web.archive.org/web/19991008092944/http://cartalk.cars.com/Survey/Results/Psychographics/caroscopes.html.
Cerquiglini, Bernard, "Variantes d'auteur et variance de copiste." In *La naissance du texte.* Ed. Louis Hay. Paris: José Corti, 1989. 105–20.
Christie's New York. "James Joyce's *Ulysses*: The John Quinn Draft Manuscript of the 'Circe' Episode." December 14, 2000. Auction catalog.
Coe, Jonathan. *The House of Sleep.* 1997. New York: Vintage, 1999. Chapter 15, pp. 263–76.
Cohen, E. A. *Getting Started with Storyspace for Macintosh.* Rev. and extended ed. Watertown, Mass.: Eastgate Systems, 1996.
Collins, Wilkie. *The New Magdalen.* 1873. N.p.: Echo Library, 2005.
Contat, Michel, Denis Hollier, and Jacques Neefs. Editors' Preface. In Contat, Hollier, and Neefs, *Drafts*, 1–5.
———, eds. *Drafts. Yale French Studies* 89 (1996).
Cosgrove, Peter W. "Undermining the Text: Edward Gibbon, Alexander Pope, and the Anti-Authenticating Footnote." In Barney, *Annotation and Its Texts*, 130–51.

Crispi, Luca. "The *James Joyce Archive* from an Archival Perspective." *Genetic Joyce Studies* (Summer 2002 Special Issue).
———. "Manuscript Timeline 1905–1922." *Genetic Joyce Studies* 4 (2004).
———. Online catalog of the James Joyce Collection at the National Library of Ireland. Forthcoming at http://www.nli.ie/.
———. Online catalog of the James Joyce Collection at the Poetry Collection, University at Buffalo. Forthcoming at http://ublib.buffalo.edu/jamesjoyce/catalog/.
———. "Sylvia Beach's Joyce Collection at Buffalo." In Maynard, *Discovering James Joyce*, 29–37.
Crispi, Luca, and Sam Slote, eds. *How Joyce Wrote "Finnegans Wake": A Chapter-by-Chapter Genetic Guide.* Madison: University of Wisconsin Press, 2007.
Danielewski, Mark Z. *House of Leaves.* 2nd ed. New York: Pantheon, 2000.
Darnton, Robert. "What Is the History of Books?" 1982. In Darnton, *The Kiss of Lamourette: Reflections in Cultural History.* New York: Norton, 1990. 107–36.
Davis, Mac. *They All Are Jews: From Moses to Einstein.* Illus. E. E. Claridge. 1937. Rev. ed. New York: Jordan, 1951.
de Biasi, Pierre-Marc. "Horizons for Genetic Studies." 1993. Trans. Jennifer A. Jones. In *Genetic Criticism.* Ed. Claire Bustarret. *Word and Image* 13 (1997): 124–34.
Debray Genette, Raymonde. "Flaubert's 'A Simple Heart,' or How to Make an Ending: A Study of the Manuscripts." 1984. Trans. Jed Deppman. In Deppman, Ferrer, and Groden, *Genetic Criticism*, 69–95.
Deppman, Jed, Daniel Ferrer, and Michael Groden. "Genetic Criticism." In Groden, Kreiswirth, and Szeman, *The Johns Hopkins Guide to Literary Theory and Criticism*, 2nd ed., 427–30.
———. "Introduction: A Genesis of French Genetic Criticism." In Deppman, Ferrer, and Groden, *Genetic Criticism*, 1–16.
———, eds. *Genetic Criticism: Texts and Avant-textes.* Philadelphia: University of Pennsylvania Press, 2004.
Derrida, Jacques. "This Is Not an Oral Footnote." Trans. Stephen A. Barney and Michael Hanly. In Barney, *Annotation and Its Texts*, 192–205.
Dettmar, Kevin. "James Joyce and the Great Books." *The Common Reader* 2.1 (2002). Online. http://web.archive.org/web/20030413150532/http://www.greatbooks.org/tcr/dettmar21.shtml.
Dickens, Charles. *David Copperfield.* Ed. Nina Burgis. Oxford World's Classics. Oxford: Oxford University Press, 1983.
Duffy, Enda. *The Subaltern "Ulysses."* Minneapolis: University of Minnesota Press, 1994.
Dunn, Mark. *Ibid: A Life.* 2004. *Ibid: A Novel.* New York: Harvest, 2005.
Eliot, T. S. *The Waste Land: A Facsimile and Transcript of the Original Drafts, including the Annotations of Ezra Pound.* Ed. Valerie Eliot. New York: Harvest/Harcourt Brace Jovanovich, 1971.
Ellmann, Richard. *James Joyce.* 1959. Rev. ed. New York: Oxford University Press, 1982.
———. Preface to *Ulysses: The Corrected Text* and *Ulysses: The Gabler Edition*, by James Joyce. New York: Vintage, 1986, 1993. ix–xiv.

———. *"Ulysses" on the Liffey.* New York: Oxford University Press, 1972.
Epstein, E. L. "Nestor." In *James Joyce's "Ulysses": Critical Essays.* Ed. Clive Hart and David Hayman. Berkeley: University of California Press, 1974. 17–28.
Every Man's Own Lawyer: A Handy Book of the Principles of Law and Equity, Comprising the Rights and Wrongs of Individuals. By a barrister. 54th ed. London: Crosby Lockwood and Son, 1919.
Fairhall, James. *James Joyce and the Question of History.* Cambridge, UK: Cambridge University Press, 1993.
Ferrer, Daniel. "Clementis's Cap: Retroaction and Persistence in the Genetic Process." 1994. Trans. Marlena G. Corcoran. In Contat, Hollier, and Neefs, *Drafts,* 223–36.
———. "Production, Invention, and Reproduction: Genetic vs. Textual Criticism." In Loizeaux and Fraistat, *Reimagining Textuality,* 48–59.
———. "What Song the Sirens Sang . . . Is No Longer Beyond All Conjecture: A Preliminary Description of the New 'Proteus' and 'Sirens' Manuscripts." *James Joyce Quarterly* 39 (2001): 53–68.
Ferrer, Daniel, and Jean-Michel Rabaté. "Paragraphs in Expansion (James Joyce)." 1989. Trans. Jed Deppman. In Deppman, Ferrer, and Groden, *Genetic Criticism,* 132–51.
Finneran, Richard J. "'That Word Known to All Men' in *Ulysses*: A Reconsideration." *James Joyce Quarterly* 33 (1996): 569–82.
Fordham, Finn. "'Circe' and the Genesis of Multiple Personality." *James Joyce Quarterly* 45 (2008): 507–20.
Frank, Joseph. "Spatial Form in Modern Literature." 1945. In Frank, *The Idea of Spatial Form.* New Brunswick, N.J.: Rutgers University Press, 1991. 3–66.
Freedman, Diane P. "Autobiographical Literary Criticism as the New Belletrism." In Veeser, *Confessions of the Critics,* 3–16.
Freedman, Diane P., and Olivia Frey, eds. *Autobiographical Writing across the Disciplines: A Reader.* Durham, N.C.: Duke University Press, 2003.
Freedman, Diane P., Olivia Frey, and Frances Murphy Zauhar, eds. *The Intimate Critique: Autobiographical Literary Criticism.* Durham, N.C.: Duke University Press, 1993.
French, Marilyn. *The Book as World: James Joyce's "Ulysses."* Cambridge: Harvard University Press, 1976.
Gabler, Hans Walter. Afterword to *Ulysses: The Corrected Text,* by James Joyce. New York: Vintage, 1986. 647–[650].
———. "The *James Joyce Archive*: A Publisher's Gift to Joyce Studies." *Genetic Joyce Studies* (Summer 2002 Special Issue).
———. "Joyce's Text in Progress." In *The Cambridge Companion to James Joyce.* Ed. Derek Attridge. Cambridge, UK: Cambridge University Press, 1990. 213–36.
———. "A Response to: John Kidd, 'Errors of Execution in the 1984 *Ulysses*.'" *Studies in the Novel* 22 (1990): 250–56. Lecture delivered at the Society for Textual Scholarship conference, New York, April 26, 1985.
———. "Textual Criticism." In Groden and Kreiswirth, *The Johns Hopkins Guide to Literary Theory and Criticism,* 1st ed., 708–14.
———. "What *Ulysses* Requires." *Papers of the Bibliographical Society of America* 87 (1993): 187–248.

Gabler, Hans Walter, George Bornstein, and Gillian Borland Pierce, eds. *Contemporary German Editorial Theory*. Ann Arbor: University of Michigan Press, 1995.

Garland Publishing Inc. Records. Firestone Library, Princeton University Rare Books and Special Collections. Consulted April 26, 2005.

Gaskell, Philip, and Clive Hart. *Ulysses: A Review of Three Texts*. Totowa, N.J.: Barnes and Noble Books, 1989.

Genesis: Manuscrits/Recherche/Invention 1 (1992–).

Genetic Joyce Studies. Special Issue: "25th Anniversary of the *James Joyce Archive*" (Summer 2002). Online. http://www.geneticjoycestudies.org.

Genette, Gérard. *Paratexts: Thresholds of Interpretation*. 1987. Trans. Jane E. Lewin. Cambridge, UK: Cambridge University Press, 1997.

Gheerbrant, Bernard. *James Joyce: Sa Vie, Son Oeuvre, Son Rayonnement*. Paris: Librairie La Hune, 1949.

Gibson, Andrew. *Joyce's Revenge: History, Politics, and Aesthetics in "Ulysses."* Oxford: Oxford University Press, 2002.

Gifford, Don, and Robert J. Seidman. *"Ulysses" Annotated: Notes for James Joyce's "Ulysses."* Rev. and expanded ed. Berkeley: University of California Press, 1988, 2008.

Gilbert, Stuart. Introduction to *Ulysses*, by James Joyce. New York: Limited Editions Club, 1935. v–xvi.

———. *James Joyce's "Ulysses": A Study*. 1st ed. New York: Knopf, 1930. Rev. ed. New York: Vintage, 1952.

Gillespie, Michael Patrick. *Inverted Volumes Improperly Arranged: James Joyce and His Trieste Library*. Ann Arbor: UMI Research Press, 1983.

Gillespie, Michael Patrick, with Erik Bradford Stocker. *James Joyce's Trieste Library: A Catalogue of Materials at the Harry Ransom Humanities Research Center, The University of Texas at Austin*. Austin: Harry Ransom Humanities Research Center, 1986.

Gillies, James, and Robert Cailliau. *How the Web Was Born: The Story of the World Wide Web*. Oxford: Oxford University Press, 2000.

Goldberg, S. L. *James Joyce*. Edinburgh: Oliver and Boyd, 1962.

Goldman, Arnold. "'Now' in the 'Post-Now' Era." Review of Richard Ellmann, *James Joyce*, rev. ed. *James Joyce Broadsheet* 10 (1983): 1.

Gorman, Herbert. *James Joyce*. 1939. Rev. ed. New York: Rinehart, 1948.

Gottfried, Roy. *Joyce's Iritis and the Irritated Text: The Dis-lexic "Ulysses."* Gainesville: University Press of Florida, 1995.

Grafton, Anthony. *The Footnote: A Curious History*. Cambridge: Harvard University Press, 1997.

Greenblatt, Stephen. "The Death of Hamnet and the Making of *Hamlet*." *New York Review of Books*, October 21, 2004, 42–44, 46–47. Also http://www.nybooks.com/articles/17483.

Grésillon, Almuth. "Slow: Work in Progress." 1992. Trans. Stephen A. Noble and Vincent Vichit-Vadakan. In *Genetic Criticism*. Ed. Claire Bustarret. *Word and Image* 13 (1997): 106–23.

———. "**Still** *Lost Time*: **Already** the Text of the *Recherche*." 1983, 1990. Trans. Jed Deppman. In Deppman, Ferrer, and Groden, *Genetic Criticism*, 152–70.

Grimes, William. "We All Have a Life. Must We All Write about It?" *New York Times*, March 25, 2005, E27, E34 (National Edition).

Groden, Michael. Afterword to *Ulysses: The Gabler Edition*, by James Joyce. New York: Vintage, 1993. 647–57.

———. "Before and After: The Manuscripts in Textual and Genetic Criticism of *Ulysses*." In *"Ulysses" in Critical Perspective*. Ed. Michael Patrick Gillespie and A. Nicholas Fargnoli. Gainesville: University Press of Florida, 2006. 152–70.

———. "Contemporary Textual and Literary Theory." In Bornstein, *Representing Modernist Texts*, 259–86.

———. "Criticism in New Composition: *Ulysses* and *The Sound and the Fury*." *Twentieth Century Literature* 21 (1975): 265–77.

———."'Cyclops' in Progress, 1919." *James Joyce Quarterly* 12 (1974–75): 123–68.

———. "Editing Joyce's *Ulysses*: An International Effort." *Scholarly Publishing* 12 (1980): 37–54. Also in *Scholarly Publishing in an Era of Change* (Proceedings of the Second Annual Conference of the Society for Scholarly Publishing). Ed. Ethel G. Langlois. Washington, D.C.: Society for Scholarly Publishing, 1981. 27–34.

———. "Foostering over Those Changes: The New *Ulysses*." *James Joyce Quarterly* 22 (1985): 137–59.

———, comp. *James Joyce's Manuscripts: An Index*. New York: Garland, 1980.

———. "'James Joyce's *Ulysses* in Hypermedia': Problems of Annotation." Online from Clemson University Digital Press: http://www.clemson.edu/caah/cedp/Tech%20Colloquium%202001/Groden%20Files/index.html. Posted August 2002.

———. "James Joyce's *Ulysses* on the Page and on the Screen." In *The Future of the Page*. Ed. Peter Stoicheff and Andrew Taylor. Toronto: University of Toronto Press, 2004. 159–75.

———. "The National Library of Ireland's New Joyce Manuscripts." In *Joyce in Trieste: An Album of Risky Readings*. Ed. Sebastian D. G. Knowles, Geert Lernout, and John McCourt. Gainesville: University Press of Florida, 2007. 13–35.

———. "A Response to John Kidd's 'An Inquiry into *Ulysses: The Corrected Text*.'" *James Joyce Quarterly* 28 (1990): 81–110.

———. *"Ulysses" in Progress*. Princeton, N.J.: Princeton University Press, 1977.

Groden, Michael, and Martin Kreiswrith, eds. *The Johns Hopkins Guide to Literary Theory and Criticism*. 1st ed. Baltimore: Johns Hopkins University Press, 1994. 2nd ed. Ed. Michael Groden, Martin Kreiswirth, and Imre Szeman. Baltimore: Johns Hopkins University Press, 2005. Also http://litguide.press.jhu.edu/.

Gunn, Ian, and Alistair McCleery, comps. *The "Ulysses" Pagefinder*. Edinburgh: Split Pea Press, 1988. Also downloadable as *The "Ulysses" Tables* and *The "Archive" Tables*. http://www.splitpea.co.uk/.

Hanna, Ralph, III. "Annotation as Social Practice." In Barney, *Annotation and Its Texts*, 178–84.

Hartshorn, Peter. *James Joyce and Trieste*. Westport, Conn.: Greenwood Press, 1997.

Hay, Louis. "Does 'Text' Exist?" 1985. Trans. Matthew Jocelyn and Hans Walter Gabler. *Studies in Bibliography* 41 (1988): 64–76. Also http://etext.lib.virginia.edu/bsuva/sb/.

———. "History or Genesis?" 1992. Trans. Ingrid Wassenaar. In Contat, Hollier, and Neefs, *Drafts*, 191–207.
Hayashi, Tetsumaro. *James Joyce: Research Opportunities and Dissertation Abstracts*. Jefferson, N.C.: McFarland, 1985.
Hayman, David. "Bringing Out the *Archive*: Memories." *Genetic Joyce Studies* (Summer 2002 Special Issue).
———. "From *Finnegans Wake*: A Sentence in Progress." *PMLA* 73 (1958): 136–54.
———. *"Ulysses": The Mechanics of Meaning*. 1970. 2nd ed. Madison: University of Wisconsin Press, 1982.
Herr, Cheryl. "Theosophy, Guilt, and 'That Word Known to All Men' in Joyce's *Ulysses*." *James Joyce Quarterly* 18 (1980): 45–54.
Herring, Phillip F. Review of *The James Joyce Archive*. *James Joyce Quarterly* 19 (1981): 85–98.
"How to Enjoy James Joyce's Great Novel *Ulysses*." *Saturday Review of Literature*, February 10, 1934, 474–75. Advertisement.
"Inside Publishing: Jousting for Joyce." *Lingua Franca* 1 (October 1991): 11.
Jackson, Shelley. *Patchwork Girl*. Watertown, Mass.: Eastgate Systems, 1995. Electronic hypertext.
James, Henry. *The Art of the Novel: Critical Prefaces*. New York: Scribner, 1934.
Johnson, Jeri. Notes to *Ulysses: The 1922 Text*, by James Joyce, pp. 763–980.
Jolas, Eugene. "My Friend James Joyce." 1941. In *James Joyce: Two Decades of Criticism*. Ed. Seon Givens. 1948. Augmented ed. New York: Vanguard Press, 1963. 3–18.
Jones, Ellen Carol. "Ghosts through Absence." In *Memory Ireland*. Vol. 4, *James Joyce and Cultural Memory*. Ed. Oona Frawley and Katherine O'Callaghan. Syracuse: Syracuse University Press, forthcoming.
———. "Memorial Dublin." In *Joyce/Benjamin*. Ed. Enda Duffy and Maurizia Boscagli. *European Joyce Studies*. Amsterdam: Rodopi, forthcoming.
Joyce, James. *Chamber Music*. 1907. Ed. William York Tindall. New York: Columbia University Press, 1954.
———. *Critical Writings*. Ed. Ellsworth Mason and Richard Ellmann. New York: Viking, 1959. Abbreviated as *CW*.
———. *Dubliners*. 1914. Ed. Hans Walter Gabler with Walter Hettche. New York: Garland, 1993; New York: Vintage, 1993.
———. *Dubliners*. 1914. Ed. Robert Scholes. New York: Viking, 1967. Abbreviated as *D*.
———. *Exiles*. 1918. New York: Penguin, 1973. Abbreviated as *E*.
———. *Finnegans Wake*. New York: Viking, 1939. Abbreviated as *FW*.
———. *Finnegans Wake*. 1939. Ed. Danis Rose and John O'Hanlon. Mousehole, UK: Houyhnhnm Press, 2010.
———. *The "Finnegans Wake" Notebooks at Buffalo*. Ed. Vincent Deane, Daniel Ferrer, and Geert Lernout. 12 vols. to date. Turnhout, Belgium: Brepols, 2001–.
———. *"Finnegans Web"* Web site. http://www.trentu.ca/faculty/jjoyce/.
———. *A First-Draft Version of "Finnegans Wake."* Ed. David Hayman. Austin: University of Texas Press, 1963. Also http://libtext-dev.library.wisc.edu/cgi-bin/JoyceColl/JoyceColl-idx?type=browse.

———. *The James Joyce Archive*. Photoreprint ed. General ed. Michael Groden. Ed. Hans Walter Gabler, David Hayman, A. Walton Litz, and Danis Rose. 63 vols. New York: Garland, 1977–79. Abbreviated in the endnotes and Table 1 as *Archive*.

———. *James Joyce: The Lost Notebook*. Ed. Danis Rose and John O'Hanlon. Edinburgh: Split Pea Press, 1989.

———. *Joyce's Notes and Early Drafts for "Ulysses": Selections from the Buffalo Collection*. Ed. Phillip F. Herring. Charlottesville: University Press of Virginia, 1977. Abbreviated in the endnotes and Table 1 as *Notes and Early Drafts*.

———. *Joyce's "Ulysses" Notesheets in the British Museum*. Ed. Phillip F. Herring. Charlottesville: University Press of Virginia, 1972. Abbreviated in the endnotes and Table 1 as *Notesheets*.

———. *Letters*. 3 vols. Vol. 1. Ed. Stuart Gilbert. New York: Viking, 1957, 1966. Vols. 2–3. Ed. Richard Ellmann. New York: Viking, 1966. Abbreviated as *L*.

———. *Occasional, Critical, and Political Writing*. Ed. Kevin Barry. New York: Oxford University Press, 2000.

———. *Poems and Shorter Writings*. Ed. Richard Ellmann, A. Walton Litz, and John Whittier-Ferguson. London: Faber and Faber, 1991.

———. "A Portrait of the Artist." 1904. In Scholes and Kain, *The Workshop of Daedalus*, 60–68.

———. *A Portrait of the Artist as a Young Man*. 1916. Ed. Chester G. Anderson. New York: Viking, 1964. Abbreviated as *P*.

———. *A Portrait of the Artist as a Young Man*. 1916. Ed. Hans Walter Gabler with Walter Hettche. New York: Garland, 1993; New York: Vintage, 1993.

———. *Selected Letters*. Ed. Richard Ellmann. New York: Viking, 1975.

———. *Stephen Hero*. Ed. Theodore Spencer. 1944. Additional pages ed. John J. Slocum and Herbert Cahoon. New York: New Directions, 1963.

———. *Ulysses*. 1922. Hamburg, Paris, Bologna: Odyssey Press, 1932; second impression, 1933.

———. *Ulysses*. 1922. New York: Limited Editions Club, 1935.

———. *Ulysses*. Paris: Shakespeare and Company, 1922.

———. *Ulysses: A Critical and Synoptic Edition*. 1922. Ed. Hans Walter Gabler with Wolfhard Steppe and Claus Melchior. 3 vols. New York: Garland, 1984. *Ulysses: The Corrected Text*. New York: Vintage/London: Penguin, 1986. *Ulysses: The Gabler Edition*. New York: Vintage, 1993; London: Bodley Head, 1993, 2008. Abbreviated as *U*.

———. *Ulysses: A Facsimile of the Manuscript*. Ed. Clive Driver. 3 vols. New York: Octagon/Philadelphia: Philip H. and A. S. W. Rosenbach Foundation, 1975.

———. *Ulysses: Annotated Students' Edition*. 1922. Ed. Declan Kiberd. London: Penguin, 1992.

———. "*Ulysses*: Episode VII." *Little Review* 5 (October 1918): 26–51.

———. "*Ulysses*: Episode Twelve (first part)." *Little Review* 6 (November 1919): 38–54.

———. *Ulysses: The 1922 Text*. 1922. Ed. Jeri Johnson. London: Oxford University Press, 1993.

Joyce, Michael. *Afternoon, A Story*. 1987. Watertown, Mass.: Eastgate Systems, 1990, 2001. Electronic hypertext.

———. "Siren Shapes: Exploratory and Constructive Hypertexts." 1988. In Joyce, *Of Two Minds: Hypertext Pedagogy and Poetics*. Ann Arbor: University of Michigan Press, 1995. 39–59.

Kelly, Joseph. *Our Joyce: From Outcast to Icon*. Austin: University of Texas Press, 1998.

Kiberd, Declan. Introduction and notes to *Ulysses: Annotated Students' Edition*, by James Joyce, ix–lxxx, 941–1195.

———. *"Ulysses" and Us: The Art of Everyday Living*. London: Faber and Faber, 2009.

Kidd, John. "Errors of Execution in the 1984 *Ulysses*." *Studies in the Novel* 22 (1990): 243–49. Lecture delivered at the Society for Textual Scholarship conference, New York, April 26, 1985.

———. "Gabler's Errors in Context: A Reply to Michael Groden on Editing *Ulysses*." *James Joyce Quarterly* 28 (1990): 111–51.

———. "An Inquiry into *Ulysses: The Corrected Text*." *Papers of the Bibliographical Society of America* 82 (1988): 411–584.

———. "The Scandal of *Ulysses*." *New York Review of Books*, June 30, 1988, 32–39. Also http://www.nybooks.com/articles/4379.

Killeen, Terence. "Seller of Joyce Trove Was Surprised by Find." *Irish Times*, May 31, 2002, 9.

———. *"Ulysses" Unbound: A Reader's Companion to James Joyce's "Ulysses."* 2004. Rev. ed. Bray, Ireland: Wordwell/National Library of Ireland, 2005.

———. "Vast Joyce Manuscript Archive Arrives in Dublin." *Irish Times*, May 30, 2002, 9.

Knowles, Sebastian D. G. *The Dublin Helix: The Life of Language in Joyce's "Ulysses."* Gainesville: University Press of Florida, 2001.

Kopit, Arthur L. *Oh Dad, Poor Dad, Mamma's Hung You in the Closet and I'm Feelin' So Sad*. New York: Hill & Wang, 1960.

Landow, George P. *Hypertext 3.0: Critical Theory and New Media in an Era of Globalization*. 1993. 3rd ed. Baltimore: Johns Hopkins University Press, 2006.

Larbaud, Valery. "The *Ulysses* of James Joyce." 1922. Trans. anon. (partial). *Criterion* 1 (1922): 94–103.

Lavagnino, John. "*Pale Fire* and the Reader of Scholarly Commentary." Chapter 3 of "Nabokov's Realism." Ph.D. diss., Brandeis University, 1998. 75–106.

Lawler, Traugott. "Medieval Annotation: The Example of the Commentaries on Walter Map's *Dissuasio Valerii*." In Barney, *Annotation and Its Texts*, 94–107.

Lejeune, Philippe. "Auto-Genesis: Genetic Studies of Autobiographical Texts." 1992. Trans. Jed Deppman. In Deppman, Ferrer, and Groden, *Genetic Criticism*, 193–217.

Lesley, Cole. *Remembered Laughter: The Life of Noel Coward*. New York: Knopf, 1977.

Levin, Harry. Introduction to Joyce, *Ulysses: A Facsimile of the Manuscript*, 1:1–11.

———. *James Joyce: A Critical Introduction*. New York: New Directions, 1941. Rev. ed. 1960.

Lewis, Wyndham. *Time and Western Man*. 1927. Ed. Paul Edwards. Santa Rosa, Calif.: Black Sparrow Press, 1993.

Lidderdale, Jane, and Mary Nicholson. *Dear Miss Weaver: Harriet Shaw Weaver 1876–1961*. New York: Viking, 1970.

Litz, A. Walton. *The Art of James Joyce: Method and Design in "Ulysses" and "Finnegans Wake."* New York: Oxford University Press, 1961.

———. "Uses of the *Finnegans Wake* Manuscripts." In *Twelve and a Tilly: Essays on the Occasion of the 25th Anniversary of "Finnegans Wake."* Ed. Jack P. Dalton and Clive Hart. Evanston, Ill.: Northwestern University Press, 1966. 99–106.
Loizeaux, Elizabeth Bergmann, and Neil Fraistat. "Introduction: Textual Studies in the Late Age of Print." In Loizeaux and Fraistat, *Reimagining Textuality*, 3–16.
———, eds. *Reimagining Textuality: Textual Studies in the Late Age of Print*. Madison: University of Wisconsin Press, 2002.
MacLeish, Archibald. "Ars Poetica." 1926. In *The Norton Anthology of American Literature*. Ed. Ronald Gottesman et al. New York: Norton, 1979. 2:1284.
MacNicholas, John. *James Joyce's "Exiles": A Textual Companion*. New York: Garland, 1979.
Maddox, Brenda. *Nora: The Real Life of Molly Bloom*. Boston: Houghton Mifflin, 1988.
Mahaffey, Vicki. "Intentional Error: The Paradox of Editing Joyce's *Ulysses*." In Bornstein, *Representing Modernist Texts*, 171–91.
Mancusi-Ungaro, Carol. "Movement as Lifeblood and Death-Knell." Introduction to Eleanora Nagy, "Calder's Once and Future Circus: A Conservator's Perspective." In Simon and Leal, *Alexander Calder: The Paris Years, 1926–1933*, 195.
Manganiello, Dominic. *Joyce's Politics*. London: Routledge and Kegan Paul, 1980.
Max, D. T. "The Injustice Collector: Is James Joyce's Grandson Suppressing Scholarship?" *New Yorker*, June 19, 2006, 34–43. Also http://www.newyorker.com/printables/fact/060619fa_fact.
Maynard, James, ed. *Discovering James Joyce: The University at Buffalo Collection*. Buffalo: The Poetry Collection, University at Buffalo, State University of New York, 2009.
Mayo Clinic. Online articles on "iritis," "uveitis," and "glaucoma": http://www.mayoclinic.com/health/iritis/HQ00940; http://www.mayoclinic.com/health/uveitis/DS00677; and http://www.mayoclinic.com/health/glaucoma/DS00283.
Mays, J. C. C. "Gabler's *Ulysses* as a Field of Force." *Text* 10 (1997): 1–13.
McCarthy, Patrick A. "*Ulysses* and the Printed Page." In *Joyce's "Ulysses": The Larger Perspective*. Ed. Robert D. Newman and Weldon Thornton. Newark: University of Delaware Press, 1987. 59–73.
McCourt, John. *The Years of Bloom: James Joyce in Trieste 1904–1920*. Dublin: Lilliput Press, 2000.
McDowell, Edwin. "New Edition Fixes 5,000 Errors in 'Ulysses.'" *New York Times*, June 7, 1984, 1, C9.
McGann, Jerome J. *A Critique of Modern Textual Criticism*. 1983. Charlottesville: University Press of Virginia, 1992.
———. "The Monks and the Giants: Textual and Bibliographical Studies and the Interpretation of Literary Works." In McGann, *The Beauty of Inflections: Literary Investigations in Historical Method and Theory*. Oxford: Clarendon, 1985. 69–89.
———. *The Textual Condition*. Princeton, N.J.: Princeton University Press, 1991.
———. "*Ulysses* as a Postmodern Work." 1985. In McGann, *Social Values and Poetic Acts: The Historical Judgment of Literary Work*. Cambridge: Harvard University Press, 1988. 173–94.
McGee, Patrick. "Machines, Empire, and the Wise Virgins: Cultural Revolution in 'Aeolus.'"

In *"Ulysses": En-Gendered Perspectives*. Ed. Kimberly J. Devlin and Marilyn Reizbaum. Columbia: University of South Carolina Press, 1999. 86–99.

McKenzie, D. F. *Bibliography and the Sociology of Texts*. 1986. Cambridge, UK: Cambridge University Press, 1999.

Miller, Arthur. *All My Sons*. New York: Reynal & Hitchcock, 1947.

———. *Death of a Salesman*. 1949. New York: Viking Compass, 1958.

Mizener, Arthur. *The Cornell Joyce Collection: Given to Cornell University by William G. Mennen*. Ithaca, N.Y.: Cornell University Library, 1958.

Moscato, Michael, and Leslie LeBlanc, eds. *The United States of America v. One Book Entitled "Ulysses" by James Joyce: Documents and Commentary: A 50-Year Retrospective*. Frederick, Md.: University Publications of America, 1984.

Nabokov, Vladimir. *Pale Fire*. 1962. New York: Vintage, 1989.

Nash, John. *James Joyce and the Act of Reception: Reading, Ireland, Modernism*. Cambridge, UK: Cambridge University Press, 2006.

Nelson, Theodor Holm. "Opening Hypertext: A Memoir." In *Literacy Online: The Promise (and Peril) of Reading and Writing with Computers*. Ed. Myron C. Tuman. Pittsburgh: University of Pittsburgh Press, 1992. 43–57.

Nolan, Emer. *James Joyce and Nationalism*. London: Routledge, 1995.

Noon, William T., S. J. *Joyce and Aquinas*. New Haven: Yale University Press, 1957.

Norburn, Roger. *A James Joyce Chronology*. Houndmills, UK: Palgrave Macmillan, 2004.

O'Neill, Eugene. *Desire under the Elms*. 1924; *The Great God Brown*. 1925; and *Mourning Becomes Elektra*. 1931. In O'Neill, *Nine Plays*. New York: Modern Library, 1954. 135–210, 305–77, 683–867.

———. *Long Day's Journey into Night*. New Haven: Yale University Press, 1956.

Owen, Rodney Wilson. *James Joyce and the Beginnings of "Ulysses."* Ann Arbor: UMI Research Press, 1983.

Peacock, Molly. *Cornucopia: New and Selected Poems 1975–2002*. New York: Norton, 2002.

———. *Original Love*. New York: Norton, 1995.

———. *Paradise, Piece by Piece*. New York: Riverhead Books/Toronto: McClelland and Stewart, 1998.

———. *Raw Heaven*. New York: Random House, 1984.

Peake, C. H. *James Joyce: The Citizen and the Artist*. Stanford.: Stanford University Press, 1977. Also http://libtext-dev.library.wisc.edu/cgi-bin/JoyceColl/JoyceColl-idx?type=browse.

Petras, Kathryn, and Ross Petras, eds. *Very Bad Poetry*. New York: Vintage, 1997.

Pierre, Arnauld. "Painting and Working in the Abstract: Calder's Oeuvre and Constructive Art." In Simon and Leal, *Alexander Calder: The Paris Years, 1926–1933*, 227–35.

Poe, Edgar Allan. "The Philosophy of Composition." 1846. In *The Norton Anthology of Theory and Criticism*. Ed. Vincent B. Leitch et al. New York: Norton, 2001. 739–50.

P[ostgate], J. P. "Textual Criticism." *Encyclopædia Britannica*. 11th ed. New York: Encyclopædia Britannica Co., 1911. 26:708–15.

Prescott, Joseph. "James Joyce's *Ulysses* as a Work in Progress." Ph.D. diss., Harvard University, 1944. Partly published as *Exploring James Joyce*. Carbondale: Southern Illinois

University Press, 1964, and as *James Joyce: The Man and His Works*. Toronto: Forum House, 1969.
Rabaté, Jean-Michel. *James Joyce and the Politics of Egoism*. Cambridge, UK: Cambridge University Press, 2001.
Radford, F. L. "King, Pope, and Hero-Martyr: *Ulysses* and the Nightmare of Irish History." *James Joyce Quarterly* 15 (1978): 275–323.
Remnick, David. "The War over 'Ulysses'" (in some editions called "Jolting the Joyceans"). *Washington Post*, April 2, 1985, B1, B4.
Riddell, John. "The People's Joyce." *Vanity Fair*, June 1934, 57, 72b.
Rose, Danis. *The Textual Diaries of James Joyce*. Dublin: Lilliput Press, 1995.
Rosen, Jonathan. *The Talmud and the Internet: A Journey Between Worlds*. New York: Farrar, Straus and Giroux, 2000.
Rossman, Charles. "The Critical Reception of the 'Gabler *Ulysses*': Or, Gabler's *Ulysses* Kidd-napped." *Studies in the Novel* 21 (1989): 154–81.
———. "The Critical Reception of the 'Gabler *Ulysses*': Or, Gabler's *Ulysses* Kidd-napped: Part Two." *Studies in the Novel* 22 (1990): 323–53.
———. "The New *Ulysses*: The Hidden Controversy." *New York Review of Books*, December 8, 1988, 53–58. Also http://www.nybooks.com/articles/4233.
———, ed. "Special Issue on Editing *Ulysses*." *Studies in the Novel* 22, no. 2 (Summer 1990).
Rowland, Wade. *Spirit of the Web: The Age of Information from Telegraph to Internet*. Toronto: Patrick Crean/Key Porter, 1999.
Rushing, Conrad L. "The English Players Incident: What Really Happened?" *James Joyce Quarterly* 37 (2000): 371–88.
Scholes, Robert E., comp. *The Cornell Joyce Collection: A Catalogue*. Ithaca, N.Y.: Cornell University Press, 1961.
Scholes, Robert, and Richard M. Kain, eds. *The Workshop of Daedalus: James Joyce and the Raw Materials for "A Portrait of the Artist as a Young Man."* Evanston, Ill.: Northwestern University Press, 1965. Also http://libtext-dev.library.wisc.edu/cgi-bin/JoyceColl/Joyce-Coll-idx?type=browse. Abbreviated in Table 1 as *Workshop*.
Schork, R. J. "The First Generation of the *JJA*." *Genetic Joyce Studies* (Summer 2002 Special Issue).
Schwaber, Paul. *The Cast of Characters: A Reading of "Ulysses."* New Haven: Yale University Press, 1999.
Schwartz, John Pedro. "'In greater support of his word': Monument and Museum in *Finnegans Wake*." *James Joyce Quarterly* 44 (2006): 77–93.
Schwartzman, Myron. "The V.A.8 Copybook: An Early Draft of the 'Cyclops' Chapter of *Ulysses* with Notes on Its Development." *James Joyce Quarterly* 12 (1974–75): 64–122.
Schwarz, Daniel R. *Reading Joyce's "Ulysses."* New York: St. Martin's, 1987.
Selley, Peter. "The Lost 'Eumaeus' Notebook: James Joyce, Autograph Manuscript of the 'Eumaeus' Episode of *Ulysses*." Sotheby's London, July 10, 2001. Auction catalog.
Senn, Fritz. "Genetic Fascination." *Genetic Joyce Studies* (Summer 2002 Special Issue).
Shakespeare, William. *Troilus and Cressida*. Ed. Daniel Seltzer. 1963. In *The Complete Signet*

Classic Shakespeare. Ed. Sylvan Barnet et al. New York: Harcourt Brace Jovanovich, 1972. 999–1049.

Sherry, Vincent. *James Joyce: "Ulysses."* 1994. 2nd ed. Cambridge, UK: Cambridge University Press, 2004.

Shillingsburg, Peter L. *Scholarly Editing in the Computer Age: Theory and Practice*. 1986. 3rd ed. Ann Arbor: University of Michigan Press, 1996.

Shloss, Carol Loeb. *Lucia Joyce: To Dance in the Wake*. New York: Farrar, Straus and Giroux, 2003.

Silver, Brenda R. "Textual Criticism as Feminist Practice: Or, Who's Afraid of Virginia Woolf Part II." In Bornstein, *Representing Modernist Texts*, 193–222.

Silverman, Oscar A. "Why Buffalo? James Joyce: Paris-Buffalo: The Joyce Collections at the Lockwood Memorial Library." 1964. In Maynard, *Discovering James Joyce*, 19–27.

Simon, Joan. "Alexander Calder: The Paris Years." In Simon and Leal, *Alexander Calder: The Paris Years, 1926–1933*, 25–59.

Simon, Joan, and Brigitte Leal, eds., *Alexander Calder: The Paris Years, 1926–1933*. New York: Whitney Museum of American Art, Paris: Centre Pompidou, and New Haven: Yale University Press, 2009.

Slocum, John J., and Herbert Cahoon, comps. *A Bibliography of James Joyce, 1882–1941*. New Haven: Yale University Press, 1953.

Slote, Sam. "Preliminary Comments on Two Newly-Discovered *Ulysses* Manuscripts." *James Joyce Quarterly* 39 (2001): 17–28.

———. *"Ulysses" in the Plural*. Joyce Studies 2004 no. 5. Dublin: National Library of Ireland, 2004.

Smith, Janna Malamud. *Private Matters: In Defense of the Personal Life*. Reading, Mass.: Addison-Wesley, 1997.

Smith, Sidonie, and Julia Watson. *Reading Autobiography: A Guide for Interpreting Life Narratives*. Minneapolis: University of Minnesota Press, 2001.

Sorrentino, Gilbert. *Mulligan Stew*. 1979. Normal, Ill.: Dalkey Archive Press, 1996.

Spielberg, Peter, comp. *James Joyce's Manuscripts and Letters at the University of Buffalo: A Catalogue*. Buffalo: University of Buffalo, 1962. Also http://library.buffalo.edu/jamesjoyce/pdf/spielberg238.pdf.

Spoo, Robert. *James Joyce and the Language of History: Dedalus's Nightmare*. New York: Oxford University Press, 1994.

———. "'Nestor' and the Nightmare: The Presence of the Great War in *Ulysses*." *Twentieth Century Literature* 32 (1986): 137–54.

———. "Tropics of Joycean Discourse: Representations of the Historical Process in *The Critical Writings*." *James Joyce Quarterly* 28 (1991): 819–25.

———. "*Ulysses* and the Ten Years War: A Survey of Missed Opportunities." *Text* 10 (1997): 107–18.

Stack, Richard. Message posted on Joyce-Ulysses Yahoo listserv, June 27, 2007. http://groups.yahoo.com/group/Joyce-Ulysses/messages. Message No. 13581.

Stauffer, Donald A. "Genesis, or The Poet as Maker." In Arnheim et al., *Poets at Work*, 37–82.

Stead, Alistair. "Great War *Ulysses*." *James Joyce Broadsheet* 71 (2005): [4].

Stoppard, Tom. *Travesties*. New York: Grove Press, 1975.
Sultan, Stanley. *The Argument of "Ulysses."* 1964. Middletown, Conn.: Wesleyan University Press, 1987.
Svevo, Italo. *James Joyce*. 1927. Trans. Stanislaus Joyce. 1950. San Francisco: City Lights, 1969.
Takács, Ferenc. "*Százharminczbrojúgulyás-Dugulás*: Bloom, Hungary, and the Spectre of the Citizen Haunting Post-Communist Europe." Lecture at Twentieth International James Joyce Symposium, Szombathely, Hungary, June 16, 2006.
Tanselle, G. Thomas. "The Editorial Problem of Final Authorial Intention." *Studies in Bibliography* 29 (1976): 167–211. Also http://etext.lib.virginia.edu/bsuva/sb/.
———. "Textual Criticism and Deconstruction." *Studies in Bibliography* 43 (1990): 1–33. Also http://etext.lib.virginia.edu/bsuva/sb/.
Thornton, Weldon. *Allusions in "Ulysses": An Annotated List*. Chapel Hill: University of North Carolina Press, 1968.
Tompkins, Jane. "Me and My Shadow." 1987. Revised ed. in Freedman, Frey, and Zauhar, *The Intimate Critique*, 23–40.
"*Ulysses*: The Text—The Debates of the Miami J'yce Conference." *James Joyce Literary Supplement* 3 (Fall 1989).
Valéry, Paul. "Ego Scriptor." 1922. In *Cahiers*. Ed. Judith Robinson. 2 vols. Paris: Gallimard, 1973–74. 1:233–319. Trans. Robert Pickering. *Cahiers/Notebooks*. Ed. Brian Stimpson, Paul Gifford, and Pickering. 2 vols. to date. Frankfurt and New York: Peter Lang, 2000. 2:455–537.
———. "Poetry." In *Cahiers*. Ed. Judith Robinson. 2 vols. Paris: Gallimard, 1973–74. 2:1057–1142. Trans. Norma Rinsler. *Cahiers/Notebooks*. Ed. Brian Stimpson, Paul Gifford, and Robert Pickering. 2 vols. to date. Frankfurt and New York: Peter Lang, 2000. 2:159–242.
Vanderham, Paul. *James Joyce and Censorship: The Trials of "Ulysses."* New York: New York University Press, 1998.
Van Mierlo, Wim. "The Subject Notebook: A Nexus in the Composition History of *Ulysses*—A Preliminary Analysis." *Genetic Joyce Studies* 7 (2007).
Veeser, H. Aram, ed. *Confessions of the Critics*. New York and London: Routledge, 1996.
———. "Introduction: The Case for Confessional Criticism." In Veeser, *Confessions of the Critics*, ix–xxvii.
Wallace, David Foster. *"Consider the Lobster" and Other Essays*. New York: Little, Brown, 2006.
———. *Infinite Jest*. Boston: Little, Brown, 1996.
Watson, G. J. "The Politics of *Ulysses*." In *Joyce's "Ulysses": The Larger Perspective*. Ed. Robert D. Newman and Weldon Thornton. Newark: University of Delaware Press, 1987. 39–58.
Weaver, Harriet Shaw. "Harriet Weaver's Letters to James Joyce 1915–1920." Ed. John Firth. *Studies in Bibliography* 20 (1967): 151–88. Also http://etext.lib.virginia.edu/bsuva/sb/.
Weininger, Otto. *Collected Aphorisms, Notebook and Letters to a Friend*. Trans. Martin Dudaniec and Kevin Solway. Version 1.12. 2000–2002. http://www.theabsolute.net/ottow/aphlett.pdf.
———. *Über die letzten Dinge*. Vienna: W. Braumüller, 1904, 1907.

Wellek, René. *A History of Modern Criticism 1750–1950.* Vol. 4, *The Later Nineteenth Century.* 1965. Cambridge, UK: Cambridge University Press, 1983.

Wellek, René, and Austin Warren. *Theory of Literature.* 1949. 3rd ed. New York: Harcourt, Brace & World, 1956.

Werner, Richard Maria. *Lyrik und Lyriker: Eine Untersuchung.* Hamburg and Leipzig: Verlag von Leopold Voss, 1890.

White, Patricia S. "Black and White and Read All Over: A Meditation on Footnotes." *Text* 5 (1991): 81–90.

Williams, Raymond. *The Country and the City.* New York: Oxford University Press, 1973.

Williams, William Proctor, and Craig S. Abbott. *An Introduction to Bibliographical and Textual Studies.* 1985. 4th ed. New York: Modern Language Association of America, 2009.

Wimsatt, William K., Jr., and Cleanth Brooks. *Literary Criticism: A Short History.* New York: Knopf, 1957.

Woolf, Virginia. "Modern Fiction." In *The Common Reader: First Series.* 1925. New York: Harvest/Harcourt, Brace & World, 1953. 150–58. Revision of "Modern Novels." *TLS,* April 10, 1919, 189.

Yeats, W. B. *The Poems.* 2nd ed. *The Collected Works of W. B. Yeats.* Vol. 1. Ed. Richard J. Finneran. New York: Scribner, 1997.

Zeller, Ursula, Ruth Frehner, and Hannes Vogel, eds. *James Joyce: "gedacht durch meine Augen"/"thought through my eyes."* Basel, Switzerland: Schwabe, 2000.

Zerby, Chuck. *The Devil's Details: A History of Footnotes.* 2002. New York: Touchstone, 2003.

Index

Abbott, Craig S., 205n13, 210n14
Adams, Robert Martin, 76
Adams, Stephen, 207n19
"Aeolus" (*Ulysses*), 1, 2, 6, 8, 11, 31, 53–56, 65–68, 115, 124, 143, 146–51, 164; headlines, 55–56, 76, 143, 147–51; Joyce's recording of, 150; manuscripts, 27, 59, 76, 200; Parable of the Plums, 2, 6, 53–56, 66–68, 146; Stephen's poem, 146
Alain, 160
Albee, Edward: "The American Dream," "The Sandbox," *Who's Afraid of Virginia Woolf?*, 48
Alice in Wonderland (Carroll), 67
"Alphabetical Notebook" (Joyce), 200, 202, 207n20, 213n1
Anderson, Chester G., 61
Anglo-Irish revivalism, 132–34
Anglo-Irish War, 128, 131–34, 143
Annotations. *See* Footnotes
Aquinas. *See* Thomas Aquinas, Saint
"Archive" Tables (Gunn and McCleery), 89
Aristotle, 5, 35
Arranger (Hayman), 111
Ascot. *See* Gold Cup race; Throwaway
Atlas, James, 8, 11
Attridge, Derek, 1, 10
Augustine, Saint, 31
Austen, Jane, 5; *Emma*, 35
Avant-texte, defined, 4, 24, 64, 106, 107. *See also* Genetic criticism

Bachelard, Gaston, 161
Bakhtin, M. M., 110, 113, 115, 118, 211n4
Barham, Peter, 130

Barrymore, John, 160n
Barthes, Roland, 4, 106, 108, 151, 211n4
Basinski, Michael, 210n6
Battestin, Martin C., 163, 165
Baudelaire, Charles, 62
Bauerle, Ruth, 207n19
BBC. *See* British Broadcasting System
Beach, Sylvia, 15, 79, 83, 91
Bechdel, Alison, 10
Beckett, Samuel, 70
Beehler, Rodger, 161
Behar, Ruth, 10, 12
Bellemin-Noël, Jean, 4, 64, 69
Benco, Silvio, 128, 129
Bénéjam, Valérie, 205n3
Bennett, Arnold, 40, 185
Bennett, Percy, 137–38
Benoîst-Méchin, Jacques, 118
Berners-Lee, Tim, 152
Bernstein, Mark, 152, 153
Best, Richard, 29, 79, 137, 189–90
Beyer, G., 182
Bien, Peter, 33–34, 40, 51–52, 70
Bishop, Ted, 7–8
Blamires, Harry, 55
Blom, Andrew, 172–73
Bloom, Leopold (*Ulysses*): error, tolerance of, 102–3; father, 37, 43–44; generosity toward enemies, 79; home, 146–47, 154, 156, 157–68; inner life vs. outer personality, 43, 185–86; Jewishness, 33, 43, 126; Joyce on, 126; known and unknown, 24, 25; letter from Martha Clifford, 144–45; love, 43; masculinity, 43;

Bloom, Leopold (*Ulysses*)—*continued*
  Molly's choice of him, 35, 77; Molly's infidelity, 33, 43, 79, 185; monuments and statues, 2; mother, 48; ordinary and heroic, 51; past and present selves, 35–36, 40–41, 65, 66, 69; personal response to, 33–34, 43–44, 48–49, 52, 78, 185, 186, 192, 193–94; privacy violated, 186–94; reading, 144–45, 146–47; watching men eat in Burton pub, 156
Bloom, Molly (*Ulysses*): body, 149–50; choice of Poldy, 35, 77; gossip about ("Cyclops" manuscripts), 122; monuments and statues, 2; mother ("Cyclops" manuscripts), 72–73, 75; personal response to, 34, 48–49, 49–50, 52, 192, 193–94; selling old clothes, 117; "yes I will Yes," 25–26, 193–94, 198
Bodley Head, 94, 101
Bolter, Jay David, 151, 153, 157
Booth, Wayne C., 111
Borden, Gavin, 85–90
Bornstein, George, 103–4, 210n14
Boully, Jenny: *The Body*, 162
Bowen, Zack, 207n19
Bowers, Fredson 57, 92
Bowman, Frank Paul, 65
British Broadcasting Corporation (BBC), 190
British Library, 16, 18, 72, 83, 84, 86, 87, 88, 107, 120, 121, 176, 196, 200
Brooks, Cleanth, 176
Brown, Ellen, 10, 11
Brown, John Seely, 153
Brown, Susan, 27
Budgen, Frank, 58–59, 82–83, 107, 112, 118, 123, 125–26, 127–31, 134–35, 139–40, 142, 214n37
Buffalo, N.Y., 32, 37, 39, 41, 49, 188, 192. *See also* University at Buffalo
Burbules, Nicholas C., 157
Bush, Ronald, 20–21, 127–28

Cadbury, Bill, 210n9
Cahoon, Herbert, 83
Cailliau, Robert, 152
Calder, Alexander, 3, 173
California Institute of Technology, 96
"Calypso" (*Ulysses*), 154, 185–86; manuscripts, 200
Canadian Broadcasting Corporation (CBC), 95
Canterbury Tales, The (Chaucer), 35

Carlton, Peter, 10, 11–12
Carr, Henry, 79, 129, 137–38, 140
Car Talk (Tom and Ray Magliozzi): Car-O-Scope, 187
CBC. *See* Canadian Broadcasting Corporation
Centre National de la Recherche Scientifique, 62
"C. G. is Not Literary, The" (Joyce), 138
Chamber Music (Joyce), 61, 86
Christie's, 14, 136
"Circe" (*Ulysses*), 30, 43, 109, 117, 132, 138, 185; manuscripts, 14, 15, 16, 19, 20, 136, 196, 197, 199, 201
Cixous, Hélène, 4
Coe, Jonathan: *The House of Sleep*, 161–63
Coleridge, Samuel Taylor: "The Rime of the Ancient Mariner," 161
Collins, Wilkie: *The New Magdalen*, 11, 206n24
Colum, Mary, 129
Cornell University, 16, 18, 28, 71, 83, 86, 87, 88, 107, 196, 200–1, 202, 211n7
Cosgrave, Vincent, 126
Cosgrove, Peter, 163
Coward, Noel, 160, 163
Crispi, Luca, 60, 206n9, 207n13, 209n15, 210n6, 210n9, 213n3, 217n88
Critical Writings (Joyce), 18, 128
Critique génétique. *See* Genetic criticism
Cross, Richard, 70
Cunard, Nancy, 141
"Cyclops" (*Ulysses*), 2, 43, 107–43, 168, 202; animal imagery in manuscripts, 110, 114; characters and speakers of dialogue in manuscripts, 109–10; "gigantism" (technic in schema), 108–18, 122, 133; "I"-narrator, 73–75, 111, 113–16, 122, 123, 133, 138–39, 143; Jews loving their country, 73, 75, 119; manuscripts, 6, 13, 16, 19, 26, 71–76, 78, 89, 105–19, 120–25, 197, 200; "Sirens," material from, used in manuscripts, 116–18; slaughter imagery in manuscripts, 114–15

Danielewski, Mark Z., 162
Dante Alighieri, 19
Darantiere, Maurice, 147–49
Darnton, Robert, 127
Dartmouth College, 32–35, 39–40, 42, 50, 52, 70
Deane, Vincent, 213n3
de Biasi, Pierre-Marc, 2, 5, 63

Debray Genette, Raymonde, 65
Dedalus, Stephen (*Ulysses*): "history is a nightmare," 130; Jews loving their country ("Cyclops" manuscripts), 73, 75, 119; known and unknown, 24, 25; mother, 41, 48; Parable of the Plums, 2, 6, 53–56, 66–68, 146; past and present selves, 36, 65, 69; personal response to, 33, 37, 39–40, 41, 44; possibilities and actualities, 5, 11, 63; Shakespeare, 28–29, 36, 79, 93, 109–11, 125, 146, 164, 189–90, 197; "silence, exile, and cunning" (*Portrait*), 133–34; static and kinetic art, 2; "word known to all men," 28–31, 93; writing a poem, 58, 146
Deppman, Jed, 4, 174–75, 178, 183, 205n7
Derrida, Jacques, 4, 47, 163–64
Dettmar, Kevin, 82, 205n1, 207n1, 209n1
de Valera, Síle, 23
Dickens, Charles: *David Copperfield*, 11
Dodd, Reuben J., 79
"Dooleysprudence" (Joyce), 128, 130, 214n37
Drafts (*Yale French Studies*), 63
Dubliners (Joyce), 61, 86, 90, 102, 121; "The Dead," 109; manuscripts, 196
Duffy, Enda, 55
Duguid, Paul, 13
Dunn, Mark: *Ibid*, 162
du Sautoy, Peter, 92

Eakin, Paul John, 8
Easter Rising, 131, 132, 133
Eastgate Systems, 153
Editing: 6–7, 8, 57, 78, 82, 91–104, 193, 203, 210n14. *See also* Textual criticism
Eglinton, John (pseud. W. K. Magee), 79
Egoist, The, (magazine), 141
Eliot, T. S., 77, 142
Eliot, Vivien, 142, 217n90
Ellmann, Richard, 5, 25, 79, 85, 92, 95, 98, 118, 126, 128, 129, 130, 138, 140, 141, 142, 156, 198
Endnotes. *See* Footnotes
English Players, 129, 137–39, 140, 143
Epstein, E. L., 215n44
Ernst, Morris, 82
Estate of James Joyce. *See* James Joyce Estate
"Eumaeus" (*Ulysses*), 35–36, 67, 102, 130, 146, 168; chairs on tables overnight, 35–36; "L. Boom," 146; manuscripts, 15, 16, 124, 136, 196, 199, 201

Every Man's Own Lawyer (anonymous), 137
Exiles (Joyce), 61, 86, 138, 140

Fairhall, James, 130, 133
Faulkner, William, 70
Feltham, Mark, 152
Ferrer, Daniel, 4, 20, 21, 65–66, 69, 116–17, 123, 143, 174–75, 183, 205n7, 207n13, 207n20, 217n11
Fielding, Henry: *Tom Jones*, 161
Finnegans Wake (Joyce), 58–59, 60, 61, 66, 82, 83, 85, 86, 90, 107, 112, 131, 143; manuscripts, 17, 19, 89, 195, 196, 197
"*Finnegans Wake*" *Notebooks at Buffalo* project, 60
Finneran, Richard J., 161, 207n27, 218n2
Fish, Stanley, 57
Flaubert, Gustave, 65
Fleischmann, Marthe, 139–40, 143
Foot, Edward Edwin, 162–63
Footnotes, 8, 12, 13, 154, 159–84
Ford, Ford Madox, 125
Fordham, Finn, 36
Fraistat, Neil, 7
Frank, Joseph, 68
Freedman, Diane P., 9, 10
Frehner, Ruth, 216n65
French, Marilyn, 1
Frey, James: *A Million Little Pieces*, 8
Frey, Olivia, 9

Gabler, Hans Walter, 86, 99, 106, 109, 118, 210n9, 210n14, 210n16; edition of *Ulysses*, 8, 12, 13, 28, 30, 56, 61, 83, 90, 91–104, 113, 117, 144, 150, 155, 156, 209n9
Gann (unreliable witness), 138
Garland Publishing, 84–90, 91, 93–95; papers at Princeton University, 86
Gaskell, Philip, 92, 94, 99
Gay, Karl, 87
Genesis: Manuscrits/Recherche/Invention (journal), 208n21
Genetic criticism, 3–6, 11, 12–13, 53–68, 90, 105–19, 174–84, 203, 205n7; described, 24, 62–66, 125; incompleteness of, 117–18, 123, 126, 143, 195–96; individual life and, 11, 36–37, 80; known and unknown, 24, 25, 31; time and, 66, 67–68, 69, 119. *See also* Avant-texte
Genette, Gérard, 160
Gibson, Andrew, 132–34

Gifford, Don: *"Ulysses" Annotated*, 5, 29, 31, 164–67, 171, 172, 173
Gilbert, Stuart, 1, 19, 67, 131, 149, 150–51, 154, 214n16
Gillespie, Michael Patrick, 127
Goethe-{#}und Schiller-Archiv, 175
Goldberg, S. L., 1
Gold Cup race, 146, 166–68, 172
Goldman, Arnold, 99, 128
Gorman, Herbert, 18, 126, 129, 132, 137, 138, 197
Gottfried, Roy, 135
Grafton, Anthony, 160
Greenblatt, Stephen, 125
Greg, W. W., 7
Grésillon, Almuth, 62, 65, 76
Gunn, Ian, 89

"Hades" (*Ulysses*), 43, 46, 173; manuscripts, 200
Hanna, Ralph, III, 163
Harry Ransom Center, University of Texas at Austin, 7, 16, 83, 84, 86, 107, 196
Hart, Clive, 86, 92, 94, 99
Hart, Elspeth, 87
Hartshorn, Peter, 134
Harvard University, 16, 81–82, 83, 85, 107, 196
Hay, Louis, 6, 24, 31, 36, 63, 107, 118–19, 198
Hayashi, Tetsumaro, 81
Hayman, David, 60, 86, 88, 111, 210n9
Henry E. Huntington Library, 84
Herr, Cheryl, 207n26
Herring, Phillip F., 18, 71–72, 90, 123–24
Hettche, Walter, 61
Hiltpold, Rudolf, 139
Home page, 153–55. *See also* Pages
Homer: *The Odyssey*, 34, 41, 54, 110, 118, 155, 156, 164; Odysseus, 2, 125–26
Hoppenot, Henri, 15
Huebsch, B. W., 83
Huntington Library. *See* Henry E. Huntington Library
Hyde, Douglas, 146
HyperCard, 151
Hypertext, 151, 153, 156, 159, 193; defined, 152, 155. *See also* Links

I Love Lucy (TV series), 38
Implied author (Booth), 111

Institut des Textes et Manuscrits Modernes (ITEM), 62, 90, 208n21
International James Joyce Symposia, 23, 88, 92, 95, 97, 101–2, 195, 215n58
Intertextuality, 76, 211n4
Isle of Man, 147
"Ithaca" (*Ulysses*), 24, 30, 43, 67, 79, 145, 148–49, 185, 193; known and unknown, 24, 25; manuscripts, 17, 19, 124, 136, 197, 201

Jackson, Shelley: *Patchwork Girl*, 155
James, Henry, 60, 61–62, 76
James Joyce Archive, The (ed. Groden et al.), 4, 6, 12, 13, 18, 50, 60, 66, 83–90, 91, 206n2, 211n7
James Joyce Estate, 90, 92
James Joyce Quarterly, 75, 85, 89, 90, 96, 99, 100
James Joyce's Manuscripts: An Index (Groden), 89, 199, 206n2
Jane Eyre (Brontë), 10
Jews and Jewishness, 32, 33, 42, 43, 49, 73–75, 119, 121, 126, 133, 168, 185
Johns Hopkins Guide to Literary Theory and Criticism, The, 176
Johnson, Jeri, 164–65, 167, 170, 172
Jolas, Eugene, 129–30
Jones, Ellen Carol, 1, 132
Joyce, Giorgio, 86
Joyce, James: Anglo-Irish War, 128, 131–34, 143; betrayal, sensitivity to, 126; colored crayons, 71–72, 74, 75, 121–22; difficult relationships, 79, 141; early scholarship on, 81–82; editions of his works, 61; English Players, 129, 137–39, 140, 143; eyesight, 80, 134–37, 139, 140, 143; heroic efforts to write *Ulysses*, 141; in Dublin, 126, 131, 139; in Paris, 202; in Trieste, 128, 202; in Zurich, 126–43; letters, 14, 17, 27, 91, 95, 112–13, 118, 126, 127, 129, 132, 134, 136, 137, 139–40, 141, 143, 214n16; manuscript collections, 83–84, 107; money, 140, 143; Nora, 95, 141–42, 143; on Bloom, 126; on Odysseus, 125–26; paragraphs as unit of writing, 65–66; reconstructing Dublin from *Ulysses*, 130–31; recording of "Aeolus," 150; revenge in *Ulysses* for wrongs in life, 79, 137–38; withdrawal into writing, 126, 141; women, 139–40, 143; World War I, 126–31, 143; writer vs. person, 79; writing, 55–56, 58, 59–60, 66–68, 76, 124,

125–43, 147–50, 195, 196–98, 199–203; writing as boring through mountain from both sides, 107; writing as elements fusing, 118, 143; writing for pages in print, 8, 146, 151. *See also* Manuscripts for *Ulysses*; *and specific episodes of Ulysses and specific works*
Joyce, Lucia, 86
Joyce, Michael, 155; *Afternoon: A Story*, 155
Joyce, Nora, 95, 126, 141–42, 143
Joyce, Stanislaus, 83, 129, 138
Joyce, Stephen James, 22, 95, 97, 206n8
Joyce Wars, 61, 96–104

Kafka, Franz, 33, 34
Kain, Richard M., 202, 213n1
Kazantzakis, Nikos, 33
Keats, John, 74; "Ode on a Grecian Urn," 44
Keep, Christopher, 152
Kelly, Joseph, 210n4
Kiberd, Declan, 39, 130, 164, 167, 171, 172, 186
Kidd, John, 96–104
Killeen, Terence, 20, 22
Kissane, Noel, 14–16, 17, 20, 21, 23
Knowles, Sebastian D. G., 103, 148, 217n90
Kopit, Arthur L.: *Oh Dad, Poor Dad, Mamma's Hung You in the Closet and I'm Feelin' So Sad*, 48
Kristeva, Julia, 4, 211n4

Lacan, Jacques, 4
La Hune. *See* Librairie La Hune
Landow, George, 151, 152, 156
Larbaud, Valery, 58–59, 214n16
Lavagnino, John, 161, 163, 165, 218n3
Lawler, Traugott, 163, 164
Lawrence,, D. H., 33, 34
LeBlanc, Leslie, 210n4
Lejeune, Philippe, 8, 11
Léon, Alexis, 20, 23, 198
Léon, Lucie, 20
Léon, Paul, 20, 83
Lerm Hayes, Christa-Maria, 216n65
Lesley, Cole, 160n
"Lestrygonians" (*Ulysses*), 34, 36, 65, 69, 156; manuscripts, 92, 94, 200; "Me. And me now," 35–36, 40–41, 65, 66, 69; men eating in Burton pub, 156

Levin, Harry, 82, 85
Lewis, Wyndham, 1
Librairie La Hune, 17, 83, 200, 203
Lidwell, J. G., 132
Limited Editions Club, 150
Linati, Carlo, 214n16
Lindey, Alexander, 82
Lingua Franca, 101
Links, 157, 163, 171. *See also* Hypertext
Little Review, The, 55, 121, 127
Litz, A. Walton, 50, 59–60, 70–71, 75–78, 85, 86, 91–92, 94–95
Loizeaux, Elizabeth Bergmann, 7
Lopate, Phillip, 10
"Lotus Eaters" (*Ulysses*), 55, 102, 144–47, 165–68, 170, 218n23; letter from Martha Clifford, 144–45; manuscripts, 200; Throwaway, 165–69
Ludwig, William, 87–88

MacLeish, Archibald, 65
MacNicholas, John, 61
Maddox, Brenda, 126, 141
Magliozzi, Tom and Ray. *See Car Talk*
Mahaffey, Vicki, 102–3
Malroux, André, 33
Mancusi-Ungaro, Carol, 3
Manganiello, Dominic, 130, 131
Mann, Thomas, 33
Manuscripts for *Ulysses*, 14–31, 53–58, 66–68, 71–80, 81–95, 97, 105–24, 142–43, 195–203; catalogs and checklists, 18, 71, 75, 89, 199, 206n2, 206n9, 209n15, 211n7; chart of extant manuscripts, 23, 199–203; collections, 83–84, 107; described, 19, 72; Joyce's notes, 16, 18, 71–72, 84, 120–22, 127, 198, 200; symbols used in transcriptions, 209n9, 212n28, 212n31; used for editing text, 78, 91–95, 97, 101
Martha (Flotow), 35
Martin, Timothy, 207n19
Matisse, Henri, 150
Max, D. T., 206n8
Mays, J.C.C., 103
McCarthy, Patrick, 146
McCleery, Alistair, 89
McCormick, Edith Rockefeller, 79, 141
McCourt, John, 23, 126

McGann, Jerome J., 6, 7, 8, 13, 26, 57, 96, 103, 119, 146, 156; linguistic and bibliographical codes, 7, 8, 13, 65, 147, 150, 157
McGee, Patrick, 55
McKenzie, D. F., 6, 7, 8
Meahan, Paul, 217n11
Melchior, Claus, 61, 99
Meyer, Richard Moritz, 177–84
Middlemarch (Eliot), 10, 11, 35
Miller, Arthur: *All My Sons*, 48; *Death of a Salesman*, 48
Miller, Nancy K., 8
Mobile, 2–3, 5, 12, 68, 69, 173. See also Calder, Alexander; Monument
Moby-Dick (Melville), 35
Modern Language Association of America (MLA), 174, 175, 184
Modern Library. See Random House
Monnier, Adrienne, 15
Monument, 1–3, 53, 63, 68, 69, 105, 173. See also Mobile
Moore, Marianne, 26, 119
Morris, William, 146
Moscato, Michael, 210n4
Müller, Hans-Harald, 179–80, 183, 184

Nabokov, Vladimir: *Pale Fire*, 161
National Library of Ireland, 6, 12, 13, 14–31, 51, 79, 84, 86, 88, 107, 120, 122–25, 136, 138, 142, 143, 190, 195–98, 213n1, 219n1; press conference in May 2002, 22–23, 195–98
National Public Radio (NPR), 186
"Nausicaa" (*Ulysses*), 79, 140, 156, 173, 202; manuscripts, 16, 26, 88, 89, 200
Nelson, Ted, 152
"Nestor" (*Ulysses*), 5, 11, 29, 54, 63, 68, 106, 121, 130, 133; "history is a nightmare," 130; manuscripts, 200; possibilities and actualities, 5, 11, 63;
"New Tipperary" (Joyce), 137
New York Public Library, 84, 176
New York Review of Books, 97, 98, 99
New York Times, 95; *New York Times Book Review*, 188
Nolan, Emer, 132
Noon, William T., S.J., 30
Norburn, Roger, 216n63

Norton (publishers). See W. W. Norton and Company
NPR. See National Public Radio

Occasional, Critical, and Political Writing (Joyce), 18
O Donoghue, Brendan, 23
Odyssey, The. See Homer
Odyssey Press, 150, 155
O'Hanlon, John, 61, 86, 213n1
O'Henly, Adrienne, 207n19
Olney, James, 8
O'Neill, Eugene: *Desire Under the Elms*, 48; *The Great God Brown*, 48; *Mourning Becomes Elektra*, 48
Owen, Rodney Wilson, 28, 121, 124, 202
"Oxen in the Sun" [sic], 89
"Oxen of the Sun" (*Ulysses*), 34, 109, 110, 119, 149, 167; manuscripts, 16, 17, 19, 89, 197, 201, 202

Pages, 8, 13, 144–58, 160. See also Home page; Print vs. screen; Web page
Papers of the Bibliographical Society of America (PBSA), 99–100
Paradise Lost (Milton), 35
Paragraphs, 65–66
"Paris Notebook" (Joyce), 18
Peacock, Molly, 18, 20, 22, 32, 39–40, 49–50, 51–52, 101, 183, 187–94; *Paradise, Piece by Piece*, 188, 191; *Raw Heaven*, 188, 190; "The Wheel," 192
Peake, C. H., 54
"Penelope" (*Ulysses*), 2, 13, 31, 49–50, 51, 67, 72, 148–49; body, 149–50; manuscripts, 17, 19, 25–26, 92, 112, 197–98, 201; monuments and statues, 2; "yes I will Yes," 25–26, 193–94, 198
Penguin Books, 94, 101
Personal criticism, 8–13, 32–52, 69–104, 185–94; alternative names for, 8–9
Petras, Kathryn and Ross: *Very Bad Poetry*, 162–63
Pierce, Gillian Borland, 210n14
Placards, described, 149
Poe, Edgar Allan, 5–6, 62; "The Purloined Letter," 177
Poetry Collection. See under University at Buffalo

"Pola Notebook" (Joyce), 18
Ponizowski, Alexander, 83
Pope, Alexander: *The Dunciad*, 161
"Portrait of the Artist, A" (Joyce), 40
Portrait of the Artist as a Young Man, A (Joyce), 2, 40, 54, 61, 82, 84, 86, 90, 91, 101, 102, 125, 133–34, 139, 141, 188; manuscripts, 88, 196; "silence, exile, and cunning," 133–34
Postgate, J. P., 91
Pound, Ezra, 77, 118, 127, 143
Prescott, Joseph, 81–82
Princeton University, 41, 52, 69, 83, 84, 85, 86, 94, 107, 196
Print: variations in presentation of text, 144, 150, 155. *See also* Print vs. screen
Print vs. screen, 144–73
Privacy, 185–94
"Proteus" (*Ulysses*), 28, 30, 39, 54, 146, 173; manuscripts, 16–17, 18, 20, 26, 27, 124, 136, 197, 200, 202, 203; Stephen's poem, 58, 146
Proust, Marcel, 33, 65

Quillian, William, 20–21
Quinn, John, 14, 93
Quinn, Lochlann, 23

Rabaté, Jean-Michel, 58, 65–66, 217n1
Rachewiltz, Mary de, 97
Radford, F. L., 132, 134, 215n58
Random House, 81, 94, 100–1, 150, 155
Ransom Center. *See* Harry Ransom Center, University of Texas at Austin
Raphael, Madame France, 213n1
Robarts Library. *See* University of Toronto
Romantic Ireland, 55, 132–34
Rose, Danis, 61, 86, 88, 213n1
Rosen, Jonathan, 153–54, 157
Rosenbach Museum and Library, 83–84, 87, 196, 197; Rosenbach Manuscript, 18, 19, 29, 56, 82, 84, 92, 93, 94, 107, 116, 123, 131, 197, 199–201, 202, 207n11
Rossman, Charles, 97, 98–99
Rowland, Wade, 153
Rumbold, Horace, 79, 137–38, 142
Rushing, Conrad, 137–38, 140
Russian Revolution, 128, 131

Saunders, Max, 214n24
Sceptre. *See* Gold Cup race; Throwaway
Scholarly editing. *See* Editing
Scholes, Robert, 18, 61, 202, 206n2, 211n7, 213n1
Schork, R. J., 210n9
Schwaber, Paul, 55
Schwartz, John Pedro, 1
Schwartzman, Myron, 75
Schwarz, Daniel R., 55
Schwarz, Oscar, 129
Scott, Tony, 23
Screen presentation of text, 144, 155, 157, 160. *See also* Print vs. screen
"Scylla and Charybdis" (*Ulysses*), 27, 28, 31, 36, 65, 69, 79, 93, 109–10, 111, 125, 146, 164; "I, I and I. I," 65, 69; manuscripts, 17, 19, 20, 28–31, 136, 197, 200, 202, 203; "word known to all men," 28–31, 93
Seidman, Robert J.: *"Ulysses" Annotated*, 5, 29, 31, 164–67, 172, 173
Selected Letters (Joyce), 95
Senn, Fritz, 97, 210n9, 216n65
Shakespeare, William, 79, 91, 125, 164, 189–90; *Hamlet*, 28–31, 125, 146, 164, 197; *Pericles*, 28; *The Tempest*, 28; *Troilus and Cressida*, 138–39; *The Winter's Tale*, 28
Shakespeare and Company, 150, 155
Sherry, Vincent, 1, 130, 133
Shillingsburg, Peter, 82
Shloss, Carol Loeb, 141
Silver, Brenda R., 211n6
Silverman, Oscar, 210n6
"Sirens" (*Ulysses*), 28, 31, 35, 115, 116, 118, 132, 140, 156, 202; fugue and *fuga per canonem*, 27, 197; manuscripts, 16–17, 19, 20, 26–28, 123, 124, 196–97, 200, 203; Molly selling old clothes, 117; overture, 27; "When first I saw" (*Martha*), 35
Slocum, John J., 83
Slote, Sam, 15, 60
Smith, Janna Malamud, 191
Smith, Sidonie, 8, 9, 12
Smith (unreliable witness), 138
Society for Scholarly Publishing, 96
Society for Textual Scholarship, 96–97
Society of Authors, 86
Sorrentino, Gilbert: *Mulligan Stew*, 162

244 Index

Sotheby's, 15, 18, 21, 136
Southern Illinois University, 83
Spencer, Theodore, 82
Spielberg, Peter, 18, 73, 74, 75, 206n2, 209n15, 211n7
Spohrer, James Henry, 178, 183, 184
Spoo, Robert, 100, 103, 130, 131
Stack, Richard, 206n24
Staley, Thomas F., 75, 85, 96, 99
Stauffer, Donald A., 57, 62
Stead, Alistair, 215n42
Stephen Hero (Joyce), 82
Steppe, Wolfhard, 61, 99
Sterne, Laurence: *Tristram Shandy*, 161
Stoppard, Tom: *Travesties*, 129, 134
Storyspace, 151
Studies in the Novel, 99
Sultan, Stanley, 55
Svevo, Italo, 128
Sykes, Claud, 130, 137, 138

Takács, Ferenc, 215n58
Tanselle, G. Thomas, 57, 210n14
"Telemachus" (*Ulysses*), 54; manuscripts, 200
Text (Barthes). *See* Work vs. Text
Textual criticism, 6, 9, 56–57, 102–3, 193, 207n13. *See also* Editing
Textual studies, 6–8, 12, 144–84
They All Are Jews (Davis), 42
Thomas Aquinas, Saint, 29–31
Thornton, Weldon, 164–65
Throwaway, 77, 165–69. *See also* Gold Cup race
Times Literary Supplement (*TLS*), 98
Tindall, William York, 61
TLS. *See Times Literary Supplement*
Tompkins, Jane, 9–10
transition (literary journal), 19
"Trieste Notebook" (Joyce). *See* "Alphabetical Notebook"

Ulysses (Joyce): annotations in, 164; annotations to, 164–65; early manuscript study of, 82–83, 90; early scholarship on, 81–82; exposure of inner life, 48–49, 185–86; fathers in, 37, 43; first U.S. publication, 81; mothers in, 30, 37, 39, 41, 48, 72, 73, 75; personal response to, 9–13, 32–37, 40–41, 43–44, 48–49, 49–50, 51–52, 69–70, 78, 80, 185, 186, 192, 193–94; privacy, violation of, 186, 194; schemas, 19, 27, 108, 114, 123, 131, 154, 203; simple solutions, avoidance of, 35–36, 157–58. *See also* Bloom, Leopold; Bloom, Molly; Dedalus, Stephen; Joyce, James; Manuscripts for *Ulysses*; *and specific episodes*
"*Ulysses*" *in Progress* (Groden), 6, 26, 50, 59–60, 63, 76, 83, 90, 105–17, 120–21, 124, 202, 211n7; three stages in development of *Ulysses*, 59, 76, 105, 202
"*Ulysses*" *Pagefinder* (Gunn and McCleery), 89
University at Buffalo: Poetry Collection, 16, 18, 26, 62, 71, 72, 75, 83, 84, 86, 87, 88, 90, 92, 120–21, 136, 142, 143, 196, 197, 200–201, 202, 211n7
University College Dublin, 84
University of Buffalo. *See* University at Buffalo
University of Miami, 99
University of Texas at Austin. *See* Harry Ransom Center, University of Texas at Austin
University of Toronto: Robarts Library, 176, 178–80, 184
University of Tulsa, 84, 98, 196
University of Western Ontario, 15, 18, 21, 35, 50, 86, 188
University of Wisconsin at Milwaukee, 84

Valéry, Paul, 5, 63–64, 175
Vanderham, Paul, 210n4
Vanity Fair (magazine), 81
Van Mierlo, Wim, 206n5, 213n1, 213n3
Vaughan Williams, Ralph, 27
Veeser, H. Aram, 9
Vintage Books, 94, 101
Vogel, Hannes, 216n65

Wallace, David Foster: *Consider the Lobster*, *Infinite Jest*, 162
"Wandering Rocks" (*Ulysses*), 28, 119, 130, 202; manuscripts, 118, 134, 200, 203
Warren, Austin, 57–58, 61
Washington Post (newspaper), 96
Watson, G. J., 132–33
Watson, Julia, 8, 9, 12
Weaver, Harriet Shaw, 27, 79, 83, 118, 140–41, 143
Weber, R. M. [*sic*], 174–84

Web page, 152–53. *See also* Pages
Weininger, Otto, 121
Weiss, Ottocaro, 79, 141
Wellek, René, 57–58, 61, 176, 177, 180
Werner, Richard Maria: *Lyrik und Lyriker*, 179–84
Wettstein, Georg, 138
White, Patricia, 161
Wilde, Oscar: *The Importance of Being Earnest*, 137
Williams, William Carlos, 77
Williams, William Proctor, 205n13, 210n14
Wimsatt, William K., Jr., 176
Wizard of Oz, The (1939 film), 72
Woolf, Leonard, 7–8

Woolf, Virginia, 7–8, 40, 70
Woolsey, John M., 81–82
Workshop of Daedalus, The (ed. Scholes and Kain), 18
Work vs. Text (Barthes), 106, 108
World War I, 126–31, 143, 215n58
W. W. Norton and Company, 101, 102, 188

Yale University, 83, 86, 87, 196
Yeats, Michael, 97
Yeats, William Butler, 74, 77, 160, 218n2

Zauhar, Frances Murphy, 9
Zeller, Ursula, 216n65
Zerby, Chuck, 150

Michael Groden is Distinguished University Professor in the Department of English at the University of Western Ontario. He is the author of *"Ulysses" in Progress*, general editor of *The James Joyce Archive*, and coeditor of *The Johns Hopkins Guide to Literary Theory and Criticism* and *Genetic Criticism: Texts and Avant-textes*.

The Florida James Joyce Series
EDITED BY SEBASTIAN D. G. KNOWLES

The Autobiographical Novel of Co-Consciousness: Goncharov, Woolf, and Joyce, by Galya Diment (1994)
Bloom's Old Sweet Song: Essays on Joyce and Music, by Zack Bowen (1995)
Joyce's Iritis and the Irritated Text: The Dis-lexic Ulysses, by Roy Gottfried (1995)
Joyce, Milton, and the Theory of Influence, by Patrick Colm Hogan (1995)
Reauthorizing Joyce, by Vicki Mahaffey (paperback edition, 1995)
Shaw and Joyce: "The Last Word in Stolentelling," by Martha Fodaski Black (1995)
Bely, Joyce, and Döblin: Peripatetics in the City Novel, by Peter I. Barta (1996)
Jocoserious Joyce: The Fate of Folly in Ulysses, by Robert H. Bell (paperback edition, 1996)
Joyce and Popular Culture, edited by R. B. Kershner (1996)
Joyce and the Jews: Culture and Texts, by Ira B. Nadel (paperback edition, 1996)
Narrative Design in Finnegans Wake: *The Wake Lock Picked*, by Harry Burrell (1996)
Gender in Joyce, edited by Jolanta W. Wawrzycka and Marlena G. Corcoran (1997)
Latin and Roman Culture in Joyce, by R. J. Schork (1997)
Reading Joyce Politically, by Trevor L. Williams (1997)
Advertising and Commodity Culture in Joyce, by Garry Leonard (1998)
Greek and Hellenic Culture in Joyce, by R. J. Schork (1998)
Joyce, Joyceans, and the Rhetoric of Citation, by Eloise Knowlton (1998)
Joyce's Music and Noise: Theme and Variation in His Writings, by Jack W. Weaver (1998)
Reading Derrida Reading Joyce, by Alan Roughley (1999)
Joyce through the Ages: A Nonlinear View, edited by Michael Patrick Gillespie (1999)
Chaos Theory and James Joyce's Everyman, by Peter Francis Mackey (1999)
Joyce's Comic Portrait, by Roy Gottfried (2000)
Joyce and Hagiography: Saints Above!, by R. J. Schork (2000)
Voices and Values in Joyce's Ulysses, by Weldon Thornton (2000)
The Dublin Helix: The Life of Language in Joyce's Ulysses, by Sebastian D. G. Knowles (2001)
Joyce Beyond Marx: History and Desire in Ulysses *and* Finnegans Wake, by Patrick McGee (2001)
Joyce's Metamorphosis, by Stanley Sultan (2001)
Joycean Temporalities: Debts, Promises, and Countersignatures, by Tony Thwaites (2001)
Joyce and the Victorians, by Tracey Teets Schwarze (2002)
Joyce's Ulysses *as National Epic: Epic Mimesis and the Political History of the Nation State*, by Andras Ungar (2002)
James Joyce's "Fraudstuff," by Kimberly J. Devlin (2002)
Rite of Passage in the Narratives of Dante and Joyce, by Jennifer Margaret Fraser (2002)
Joyce and the Scene of Modernity, by David Spurr (2002)
Joyce and the Early Freudians: A Synchronic Dialogue of Texts, by Jean Kimball (2003)
Twenty-first Joyce, edited by Ellen Carol Jones and Morris Beja (2004)
Joyce on the Threshold, edited by Anne Fogarty and Timothy Martin (2005)

Wake Rites: The Ancient Irish Rituals of Finnegans Wake, by George Cinclair Gibson (2005)
Ulysses *in Critical Perspective*, edited by Michael Patrick Gillespie and A. Nicholas Fargnoli (2006)
Joyce and the Narrative Structure of Incest, by Jen Shelton (2006)
Joyce, Ireland, Britain, edited by Andrew Gibson and Len Platt (2006)
Joyce in Trieste: An Album of Risky Readings, edited by Sebastian D. G. Knowles, Geert Lernout, and John McCourt (2007)
Joyce's Rare View: The Nature of Things in Finnegans Wake, by Richard Beckman (2007)
Joyce's Misbelief, by Roy Gottfried (2007)
James Joyce's Painful Case, by Cóilín Owens (2008)
Cannibal Joyce, by Thomas Jackson Rice (2008)
Manuscript Genetics, Joyce's Know-How, Beckett's Nohow, by Dirk Van Hulle (2008)
Catholic Nostalgia in Joyce and Company, by Mary Lowe-Evans (2008)
A Guide through Finnegans Wake, by Edmund Lloyd Epstein (2009)
Bloomsday 100: Essays on Ulysses, edited by Morris Beja and Anne Fogarty (2009)
Joyce, Medicine, and Modernity, by Vike Martina Plock (2010)
Who's Afraid of James Joyce?, by Karen R. Lawrence (2010; first paperback edition, 2012)
Ulysses *in Focus: Genetic, Textual, and Personal Views*, by Michael Groden (2010; first paperback edition, 2012)
Foundational Essays in James Joyce Studies, edited by Michael Patrick Gillespie (2011)
Empire and Pilgrimage in Conrad and Joyce, by Agata Szczeszak-Brewer (2011)
The Poetry of James Joyce Reconsidered, edited by Marc C. Conner (2012)
The German Joyce, by Robert K. Weninger (2012)
Joyce and Militarism, by Greg Winston (2012)
Renascent Joyce, edited by Daniel Ferrer, Sam Slote, and André Topia (2013)
Before Daybreak: "After the Race" and the Origins of Joyce's Art, by Cóilín Owens (2013)

www.ingramcontent.com/pod-product-compliance
Lightning Source LLC
Chambersburg PA
CBHW020834160426
43192CB00007B/647